P9-EFG-092

DISCARDED

AFTER-EDUCATION

AFTER-EDUCATION

ANNA FREUD, MELANIE KLEIN, AND PSYCHOANALYTIC HISTORIES OF LEARNING

DEBORAH P. BRITZMAN

STATE UNIVERSITY OF NEW YORK PRESS

Published by
STATE UNIVERSITY OF NEW YORK PRESS,
ALBANY

© 2003 State University of New York

All rights reserved

Printed in the United States of America

No part of this book may be used or reproduced in any manner whatsoever
without written permission. No part of this book may be stored in a retrieval
system or transmitted in any form or by any means including electronic, elec-
trostatic, magnetic tape, mechanical, photocopying, recording, or otherwise without the prior permission in writing of the publisher.

For information, address
State University of New York Press
90 State Street, Suite 700, Albany, NY 12207

Production, Laurie Searl
Marketing, Anne M. Valentine

Library of Congress Cataloging-in-Publication Data

Britzman, Deborah P., 1952–
     After-Education: Anna Freud, Melanie Klein, and psychoanalytic histories of
learning / Deborah P. Britzman.
     p. cm.
     Includes bibliographical references and index.
     ISBN 0-7914-5673-0 (alk. paper) — (ISBN 0-7914-5674-9 (pbk. : alk. paper)
     1. Psychoanalysis and education.   2. Learning, Psychology of.   3. Freud, Anna,
Klein, Melanie.   I. Title.

LB1092.B75 2003
370'.15—dc21   2002075880

10 9 8 7 6 5 4 3 2 1

CONTENTS

ACKNOWLEDGMENTS

The ideas that became this book were first expressed as a promise in a 1997 grant application to the Social Science and Humanities Research Council of Canada (SSHRC), written with Professor Alice Pitt. "Difficult Knowledge in Teaching and Learning: A Psychoanalytic Inquiry" proposed a series of projects for a three-year period, organized to examine the status and work of "difficult knowledge" in the postmodern university: how teachers and students represent it, how theory contains it, and how practices of teaching and learning in the field of psychoanalysis and education emerge from and elaborate it. This manuscript belongs to the labor of the third project—an inquiry into the relevance of controversies in the field of child psychoanalysis to the large field of education. While in each project "difficult knowledge" emerged in places where we least expected it, in this manuscript there was another surprise: it became a metaphor for the vicissitudes of education.

The research and the technical support for writing this manuscript were supported by the Council, under the standard SSHRC grant #410-98-1028. While the views do not represent those of the Council, I am grateful for its support. I also thank the following: Wellcome Library for the History and Understanding of Medicine in London (aka Wellcome Library), where the personal papers of Melanie Klein (1882–1960) are housed; Dr. Lesley A. Hall, the archivist who catalogued the Klein papers; and, the Melanie Klein Trust for permission to reproduce in chapter 6, some unpublished material on loneliness found in the Klein papers. Working with the Melanie Klein archive was, for me, a deeply moving experience.

Over the course of writing this book, I have benefited from lively conversations and symposiums, where some of this work has been presented. More intimately, there are others to thank directly: I thank William

Haver for encouraging a more insistent prose and for his friendship, and Pattie Lather, who has, throughout this project, offered keen advice, scholarly discussion, and lovely encouragement.

Throughout the thinking and the writing of this book, I am indebted to Alice Pitt, my partner in research and in life, whose knowledge and grace are only matched by her keen understanding of education and psychoanalysis.

For her ongoing help with new ways to express and understand the drama of learning, I remain grateful to Dr. Michelle Flax.

The photograph for the book cover is titled "After education," by Sharon Sliwinsky. I thank her for this work.

In preparing this manuscript, the following individuals provided editorial assistance: Jen Gilbert, Sarah Dingle, and Kate Kaul. I also want to acknowledge Laurie Searl, Senior Production Editor and Priscilla Ross, director of State University of New York Press, for seeing this project through its completion.

I take this opportunity to acknowledge that an early version of chapter 3, originally published as "Why Return to Anna Freud? Some Notes from a Teacher Educator," in *Teaching Education* 10:1 (1998): 3–16; an earlier version of chapter 4 with the same title, originally published in *International Journal of Leadership in Education* 14:2 (1999): 313–35 (http://www.tandf.co.uk/journals); and an earlier version of chapter 5, in *Regarding Sedgwick: Essays on Queer Culture and Critical Theory*, edited by Stephen Barber and David L. Clark, Routledge 2002.

CHAPTER ONE

DIFFICULT EDUCATION

Something about education makes us nervous. In fact, Sigmund Freud accords to education and civilization the development of various neuroses and unhappiness. Yet to imagine this view, the narratives of education must be conceived broadly as the means of both expressing and encountering reality and phantasy. All at once, the time and reach of education can move backward and forward when we recall our history of learning through our childhood, through friendship and love, through the force of ideas, through encounters with cinema, books, and ordinary accidents, and through our hopes for influencing others and being influenced. This particular education is a play between the present and past, between presence and absence, and then, by that strange return that Sigmund Freud (1914a) describes as deferred: it is registered and revised by remembering, repeating, and working through. If we make education from anything, we can make education from experiences that were never meant to be education, and this unnerves our educational enterprise.

When Sigmund Freud (1930) argued that education carries psychical consequences, not many people were convinced. After all, a great deal of the official history of education depends upon confining its sphere to concrete manifestations: the school, the textbook, and the objectives. It would take the child analysts—particularly Anna Freud and Melanie Klein—to draw us deeper into the psychical drama both of having to be educated and trying to educate others. But even for these women, whom I will

1

introduce shortly, a certain incredulity—a resistance—persists toward their work and their world. Freud, however, brought the enterprise of education and the vicissitudes of its phantoms to everyday problems of reality testing and saw in this relation a constitutive failing. In *Civilization and Its Discontents*, he warned educators that idealizing the world for children and promising them happiness in a life without conflict would only incur helplessness and future disappointment. This book was written between the World Wars, and Freud felt that education would be more relevant, more useful to those subjected to it and to the world, if educators could prepare students for the harshness and difficulties of life and for the inevitable problems of aggression and violence. This plea to educators was the least of his worries, for Freud's critique of education draws him into a deeper psychoanalytic paradox. If aggression is unavoidable, if it is not just a problem between people but, more pertinently, an operative within each person, how can anyone prepare for what is already there? And, can education even know its own aggression? These questions returned Freud to the profession of psychoanalysis. Can psychoanalysis, itself a helping profession, avoid the dangers of trying to educate? What is the difference between psychoanalysis and education? Does psychoanalytic education, for example, avoid Freud's critique? How does one think about education without calling forth or stumbling upon the force of history made from one's own education?

In Freud's writing, for instance, in his discussions on group psychology and psychoanalytic technique, and even in his reminiscence over his own susceptibility to teachers, education persists as being necessary to the very construction of psychoanalytic theory. It may be that both fields have the same trouble: that which makes the heart beat and break belongs to the question of learning and not learning at all. However, responses to not learning in formal education and not learning in the analytic setting differ dramatically. It seems as though in analysis one can wait patiently for education to become meaningful. In an early paper on psychoanalytic technique, Freud (1914a) suggests this lingering time, barely touching on the question of education: "The doctor has nothing else to do than to wait and let things take their course, a course which cannot be avoided nor always hastened. If he holds fast to this conviction he will often be spared the illusion of having failed when in fact he is conducting the treatment on the right lines" (155). Still, the uncertain question of education returns, now as a sustaining illusion. If education makes us nervous, if its effects are felt before they can be known, and if, at times, it is difficult to distinguish failure from learning, education also offers Freud a way to configure the influence of central psychoanalytic relations: the playground of transference, the resistance, and the working through. We can put the psychoanalytic paradox in this way: education makes us nervous, and psychoanalysis touches on raw nerves, but its touch requires something other than our nervous conditions. It will take a vicissitude of education to call education into being.

Can we do without education? Certainly Freud cannot. After all, his method of the talking cure is a strange exploration of a formal and an imagined upbringing. And these psychoanalytic narratives offer a more difficult sense of the workings of history for the psyche and so call attention to the sporadic qualities of learning itself. From a psychoanalytic view, André Green (2000, 2–3) describes our history of learning as a condensation of many fragments of events, even as shards of experience that return when least expected. This leads him to describe history for the psyche through its absences and gaps and as drawing into its narrative what has happened, what we wish had happened, what happened to others but not to us, what happened but cannot be imagined, and what did not happen at all. Such is the creative expression of what we do with the meeting of phantasy and reality. Here and there, history is the return of affect: pining, disappointment, envy, and wish. It also is the narration of and resistence to these shadowy experiences. And it is precisely with this strange and estranging mixture that the otherness of our educational archive returns, now as psychoanalytic inquiry.

While the relation between analyst and analysand can be likened to a voluntary school for analysis, to compare formal education to the psychoanalytic experience meets a psychoanalytic resistance. Whereas formal education and upbringing are organized by deliberate actions and advanced plans, these ideal assumptions are obstacles to the only rule in psychoanalytic work—free association, allowing anything to come to mind without the confines of having to make sense. Formal institutional education may be seen as opposing phantasy, but psychoanalysis views phantasy as central to its work and to one's capacity to think. Analytic time is quite different from the ordinary chronology of classrooms, grades, semesters, and years. It is a play between reality and phantasy, between time lost and refound, and between the meeting of the unconscious and the narrative. Analytic time is recursive and repetitious, reconstructed from psychoanalytic theories of deferred action, resistance, and the transference, and from the interpretation of the defenses. And yet even this fictive time returns us to education, indeed, to the work of culture: where interpretation was, there education shall become.[1]

Freud tried to separate education and psychoanalysis over his long career, and nowhere did this labor feel more painful than when he tried to comment on the question of child analysis. He became caught in debates over whether child analysis can be psychoanalysis when the child is under the continuous influence of education. At one point, Freud (1925c) tried to settle the dilemma with what he called "a conservative ring": "It is to the effect that the work of education is something *sui generis*: it is not to be confused with psycho-analytic influence and cannot be replaced by it . . . after-education is something quite different from the education of the immature" (274). This was Freud's second attempt to distinguish the difference. A few years earlier, he (1916) had tried to separate these fields, only to bring them together again: "This work of overcoming resistances is the essential function of analytic treatment; the patient has to accomplish it and the doctor makes this possible for him with the help of suggestion operating in the *educative* sense. For that reason psychoanalytic treatment has justly been described as a kind of *after-education*" (451, emphasis in original). The editors of the *Standard Edition* offer a footnote on this term: "where, incidentally, the German word '*Nacherziehung*' ('after-education') is wrongly translated [in Freud's text as] 're-education' " (451).[2]

The problem is that translating after-education as re-education confines to indoctrination experiences of being influenced and of influencing others and so cannot wrest the transference—or the unconscious ways we use our history to encounter what is not yet history—away from hypnotic suggestion. It also suggests there is something wrong with being susceptible to events that may or may not address us, and so re-education does not describe the work of reconstruction that our histories of learning require. Two dynamic actions allow after-education its diphasic qualities. After-education refers us back to an original flaw made from education: something within its very nature has led it to fail. But it also refers to the work yet to be accomplished, directing us toward new constructions.

After-education refers both to past mistakes and to the new work of constructing one's history of education after the experience of education. In one sense, the concept of after-education signifies a kind of correction. Habits of avoidance—inhibitions of curiosity—are cultivated in education as a defense against its structures of authority, dependency, and interference. And these strategies, affected by what they defend against, also preserve anxiety in learning. So to move the idea of after-education beyond re-education, the methods that make education—explicit instruction, didacticism, moralism, and so on—must be doubted and set aside for a new learning disposition to be constructed.[3] If Freud tried to undo the aftereffect of education without educating, his understanding of education was made from trying to distinguish learning from indoctrination, influence from hypnotic suggestion, and working through from acting out. So he offered a compromise that would conjugate both fields in ways we are still trying to understand—*after-education*, a strange tense of grammar that associates but does not complete the fragments of experiences made when two dimensions of time communicate: the reconstructed time of psychoanalysis and the exigency of education.

What is education that it may need an afterward? Freud (1911) offers one glimpse of this dilemma in an early essay when he ties mental functioning to the pleasure and reality principles and then catches education in that knot. Education, at least at first, is caught up in the harshness of reality *and* the oceanic pleasures of love, a combination that animates libidinal tension for both the educator and the student:

> *Education* can be described without much ado as an incitement of the pleasure principle and to its replacement by the reality principle; it seeks, that is, to lend its help to the developmental process which affects the ego. To this end it makes use of an offer of love as reward from educators, and it therefore fails if a spoilt child thinks that it possesses that love in any case and cannot lose it whatever happens. (224)

If education is indeed a necessary part of the human condition, it must be conditional in its mode of exchange. The very conditions of education are subject to the yearnings and dreams that animate existence. In Freud's view, education and love are intimates, but their exchange is as precarious as are the realities proffered. At times, the influence that is also education can sustain relations of dependency and helplessness. If it promises unconditional love, then the inevitable withdrawal of that love will incur resentment and misunderstanding. Freud suggests that if education incites pleasure, and if it also attempts to move pleasure closer to reality, then this very trajectory requires that we think about education after the experience of education.

Near the end of his life, Freud (1940a) returned to the work of thinking made after education, as a corrective to relations in education and to the educator herself or himself. Education continues to appear as a problem of self/other relations and of interiority, and nowhere is this more evident than in an unintended consequence of having to learn: the superego springs from the history of these relations of love, dependency, and authority. The superego is made from, contains, and expresses the strange history of love and authority encountered and imagined. But this psychical agency also is aggressive. Its aggression legitimates itself through the very process of rationality and guilt that education also must employ. Yet the superego also is another site for after-education, and so Freud's advice to the analyst is worth considering, because it recognizes the difficult cost of educational temptation:

> However much the analyst may be tempted to become a teacher, a model and ideal for other people and to create men in his own image, he should not forget that is not his task in the analytic relationship and indeed he will be disloyal to his task if he allows himself to be led on by his inclinations. . . . In all his attempts at improving and educating the patient the analyst should respect [the patient's] individuality. (175)

Something difficult occurs in helping relationships. We are apt to forget our differences. That respect of the other's otherness is, for Freud, precisely where education founders and begins.

Freud is not the only one who is uncertain in our uses of education, how education can reverse its content and turn against itself, and indeed, how to analyze its mechanisms of defense, its symptoms, and its dreams. We find discussions of education and its nervous conditions in the most unusual places: in a spate of contemporary novels, where the university is the stage for betrayal and misunderstandings; in popular films, where heroic teachers, aliens, and teenagers vie for glory; in comic sketches that exaggerate the absurdity of school rituals; and, most intimately, in our dreams. In dream time, the school itself is the stage for revenge and rescue fantasies, sexual intrigue, and the return of all forms of forgetting usually concealed in waking hours. Made from that difficult combination of love and hate, from excess of affect that experience cannot complete, these narratives of education draw their force from literary design: the epic, the tragedy, the comedy, and the *Bildungsroman*. Expelled by education, phantasy artfully returns to invite second thoughts through the reconstruction of events in education. We can read these literary expressions as symptoms, as a compromise between the wish and the need, as a return of the repressed, and as a placeholder for what has been missed. Then we might also interpret the fictions of education as trying to say something difficult about determining what belongs to the inside of education and what belongs to its outside, what is conviction and what is imposition, and what belongs to the immediacy of education and what comes after education. We need the tropes of fiction to lend a quota of our affect to symbolizing the forces and expressions of education, because when we are trying to say something about education, this education and that phantasy are difficult to pry apart. And that makes us nervous.

Throughout this book, I explore a series of psychoanalytic arguments over the uses of reality and phantasy for thinking through the experiences of education by way of the question, *what is education that it should give us such trouble?* The question first arose from a certain exasperation I experienced while studying the work of some difficult figures in the history of child psychoanalysis—beginning with Anna Freud and Melanie Klein— who seemed to haunt, sometimes explicitly and other times almost imperceptibly, the history of dilemmas in representing education. Their arguments are instructive, because both analysts attempted to influence and undo both the education of children and the education of psychoanalysts.

These analysts also argued over timing, offering different emphases on what can happen before, during, and after education. Each offers fascinating and at times fantastically cruel narratives of education. When they faced one another, their controversial debates opened educational reasoning to all that can confuse it: where to put the vicissitudes of reality and phantasy in learning to live with others. I began to surround these analysts with distant others, juxtaposing people who never actually met but when imagined together allowed me to raise crucial questions about the reach, timing, and limits of contemporary education. These two analysts invite the idea that any education does not just require crisis but is, in and of itself, an exemplary crisis: that events both actual and imagined are forcibly felt before they can be known. This, for them, provokes the design we come to call "learning" and what we come to understand, in retrospect, as "history." Their work begins with the insight that making a signature on knowledge through our thoughts and social relations is, at first, an arduous affair. Each explores the idea that learning and terror are not easily distinguishable from curiosity and pleasure. They warn that devastating experiences within the self occur when education bonds with idealization, denies its own difficulties and the difficulties of others, and involves the absolute splitting of good and bad and of failure and success in terms that disregard human complexity. Simply put, their thinking about the difficulties of education might be used to encourage us to explore our own associations with education.

What then is education that it should give us such trouble? This question is a central leitmotif, and while I will offer a wide-ranging sense of what education becomes affixed to, I use the notion of trouble to consider two related difficulties, drawn throughout this book. One difficulty is with opening the definition of education to include events that resist but nonetheless shape education, such as not learning, ignorance, aggression, and even phantasies. The qualities of this first difficulty also will appear when I use the term *education* to characterize the formation of psychic structures and strategies shaping this inner world. I will depend upon the theories of Melanie Klein to consider what can best be thought of as an education that comes before education, a potential trouble, a precociousness found in psychological knowledge that Klein named as phantasy. The second trouble concerns trying to know the outside world. Education will be a means to enlarge one's sense of reality. It will focus on the practices and theories of education writ large, and so education will be used to signify, for all ages, both crisis and promise. The difficulty of making a relation to reality will be dependent upon some of Anna Freud's theories on the necessity and dangers of education. With this turn of affairs, education will stand in as a shortcut for describing the maturation of children and the experience of development. Then it will be akin to the German notion of *Bildung*, thus signifying the simultaneous tensions of formation, process, and its results. With the help of Anna Freud, education will be the trouble made from relations between parents and children and teachers and students. It will inaugurate, for the adult, a crisis that gradually calls for thinking.

Education then reappears as a social relation, as a quality of the psychical, and also as an institution that draws upon, even as it influences and is influenced by these events. It will refer to how adults learn a profession and how a profession comes to affect itself. In that context, education is the result of what happens when institutional policies meet group psychology and when education is experienced without being consciously thought. And, when used in its institutional sense, education will refer to a social imaginary. I juxtapose arguments in the field of psychoanalysis over the education of analysts with discussions that concern the education of teachers in schools and in the university. There, education becomes a series of theories, strategies, and relations with self and others, an argument over which knowledge serves its intentions, and even as a defense against the uncertainty of existence made from not knowing what to do but still needing to think.

Most generally, however, I will refer to education in terms of the animation, elaboration, and perhaps refinement of psychological knowledge made through psychical dynamics and its psychical representatives. In its ineffable sense, education will feature in the internal world of object relations. Education will then reemerge as a means to symbolize and construct the significance of this other history, and it will be made from a particular revision of psychical life: the wavering between breakdowns in meaning and our urges for their reparation. Education is thus a drama that stages the play between reality and phantasy and a question that leaves its trace in something interminable about our desire to know and to be known.

My orientation to the trouble in education is a patchwork of Anna Freud's insistence that education is made from all sorts of interference, and Melanie Klein's argument that the desire for creativity and construction emerges from destruction and negativity.[4] While Anna Freud emphasizes the work of reality testing and sees in this work the means for the ego to transform its expectations, anticipations, perceptions, and even its worries over what might count as interference from the outside, Melanie Klein privileges the importance of an interior interference she calls "phantasies." Klein believes a certain freedom can be achieved by elaborating phantasies through a knowledge of their workings and uses. In her view, phantasies come first, and thinking comes afterward. Anna Freud's direction is otherwise; the ego's freedom is intimately bound to its interest in the world, its relations with others, and to its capacity to question and adjust the reach of its defenses. If internal conflicts come before they can be understood, sublimation makes an afterward. They do agree on one point, a commonality that is worked upon throughout this book but highlighted in the concluding chapter, where I explore their shared views on the importance of loneliness to thinking. Both analysts, albeit in different ways, maintain the view that the ego's mechanisms of defense are just different ways of thinking. Together, their respective orientations narrate as contention the theater of education. It will be the staging of that strange encounter with reality and phantasy and so this will rewrite our very capacity to construct knowledge of the self and others.[5]

Education staggers under the heavy burden of representing its own cacophony of dreams, its vulnerabilities, and its incompleteness. If, in education, we must experience a confusion of time that makes distinctions among the past, present, and future difficult to maintain, if the love being offered heralds an impossible and a tantalizing promise and, then, if the thought of education must suffer from the grief of retrospection, from an after-education, then these processes are uncanny. Humans, after all, work both their breakdowns in meanings and their repairs of significance in similar ways. To think the thought of education, we must argue over what counts as education and miseducation, as neurosis and insight, as idealization and disillusion, as progress and regression, and as human and inhuman. We also must argue, as the analysts did, over the nature of the educational relationship and how emotional ties between people both allow and inhibit our understanding of what becomes of the work of learning. All of these vacillations of education, made from something in excess of deliberate planning, predicable outcomes, or translatable theory, are its nervous systems.

There was a moment in the history of child psychoanalysis when two schools of thought—Anna Freud's and Melanie Klein's—clashed over problems of research strategies, knowledge claims, techniques of practice, training regimes, and the ways in which the adult and child might be imagined and enlivened. This clash tied the problem of uncertainty in practices to debates on the nature of reality and phantasy. Readers will encounter what are now known as the "Freud–Klein Controversies" in chapter 2. Beyond the explicit history that these disputes offer, however, and in much of this book, their insistent arguments also are emblematic of the problem of thinking about education. This is because they argued over the status of reality and phantasy in learning to live and in the very poesies and processes of knowledge and its authority.[6] More than glimpsing the differences between what are roughly thought of in psychoanalysis as the schools of ego psychology and object relations,[7] beyond attempting any synthesis of a contentious and lively history that continues to haunt our contemporary efforts, and beyond putting certain figures to rest in peace, my purpose is to bring the difficulties psychoanalytic views suggest to education with the difficulties education brings to psychoanalysis. In doing so, I will propose that if education makes us nervous, it need not end in neurosis.

Readers may notice that my arguments carry an ambivalent tone, and perhaps, occasionally, touch on raw nerves. At times, I verge on unfashionable claims by arguing for the importance of confronting knowledge in excess of personal experience, of accepting our constitutive asocial vulnerabilities, and of posing education as difficult, as other to the dream of progress and mastery, even as we also must risk a theory of history, sociality, and education. While researching for this book, I found myself in the ambivalent position of becoming utterly persuaded first by Anna Freud and then by Melanie Klein. Here are just a few stumbles: *Yes, of course, it is crucial to center the problem of anxieties that are in excess of social causes. Yes, of course, reality causes misery. Yes, misery requires neither reasons nor rationality. Yes, of course, it is crucial to center the influence of actual others over the phantasy life of the individual. Yes, analysis should have an educational core. Yes, it is best to keep education away from the analytic setting and analysis away from education.* And yet, while reading their work alongside those who argued with it and supported it, I also experienced a certain fear and incredulity toward them both. I disagreed with parts of their theory that rendered sexuality in homophobic terms,[8] or that affixed gender too easily to the dictates of social convention. My resistance to some of their theories also was made from a desire to escape their respective gambles over the reach and strange returns of psychical reality.

Despite these protests, however, I found myself feeling pathos in and attraction to their long years of research and their respective lives.[9] After all, their lives were made in what Kristeva (2001b) calls "the psychoanalytic century,"[10] where the line between madness and sanity became more faint and, where the speaking subject, testimony, and witnessing became associated with justice and working through. These women were caught not just in the nexus of the contentious early history of child psychoanalysis and, then, in how it would be chronicled, remembered, and disputed, but their lives and theories spanned much of the history of the twentieth century: its World Wars, its technological revolutions, its universalization of education and human rights, its gender and sexual revolutions, and its long-standing disputes over what it means to be human, to be subject to both history and phantasy. To figure the history of education through its controversies over the status of learning, knowledge, and authority and through philosophical and literary discussion of the problems of understanding self/other relations may mean reconsidering the relevance of psychoanalytic theories from the vantages of Melanie Klein and Anna Freud. It also may mean returning to the status of phantasy and reality in our educational thinking and, perhaps like Sigmund Freud, trying to figure their educative and miseducative senses.

It is useful to reconsider Anna Freud and Melanie Klein together, because they not only emphasize different qualities of reality and phantasy but suggest divergent methods for how these qualities can even be known. Their arguments are not just about which woman might be seen as carrying the authority of Freud, although, as we will see in chapter 2, Freud tried to settle this competition before his death. Both women also establish the relevancy of psychoanalytic theory to children by their witnessing the child's psychical complexity; in doing so, they may have inadvertently offered something quite stunningly difficult, even audacious to the ways we can now imagine education and the relations that compose it. That something has to do with the ways in which love and

hate—through the dynamics of loss and mourning—animate the poten-
tiality of psychical and historical reality and our capacity to be susceptible
to education. They allow us theoretical speculations on the nature of
aggression but urge us to do so with a curiosity and patience that can
provoke us to think with creative reach and to inquire with compassion.

If noting such grand purposes could not help my wavering, considering the way their arguments resemble our contemporary breakdowns
did give me a pause.[11] After all, a great deal of their fight concerned the
problem of splitting: choosing sides, being recognized, expelling that
which a theory cannot configure, and, most problematic of all, resisting
free association, perhaps the only rule that makes psychoanalysis, well,
psychoanalysis.[12] And yet, both women and their schools do require dis-
cretion, as they try, in very different ways, to characterize the neglected
relations between reality and phantasy, consciousness and the unconscious,
adult and child, and practice and theory. They ask us to accept the incredulous reach of psychical life—our own and that of others—and still hold
onto varying degrees of the world outside of our psychical realities, to its
constraints and possibilities, and the conditions we confront that are not
of our own making, yet still require something from us. If each of their
orientations, to child analysis and, to some extent, to the education of
teachers and analysts, acts out the very wish for knowledge that they tried
to analyze in others, then reconsidering their methods also can mean raising new questions for what we take to be the workings of reality and
phantasy in our education, provided that we can tolerate what both women
have to say.

Melanie Klein asks us to accept an inaugural negativity at the heart
of psychical design—a time before education that nonetheless still exerts
influence. This kernel of negativity creates, for Klein, our urge for reparation, the gradual translation of inchoate demands and feelings of persecution into affectation, the desire to think of and care for the other. It
is a process that can never be completed. In her view, there is a destructive force within that must, over the course of one's life, be overcome and
affected by another of our nascent promises: the capacity to love and
experience gratitude. She offers a theory of psychical positions as the
beginning of thinking, made from a primary anxiety and terrible helplessness. Becoming thoughtful toward the self and others entails finessing,
not limiting, the creative elaboration of phantasy. Klein believed this is
best accomplished through developing knowledge of phantasy and learning to respect the workings of one's own psychical reality. Without this
respect for interiority, Klein would maintain, there can be no relation to

reality. For Klein, the psychoanalytic problem concerns our phantasmagoric creations and how these originative creatures, what she called "persecutory and part objects," structure and are themselves structured by perception, desire, and experiences of being alone and with others.[13]

For Anna Freud, what makes the psychic heart beat and break belongs to instinctual conflict and then to the ego defenses that evolve slowly and in relation to, or in tension with, dramas staged between the actual world and the inner conflict. Anxiety plays a starring role in the theater of our psychical world, and its character is elaborated as ego defense mechanisms. Anna Freud's analytic technique with children has a normative goal: adaptation to the reality principle, sublimation of the pleasure principle, and an interest in using ego defenses more flexibly. After all, she might observe, our ego is rather fragile, because it evolves in relation to others and arrives before the self can stage understanding. And so, the ego must, in many senses, defend itself against overwhelming stimuli. We can become better reality testers, but this need not mean that we become compliant, conformist, or resistant to changing the very reality that we try to apprehend. Indeed, for Anna Freud, compliance and conformity represent defenses against the anxiety of loneliness, worries over being left out, and worries that one cannot change. It also means that the more rigid the defense mechanism, the harsher reality can seem, which leaves a question for Anna Freud concerning the evolving relation between the ego and its reality. Chapter 3 returns to these particular dilemmas by considering the working of ego defense mechanisms in experiences of learning to teach. There I explore some small controversies of learning that occurred when I tried to teach something about the theories of Anna Freud to undergraduate university student teachers.

Quite differently, the psychoanalytic theories of Anna Freud and Melanie Klein take what we imagine to be education to its limits by opening its borders of reason and rationality to unconscious phantasy and to ego demands that meet these processes in the other. Education is lost and found, they remind us, somewhere between intellectual inhibition and social prohibition, somewhere between the search for pleasure and the confrontation with reality, somewhere between the negativity of the death drive and the integrating work of the Eros and of reparation. The vacillations between self and other, perception and desire, phantasy and reality, and "primary processes" and "secondary processes" begin in phantasy.[14] While these speculations can seem to dispute the force of outside circumstances and of conditions not of our own making, they also may be used to heighten our attention to the problem of how the world is noticed, lived in, and used, to what it is to make lively and relevant selves, and to figuring out something new about the difficult work of learning to live with others. These tensions are the subject of chapter 4, animated by the dilemmas of thinking within the dynamics of group psychology.

Rather than view one school of thought as being more important or more true than its adversary, and rather than decide, once and for all, whether the views of Anna Freud or Melanie Klein are beyond the pale of contemporary education, readers are asked to consider both orientations: when they meet, when they seem far apart, and when they transform something of their respective insistencies. Read through the exemplary conflict of the Freud–Klein Controversies, education proffers narratives of lives that one will never live and glimpses of histories that require something unanticipated from our present encounters with them; education also is the place where individuals are asked to imagine something about realities that they do not yet know or know so well. These gambles, that knowledge matters, mean that education can be thought of more vitally as residing between phantasy and reality, between the breakdowns of meaning and the afterward urges for reparation.

So the ghosts of Anna Freud and Melanie Klein haunt each of these chapters: we will find them in their own controversial discussions, in classroom discussions about their work, in theories of group psychology, and in thinking with other theories and in contexts that they never would have entered and, more than likely, would have avoided. Let us try to see what these tensions they called "education" can mean for our own time. For the rest of what follows, I sketch a series of dilemmas in psychoanalysis, curious problems for education really, that preoccupied our key protagonists and their worthy adversaries. I consider some key debates over the theoretical nature of learning: the philosophical nature of subjectivity and, while not so popular in times of social construction theory, the ontological capacity of humans to transform themselves and others through an original suceptibility to knowledge, social relations, and libidinal bonds. These dilemmas return to help us think about group psychology in chapter 4 and the question of theory and affect in chapter 5. The last chapter continues these themes, from the vantage of theories of loneliness. There, both Melanie Klein and Anna Freud try to construct psychoanalytic histories of learning by their meditation on the relation between loneliness and poignant thinking. How curious, then, that it would take a concept called "loneliness," made from what Kristeva (2001b) calls "the fate of being a stranger" (194), for them to finally meet and for us to reset the time of after-education.

IMPOSSIBLE PROFESSIONS

If each of us holds intimate views on what counts as bad education, ill-prepared teachers, and miserable school settings, then we may also try, at times, to imagine an education that can make the world better and people more generous, encourage tolerance, and banish humiliation to nightmares. And yet, however we try to characterize education, there is a nagging sense that even this work resists any understanding of the uncertainties of our lives and what becomes of our knowledge when we try to communicate it to another. Sigmund Freud may well characterize the problem of education most openly when he calls it, more than once, one of the "impossible professions." How can one stay close to Freud's difficult insistence upon the impossibility of teaching and learning without using it to express tired cynicism, or to represent a certain exhaustion teachers and students make from trying to sort out the problem of what education can and should signify?

Consider the notion of impossibility as a metaphor, as a work of language, that tries to associate education with a constitutive difficulty at the heart of trying to teach and to learn: our idiomatic selves. The concept of impossibility signals a certain excess and distress, which results when the qualities of trying to learn and to teach, namely, the desire to persuade, believe, and transform the self and the other, encounter uncertainty, resistance, and the unknown. All of these remnants are indices of new editions of old conflicts that allow psychical demands to do their strange work. What makes this work both estranging and strange is the paradox in which learning begins in the breakdown of meaning, while these fragments animate the wish that knowledge settles distress and erases what cannot be understood. This is the tension at the heart of psychoanalytic method, described quite beautifully by Christopher Bollas (1999):

> The wish for knowledge must not interfere with a method that defers heightened consciousness in favor of a dreamier frame of mind, encouraging the free movements of images, ideas, pregnant words, slips of the tongue, emotional states and developing relational positions. (35)

The method of free association itself meets an incredible resistance for Freud—there is something maddeningly obdurate, irrational, really, about the human. The early Freud names this madness "sexuality" or "libidinality," the insatiable search for pleasure and the avoidance of pain. A later Freud reaches into something far more frightening: the death drive, the reduction of all tension, the annihilation of conflict. In placing education in the realm of impossible professions, he suggests that the work and workings of education are not immune to their own psychical consequences: narcissism, masochism, sadism, regression, omnipotence, denial, undoing, and all of the forms of aggression that work in the service of destruction. What seems impossible, then, is not so much that we have education. Rather, the impossibility is that however good and intentional our methods may feel, we cannot guarantee, for either ourselves or others, the force, experience, or interpretation of our efforts once they become events in the world of others. That provisional knowledge arrives belatedly, in the form of an existential question such as, what have I really made? After the experience of education, there is still the problem of education.

Sigmund Freud (1925c) first called education one of the "impossible professions" in his foreword to the now almost forgotten study of delinquency, *Wayward Youth,* by August Aichhorn. Aichhorn was a colleague of Freud's and worked closely with Anna Freud in designing after-school programs for working-class youth in Vienna. Freud understood that psychoanalysis, because of its emphasis on the prehistory of the adult, on repressed infantile wishes, and on a prophylactic child psychoanalysis, would offer a great deal of hope to the field of education in terms of preventing neurosis from having a future and in terms of freeing children and adults from superstitious thought, the censoring of sexuality, and crude authoritarian social relations.[15] Indeed, from its inception, child psychoanalysts could not help but talk about neurotic tendencies made from the experience of school: school phobias, running away, not being able to read, early stuttering, school pranks, and even cases of uncontrollable laughter. And by the early 1930s, in Europe, the United Kingdom, North America, and Latin America, the thought experiment known as "psychoanalysis" was influencing—particularly through the work of Anna Freud, August Aichhorn, Siegfried Bernfeld, and Melanie Klein—the ways education could be designed.[16] Freud, however, was ambivalent about what it meant for the human to learn, and he tried to separate himself from both child analysis and education.

And yet, over the course of his long career, Freud returned continually to the dilemmas of educating: he wrote of difficulties made from psychoanalytic technique and of the problems in learning from, as opposed to about, psychoanalysis; he questioned the problem of when analysis is said to be over; and, in debating the meanings of psychoanalysis, he acknowledged its limits. Near the end of his life, he was still struggling with justifying the diverse potential of psychoanalysis and the possibility that the talking cure might offer a means of reconstructing the significance of a history that is no longer available but that still exerts pressure on the ways the present can be experienced. If Freud feigned reticence in transposing psychoanalytic methods beyond the analytic setting—and in the conclusion of this chapter, I will return to the tensions that psychoanalysis offers to social commentary—he also saw his method as offering new constructions to "kernels of historical truths" that could illuminate, even by psychoanalytic myths and its theoretical fictions, larger cultural regressions, historical breakdowns, and societal repressions.[17] That is, he felt that psychoanalysis might have a great deal to say about the human's proclivity to violence, to unhappiness, to charismatic leaders, to group psychology, and to forgetting one's own traumatic origins.

Analyzing the failures that belong to education is not, for Freud, an academic exercise of application, where the thinker is somehow immune to the implications of her or his own argument. In defending the qualifications of lay analysts—or of those who practiced psychoanalysis without a medical degree—Freud (1910) also insists that utilizing psychoanalytic views without oneself being subject to the demands of a personal analysis can only be "wild analysis." The wildness is not because the claims made are out of control, although they can be, but unless psychoanalytic claims direct self-understanding, they can easily become an occasion to act out one's own aggression and disclaim one's own experience. Freud (1925c) suggests this resistance to learning from psychoanalysis when he urges educators to undergo a personal analysis: "A training of this kind is best carried out if a person . . . undergoes an analysis and experiences it on himself: theoretical instruction in analysis fails to penetrate deep enough and carries no conviction" (274). We are back to the problem of conviction: how it is made, what rules its passions, and even why theoretical instruction stops it short. We carry conviction, Freud seems to suggest, when we experience the limit and doubts of trying to construct self-understanding. We carry conviction when we can encounter the vicissitudes of suffering.

Despite Freud's attempts to control the reach and relevance of psychoanalysis to the world beyond the intimate analytic setting, his (1925c) preface to Aichhorn's *Wayward Youth* seems to leave the field of education to others:

My personal share in this application of psycho-analysis has been very slight. At an early age I accepted the *bon mot* which lays it down that there are three impossible professions—educating, healing and government—and I was already fully occupied with the second of them. But it does not mean that I overlook the high social value of the work done by those of my friends who are engaged in education. (273)

And yet, a cursory look through the index of Freud's twenty-four-volume *Standard Edition* complicates his claim to have left the dilemmas of education to others. The index entry under the heading "education" is not half as long as the one under the word "ego," but there are wide-ranging associations: "sexuality," "inhibitions," "prevention of war," and "unsolved problems of." Oddly, Freud's "after-education" is not cross-referenced, although it appears in his preface for Aichhorn. If education is impossible, part of its common impossibility emerges when one tries to consider what education should be responsible for, and whether education can prevent and solve human suffering.

Freud's (1937a) second mention of the impossibility of education is found in one of his last essays, "Analysis Terminable and Interminable," in which he returns to the problem of psychoanalytic technique. Here, education is bleak, entangled in what he calls "negative therapeutic reaction," or the analysands' participation in her illness through the resistance to cure, by which Freud means the painful refusal to risk love and work, even if these chances are utterly vulnerable to loss, disillusion, and melancholia and mourning. The negative therapeutic reaction is a notoriously misunderstood concept, one that posits unconscious investments in not changing and in suffering. These efforts do not belong to rational thought, and they are communicated indirectly, through the symptom. Freud considers the special efforts of the analyst, herself not immune from the negative therapeutic reaction, in trying to practice:

Here let us pause for a moment to assure the analyst that he has our sympathy in the very exacting demands he has to fulfil in carrying out his activities. It almost looks as if analysis were the third of those "impossible" professions in which one can be sure beforehand of achieving unsatisfying results. The other two, which have been known much longer, are education and government. (248)

Shoshana Felman's (1987) exposition of the teachings of Freud and Lacan begins with the difficulty of self-transformation and the transformation of the other. Her sense of the negative therapeutic reaction begins with a passion for ignorance, indeed, the commitment not to know what one already knows! Felman is interested in why there is resistance to knowledge and what this resistance means for pedagogy. She too suggests that unsatisfying results are the very heart of the pedagogical exchange, not because nothing can be known "not so much with lack of knowledge as with resistance to knowledge. Ignorance, suggests Lacan, is a passion" (79). But a passion for what?

"BETWEEN THE THUMB AND THE TEDDY"

Try going back to a time before education. This imaginative effort preoccupied many analysts influenced by Melanie Klein, and it characterized the creative work of D. W. Winnicott.[18] To consider education through Winnicott's (1992b) paradox of indebtedness allows us to meet illusion: education is a relation that exists and does not exist at the same time. Before there is education, there is potential space. In writing about transitional objects, Winnicott's curiosity turns to the not-yet social space that the baby makes between the thumb and the teddy, an early instance of what he calls "the intermediate area of experience" (230). This complex emotional geography is already full of all sorts of experiences, even before it is entered into, and this fullness totters precariously between the subjectively and objectively perceived. Two experiences are confused in this area: the baby is projecting and introjecting objects. We are imagining the chaotic world of phantasy: here, condensed affect that wants before it can know. Along with this internal work, Winnicott points to a potential relation that is neither internal nor external; he describes this as indebtedness, as somewhere "between primary awareness of indebtedness and the acknowledgment of indebtedness ('Say: ta!')" (ibid.). The area is an illusion, and it is tentative; provided that the baby does not have to defend it, this intermediate experience will become creative.

If we cannot know from this forgotten space what the baby experiences as indebtedness, we can speculate about what ruins it. If any outsider makes a decision about the nature of this space, the baby's illusion that experience is hers or his to make will be spoiled. We also can wonder about the nature of this debt—how it will come into awareness, be played out, and even become a relationship, what Winnicott calls "indebtedness." We can imagine as well these qualities as composing education, where the student and teacher come into existence and then accumulate debts of their own. The paradox is that education exists and does not exist at the same time; it is a space already filled with the meanings of others, and yet it still needs to be thought.

Is it only the psychoanalyst who is concerned with the thumb and the teddy? Or is there something essential about the fact of natality that absorbs all sorts of discussion? In his study of philosopher Levinas, Richard Cohen (2001) enjoys the gift of the introduction. That first introduction, the fact of natality, opens our lives to others with promise and vulnerability. From this relation, Cohen sees the question of freedom as inextricably tied to obligation; this emerges from the fact "that we are *born* and not *caused*, and that we necessarily have parents" (22). To narrate what comes after this fact of natality, that a life comes into the world of other lives, that this new life requires introductions, even as it introduces itself, brings education closer to ethics. Cohen's view is not so far away from Winnicott's insistence on the ways baby makes the parent. And both the philosopher and analyst are occupied with the question of how, from such inarticulate beginnings, does the human become humane?

If Cohen brings the necessity of parents into the miasma of beginnings, then Lyotard (1991) stresses not the introduction but the problem of having to learn. The human must learn to become human. Lyotard's argument is deceptively simple: "If humans are born human, as cats are born cats (within a few hours), it would not be . . . possible to educate them. That children have to be educated is a circumstance which only proceeds from the fact that they are not completely led by nature, not programmed" (3). Here is the paradox: We are not led by nature, but without our nature we would not need to be educated. Our helplessness and dependency are the very conditions that make us so susceptible to education. We are born, and this fact of natality creates the baby and the parents. It also turns introduction into obligation. Lyotard provides us with one dilemma that this nature archives, now from the vantage of the adult's awareness of her or his indebtedness to the baby:

> Shorn of speech, incapable of standing upright, hesitating over the objects of its interest, not able to calculate its advantages, not sensitive to common reason, the child is eminently the human because its distress heralds and promises things possible. Its initial delay in humanity, which makes it hostage of the adult community, is also what manifests to this community the

lack of humanity it is suffering from, and which calls on it to become more human. (3–4)

Lyotard's characterization of the relation of the inhuman to the human is such that if the child wants before it knows, others do not just have difficulty in this delay but must use this very distress to educate. Our humanity is that distress that allows for all that will follow, even education: "All education is inhuman," writes Lyotard,

> because it does not happen without constraint and terror; I mean the least controlled, the least pedagogical terror, the one Freud calls castration and which makes him say, in relation to the "good way" of bringing up children, that in any case it will be bad . . . everything in the instituted which, in the event, can cut deep with distress and indetermination is so threatening that the reasonable mind cannot fail to fear in it, and rightly, an inhuman power of deregulation. (4–5)

This melancholy education is made from the least pedagogical experiences, namely, processes of psychical growth: learning to give up magical and omnipotent thinking, noticing when the desire for mastery and absolute knowledge domesticates curiosity and our capacity to be surprised, having to enter into a law greater than the self, and accepting our own fragility, dependence, and faults. These qualities—for both the child and the adult—are the least pedagogical, because they are made from distress, vulnerability, and chance. The terror and constraint of education come from within, even as these impositions are found outside. If psychical development is the least pedagogical experience because it is so subject to the helplessness of our beginnings, to the passion for ignorance, in short, to the unconscious and the return of this repressed, then these modes of resistance offer us another sense of the difficulties of that other development, namely education.

How the human learns is, of course, a very old problem in education, one that is difficult to separate from its other side: upbringing, pedagogical exchange, and how (or whether) one teaches the human to become human. Is there something implicit in or natural to the human that should be honored, or from which we ought to learn? Is nature the place where learning imposes itself? Is there something monstrous, even gothic, about the human that requires drastic prohibitions? These questions still plague our pedagogical imagination. In 1762, Rousseau (1979) offered to his public a "natural" guide that linked child rearing to the bringing up of culture. He created a paper-boy-child—Emile— and tutored him, provided for him, selected only a few books for him, and arranged for his gradual confrontation with the world. Rousseau's was an experiment to help Emile lose time with his own development. On the way to becoming a human, at least in paper form, Emile also served as a foil; Rousseau used Emile as a critique for how children were brought up in his own time, and one of his biggest arguments had to do with when children were thought to be able to reason:

> If children jumped all at once from the breast to the age of reason, the education they are given might be suitable for them. But according to the natural progress, they need an entirely contrary one. . . . The first education ought to be purely negative. It consists not at all in teaching virtue or truth but in securing the heart from vice and the mind from error. (93)

While Rousseau's thought experiment on how to raise a child for eventual self-sufficiency became the grounds for what we now know as progressive and child-centered education, Alan Bloom's (1979) introduction to this classic reminds us of the paradox of Rousseau's moral pedagogy: "What is forgotten is that Rousseau's full formula is that while the child must always do what he wants to do, he should want to do only what the tutor wants him to do" (13).

Freedom, it seems, is not quite free but rather binds obligation and indebtedness to constraint and terror. This difficult equation was made years later by Mary Shelley's (1996) cautionary tale on the impossibility of education, this time through a confrontation with science and poetry. Perhaps the novel *Frankenstein; Or, The Modern Prometheus* should be read as a rejoinder to Rousseau's *Emile*. Shelley offers us a mad scientist's sublime creation, a nameless creature who learns to speak and read on his own and then, because of language and literacy, suffers from loneliness so profound that it drives this inhuman being into human madness. In one conversation with Victor Frankenstein, the creature compares himself to the first biblical man, Adam. Much too late, he demands of his creator: "Make me happy, and I shall again be virtuous" (57). The lonely creature requires his distresses be acknowledged by way of being loved. But the creature also may be mistaken in his hope that being happy leads to virtuousness. The other side of this equation is spoiled by Victor

Frankenstein, whose manic triumph, after the creature was given life, turns into a disillusionment in which he feels only horror toward his own awful experiment. Without a sense of indebtedness made from this terror, education would remain inhuman and our creature, along with Victor, would remain all too human.

The preoccupation with what exactly the baby or the child is capable of, and with what adults ought to do with it, belongs to our modern sensibilities. The baby returns us to the nature of being and to the question of history.[19] When Hannah Arendt (1993) wrote of North American education, she too returned to the baby and to our fact of natality, but only to appeal to the adult's indebtedness to the child. The fact of natality is actually three facts for Arendt. New events enter the world, and so natality consists of a promise. Second, natality also is a state of extreme dependency and vulnerability. This gives rise to its third feature, natality ushers in obligation. It requires something from those already in the world, just as those already in the world require something from the new. The fact of natality thus references the promise of sociality for renewal and continuity, a promise easily broken. Kristeva's (2001a) meditation on Arendt's thinking centers on this very human condition, and she may as well have been referring to processes of education: "Arendt reconstructs the political realm from scratch based on two key notions— the birth of individuals and the frailty of actions—and on two psychopolitical interventions—forgiveness and the promise" (204). These dilemmas of the unknown are, for Arendt, the crisis of education. And just as in the fact of natality, there is something utterly ordinary about the crisis of education, even if the demands of responding to the human condition are extraordinary.

Arendt's move is bold, for she is addressing the situation of education in North America. She asks, how can one suggest, for all of the devastations of the twentieth century, that North American education is in crisis? One sees in newspapers daily laments over standards, over literacy attainment, and over a certain lack of discipline, whether it is found in the students, the curriculum, or the community. But when compared to the wars in Europe, Arendt goes on, and perhaps in reference to Adorno's (1998) question, what can education be after Auschwitz?, such worries seem irrelevant. Still, for Arendt, education is a promise, a responsibility, and a social obligation; precisely because these are its vulnerable conditions, it must, by its very nature, inaugurate itself through the crisis of sociality. Like Lyotard's, Arendt's suggestion for thinking education as crisis also is deceptively simple:

Aside from these general reasons that would make it seem advisable for the layman to be concerned with trouble in fields about which, in the specialist sense he may know nothing (and this, since I am not a professional educator, is of course my case when I deal with a crisis in education), there is another even more cogent reason for his concerning himself with a critical situation in which he is not immediately involved. And that is the opportunity, provided by the very fact of crisis—which tears away facades and obliterates prejudices—to explore and inquire into whatever has been laid bare of the essence of the matter, and the essence of education is natality, the fact that human beings are *born* into the world. (1993, 174, emphasis in original)

If Arendt reminds us of our big obligations toward strangers and even in caring about fields in which we are not specialists, Winnicott brings us to the smaller responsibilities that perhaps allow us to notice the crisis differently. For Winnicott as well, there is something absolutely delicate that must be respected from this fact of being born. It has to do with the work that the infant does, along with the work that the adult must do to allow the infant its explorations. The indebtedness that an adult makes with the infant begins from the adult's willingness to not ask a certain question about the infant's experience. Winnicott (1992b) warns us against pedagogical intrusions: "*Of the transitional object it can be said that it is a matter of agreement between us and the baby that we will never ask the question 'Did you conceive of this or was it presented to you from without?' The important point is that no decision on this point is expected. The question is not to be formulated*" (239–40, emphasis in original). This careful indecision depends upon the nature both of the baby and the transitional object: with the transitional object, the baby is participating in the adventure of symbolization and also designing what Winnicott calls the "first not-me possession," the nature and use of an attachment. With the transitional object, reality and phantasy can be safely confused. It is the allowance for this confusion that ushers in curiosity and thinking.

Winnicott's description of the use of the transitional object matches later uses of knowledge in academic work: attachment to the object includes both cuddling and mutilation; it seems to survive the baby's aggression; it cannot change unless the baby makes it change; it seems to have a reality of its own; it is close to the baby's point of view; and, in the end, it is discarded when eventually it loses these meanings

(1992b, 233). If all goes well, and this is Winnicott's phrasing, then this loss is not to be mourned. But neither is the discarded object just forgotten. The transition does take some time to play out, because the qualities that Winnicott notes and the naïveté of the claimed authorship fray the borders of the passion for ignorance and knowledge. Because the transitional object is bestowed with this peripatetic passion, it would break the illusion to ask, did you find it, or did you create it? For to ask the baby if she or he found or created the teddy, or the blanket, or the cotton would impose a point of view that would simply devastate the attachment so painstakingly made, the attachment that consoles distress and heralds indebtedness. The transitional object cannot be separated from its use and, in a certain way, its user: the play of the transitional object vacillates between madness and care, ruthlessness and petting, biting and kissing, banishing and cherishing. Its point of view is not yet a point of view but rather symbolizes a reality so magnetizing that it absorbs and survives the owner's affect.

"MINUS K"

If some are questions best left unasked, then others are worth asking. While Winnicott offers us a way to conceive of how the baby makes and finds knowledge, Wilfred Bion wonders what inhibits the capacity of adults to attach passionately to new ideas and people.[20] He asks the startling question, why is there a hatred of learning? Bion considers the psychical experience of thinking in groups and the phenomena of what he calls "thoughts awaiting thinkers." "The problem is simplified," Bion (1994b) writes, "if 'thoughts' are regarded as epistemologically prior to thinking and that thinking has to be developed as a method or apparatus for dealing with 'thoughts' " (83). Bion was interested in designing a system of notation used when listening to his analysand's free associations and when studying how individuals think in groups. One of these symbols was called "Minus K," where K stood in both for the problem of realizing "knowledge" and for accepting new ideas and new people as valuable and worthy. "Minus K" is a destructive attack upon links between ideas and people. It overtakes thoughts when groups feel somehow devalued by new members, and when ideas that have not yet been thought are felt as if they were sent to ruin a pristine reality. More devastatingly, the group's sense of its own moral superiority feels attacked, and thereby the group creates the conditions for "Minus K" to stand in for the group's own hatred of development. Symptoms of this hatred are conceptual: the group splits ideas into rigid formulations of good and bad, and this splitting fuels its aggressive moralism toward new ideas or what it does not understand. All of this aggression is sustained as a group necessity, for in "Minus K," the group feels attacked by ideas, language, and potential differences within the group. What, Bion wonders, makes new knowledge so threatening? Why are new ideas so difficult to digest that they seem to provoke mental indigestion and even regurgitation?

Bion's attempt to answer these questions draws on the work of his analyst, Melanie Klein, and her concepts of envy and gratitude. Envy is a particularly violent affect, different from its more common usage offered perhaps as a backhanded compliment of admiration, such as when we "envy" a colleague's success or vacation. Klein's (1957) essay, "Envy and Gratitude," sketches a series of confusions in thinking that inhibits or undermines the capacity to craft meaningful relations with others. She proposes that confusion itself is a defense, the key confusion being between good and bad. Indeed, Klein's concept of envy does not include outside rivalry but rather an internal drama that has to do with what Likierman (2001) noticed as "a malign resentment of [the object's] goodness" (175). Envy is a violent affect in which goodness itself is rejected, and Bion viewed this violence as "Minus K."

Klein returns to our earliest object relation, her first fact of natality: the breast.[21] To the infant who experiences bodily sensations before meaning arrives, the breast offers both good and bad phantasies: it is blamed and hated when needs are felt but not satisfied. This is Klein's model for splitting.[22] The good breast assuages the infant's anxiety, and the bad breast persecutes the infant by holding its nourishment back, by not being available. Splitting, for Klein, is one of the human's earliest defenses against unbearable anxiety; from this severe phantasy the confusion of good and bad emerges to create the conditions for the painful problem of integration, of acceptance of both good and bad. This acceptance is made through the development of gratitude, a poignant form of thinking indebted to the creativity and separateness of the other. But for the other to be seen as separate, the self must learn to acknowledge her or his own psychical reality, including phantasies of destruction and the guilt left in their wake. These painful realizations are, for Klein, the material from which we construct reality. "Together with happy experiences," she writes,

> unavoidable grievances reinforce the innate conflict between
> love and hate, in fact, basically between life and death instincts,

and result in the feeling that a good and bad breast exist. As a consequence, early emotional life is characterized by a sense of losing and regaining the good object. In speaking of an innate conflict between love and hate, I am implying that the capacity both for love and for destructive impulses is, to some extent, constitutional, though varying individually in strength and interacting from the beginning with external conditions. (1957, 180)

The confusion of love and hate exists from the beginning, and the raw combination of this primal or one can even say prehistoric, conflict is the material from which thinking is gradually made. Paradoxically, thinking is aroused from conflict and so carries traces of its own difficult emergency. It may seem, at first glance, as if Klein is suggesting an absolute boundary between love and hate, that hate is something we must stop feeling, and love is something we must feel in spite of ourselves. However, to idealize these affective relations, or better, what Klein calls "object relations," is to forget what in the human is least pedagogical and, at the same time, utterly susceptible to influence: phantasy. For Klein, envy "is the angry feeling that another person possesses and enjoys something desirable—the envious impulse being to take it away or to spoil it" (1957, 181). The breast is the baby's first object of love and hate, and so of envy. It will be the experience that allows the baby to move from "*deprivation* into *frustration*" (Kristeva 2001b, 142; emphasis in original). But it also will be the first object where enjoyment and, hence, gratitude is made. From gratitude, Klein believes that the "capacity to make reparation" (1957, 189) gradually becomes stronger. If the infant can come to tolerate frustration, to understand the other as offering new experiences, to enjoy the feeling of making a bond, and to accept that both frustration and satisfaction are needed parts of life, then she or he will slowly make from this anxiety feelings of gratitude, something needed in later life for the capacity to make reparation, indeed, to feel indebtedness to the other. The hopeful trajectory that Klein sets for thought, her sense of promise and obligation, begins in anxiety and splitting, progresses to envy, and then to gratitude, and the urge for reparation. Then there can be an acceptance of mourning. For Klein and Bion, thinking is just another word for symbolizing and working through crisis. Perhaps the same trajectory can be said for what becomes of our education, provided that we can tolerate a frustration that is also education.

We have almost come full circle, seeing the fact of natality from the perspectives of baby, parent, and then theorists. From the paper child to the paper monster, philosophers and novelists try to invoke something of the dilemmas of the duration and aftermath of education. Perhaps Arendt comes closest to the crisis: We are born, and we need education. If both education and natality are in the realm of the fragility of actions, neither being born nor having to learn is an experience that can be known in advance. And this radical uncertainty—what Arendt called "crisis"—is the structuring tension in education. On the one side, there are passionate scenarios of love, hate, and aggression; on the other side, indebtedness, promise, and forgiveness. The work of thinking carries the traces and disturbances of both sides, but what invokes the need to think, as opposed to the capacity to think, is the presence of the other. This too is a fact of natality: there needs to be another. Likierman's (2001) discussion of Melanie Klein concludes with her view that, like other analysts, Klein wandered into the dramatic scenarios of inner worlds and saw in this theater the promise and perils of natality, but not of education per se. Klein's theories are not prescriptions and so, in Likierman's words, "There is no general message in this about whether humanity is destructive or benign, only the idea that it needs to battle with destructive and loving tendencies" (196). The same battle belongs to education.

EDUCATION, TERMINABLE AND INTERMINABLE

What difference can a return to these debates on the nature of the mother-child relation, on child psychoanalysis, and on a psychical life make for the problems of representing education? Sometimes none at all—particularly if these debates are taken as irrelevant to thinking about the outside world, or if the fact that we have parents is rendered idealized and emptied of the conflicts that make psychoanalytic inquiry possible: ambivalence, love and hate, and having to learn. Much about the contemporary self-help industry forecloses these tensions, taking up residence in the romance of childhood, the refinding and reclamation of the lost inner child, and even in the idealization of knowledge in such places as kindergarten, with the claim that all the human needs to know can be found there. These calls for reclamation can also be found in discussions of the university, where demands for a nonconflictive and objective knowledge—better preparations for the world of work—foreclose problems of indebtedness, the work of self-exploration that allows for the existence of the other, and our grasp of what destroys this relation.

And yet, how can one understand the crisis of education without reference to the lives of those in it and without a concern for what happens when education loses its urgency and creativity, indeed, its language? Ten days after the Columbine High School shootings in Littleton, Colorado, in April 1999, a *New York Times* reporter held a two-hour discussion with eight students from that school.[23] They were asked to talk about violence in schools, their sense of cliques and hostilities between groups, and how they were making sense of the terrible event, not just from the continuous media coverage but from reflecting on the quality of life in school before the murders. Would any of these students, the reporter seemed to ask, think the murders would happen in their school? Here is what some of those interviewed remembered about how the two students who killed others and then turned guns upon themselves were treated at the high school:

> *Meg:* They'd call them freaks, weirdos, faggots. It was just stupid name-calling, acting like little children.
>
> *Devon:* People called them fags. People thought they were gay. And that's not right. I mean, even if they were—which they weren't—it's not right to say that.
>
> *Dustin:* When they call them fag, I think it's just a slang term for, like loser. I don't think they really meant that. They were like nerds. (*New York Times,* April 30, 1999, p. A25)

In reading through this interview, there is a terrible sense that language and knowledge have lost their objects, indeed, have lost the qualities of the transitional object, and so that transitional space is filled with nothing that matters, including the disclaimed hatred and hostility of empty words. This is the painful condition of what Bion called "Minus K," in which symbolization becomes the enemy and where envy of the other forecloses the other's capacity to exist as a separate being. Note how difficult it was for these interviewed students to represent these boys, how their anxiety over meaning contributed to their own helplessness in having to make sense of what in fact happened to them. Words fail, because there is no difference between the word and what it signifies.

Then there is the horrible surprise that hostility in everyday school life can accrue to its breaking point, exploding in an inchoate and a traumatic murderous rampage. The school spirit that provoked profound isolation for some and community for others could not be invoked to help those who survived. The more the students spoke in this interview, the less meaning could they make and the more, perhaps, they felt excluded from their own narratives. So too was this the case with what can only be called an avalanche of reportage: repetitions of the traumatic event through video replays, talk shows, and the daily news. In trauma, acts are repeated but carry no psychological significance.[24] In our media, acts are repeated but carry only incredulity. There is incredulity, a repetition of the refusal to believe what has actually happened, a refusal as well of any indebtedness or obligation to engage or respond, because the event has become a simulacrum, an instant replay.

Reconstructing this horrible event is something education must do, but everything is at stake in how the fragments that return from this event are narrated, how we make education from an experience that was never meant to be education. For if the core of an event is bounded by the time of its occurrence, then the resistance of an event to symbolization, what Klein called "phantasy," also is a part of what is transposed afterward. This belatedness, the fragile time of interpretation, thus obligates education to crafting an afterward. After World War II, there was and must still remain discussion on how to think of education after Auschwitz. Theodor Adorno's (1998) essay, "Education After Auschwitz," begins, "The premier demand upon all education is that Auschwitz not happen again" (190). And yet, if Adorno is puzzled as to why this demand cannot be met, he also understands that education is not a prevention but a social practice. He speaks of the two times of education, returning us to Freud's distinction between the education *sui generis* and after-education. Each time holds psychological consequences. To figure the work of after-education, we are brought back again to the arguments between Melanie Klein and Anna Freud, in which reality and phantasy and love and hate are the subjective conditions that allow education to disclaim the ways in which it also can be the grounds for social violence, thoughtlessness, and inhumanity.

Giorgio Agamben's (1999) meditation on the testimonies of Holocaust survivors offers a glimpse of the utter difficulty of making knowledge from traumatic devastation: "The aporia of Auschwitz is, indeed, the very aporia of historical knowledge: a non-coincidence between facts and truth, between verification and comprehension" (12). This is the noncoincidence of psychical and historical reality as well. While Auschwitz can scarcely be compared to the events at Columbine, my juxtaposition of what knowledge of Columbine can mean for education with Adorno's demand for education to learn from its history recalls the breach that was first discussed when educators and others began to consider the ravages of World War II. What meaning can this devastating history offer to an understanding of our present? Where does the urge for reparation begin? We must ask that education take on all modes of inexplicability and still, somehow, allow for those who come after, the potential space: to think through their own affectation made from social breakdown, profound hatred, and woeful disregard in relation to the affectations of others no longer present. When Shoshana Felman (1992) asked about the relation between education and crisis, whether there is anything that education can or should learn from the ravages of the twentieth century, she too wondered how knowledge can be made from traumatic events, and how difficult knowledge is used, related to, and learned from. But to ask what can we learn does not mean supplying a lesson that can somehow stabilize the utter difficulty of this interminable question.

Alain Finkielkraut (2000) ends his reflection on the twentieth century by lamenting over the utter difficulty of changing the self and the power of "Minus K":

> Life goes on, things happen, but nothing seems exciting enough to change modern man. Feelings reign freely, and ideology is defeated—at least for the time being—but the new age has not conquered the empire of resentment. Has the twentieth century therefore been useless? (112)

Finkielkraut also may be asking something about education. Has education been useless? Is there something that comes after education? Is learning to think about the difficulties of education, from the vantage of psychoanalytic controversy and historical crisis, as useless now as the century that ushered in psychoanalysis? Freud seems to ponder something similar when he characterizes education as one of the impossible professions and as invoking neurosis. Near the end of his study, *Civilization and Its Discontents*, Freud (1930) also wonders about the usefulness of analyzing cultural neurosis, particularly because there would be no accompanying therapy, even if the diagnosis were correct.[25] Is there any use in trying to understand the theoretical significance of aggression and reparation in education? If, as William Haver (1996) writes in his study of AIDS, "Not even education can save us now," (23) he insists as well on our obligations to respond to "a call . . . of the ethical" (24). It will then be the heart of this book to respond to and imagine the call of the ethical as that which obligates us to education. If education is no longer the cure, if it is to have a destiny, then our responsibility to the present becomes greater than what we have previously imagined.

Can the sense of the utter difficulty of learning to live, which psychoanalytic theory offers, be of any use in thinking about why, in a place called education, language loses all meaning, and the intermediate space of culture fills itself with "Minus K"? Can a reconsideration of controversies that are not our own, and of those that are not yet claimed, both enlarge the ways education can be represented, interpreted, and learned from, and so construct another condition for what Melanie Klein calls the "work of reparation"? To think about what we inherit as neither tradition nor as the culmination of irreversible processes (or even fate), called "history" means returning to the persistent and, in all respects, difficult questions that education presents. After the experience of education, there is still the problem of working through the distress and the promise that education heralds. To suggest that the urge to make reparation will be a central part of our work in education may mean reconsidering what makes education terminable and interminable, and still wonder, what might come after education.

CHAPTER TWO

THE FREUD–KLEIN CONTROVERSIES AS A PROBLEM OF EDUCATION

Between 1942 and 1944, a series of "Extraordinary Meetings" occurred in the British Psychoanalytical Society in London over the future direction of child psychoanalysis. The integrity of the Society would be at stake, because a crucial decision that members would face was whether a single society could hold conflictive theoretical orientations to psychoanalytic practice and still recognize itself. Known as the "Freud–Klein Controversies," these meetings and the papers read at them took their name from the key protagonists involved: Anna Freud and Melanie Klein.[1] Ironically, these analysts were behind the scenes as their emissaries aired grievances, revised theories, and sometimes switched sides. It would be behind these scenes that Anna Freud and Melanie Klein would come to a kind of truce that allowed the Society its life and, some would add, its future creativity.[2]

The Controversies occurred in the midst of the Second World War, during the historic exile and dispersal of psychoanalysis from cities such as Vienna, Budapest, and Berlin to locations in London, Toronto, and New York. Indeed, the immediate timing of the Freud–Klein Controversies was profoundly difficult for those involved and mirrored much larger social traumas and hostilities. From the outside, the world collapsed into war; London was being bombed, exiled Viennese Jewish analysts (recently arrived in London), who were designated "enemy aliens" and so were not permitted to travel beyond city limits clashed with their British

33

and Viennese counterparts, and economic insecurity and social displacement were rampant. Within the British Society was the question of how psychoanalysis was to survive the death of Sigmund Freud and the attempt by Nazi Germany to destroy its theories, institutes, journals, and books.[3] Within psychoanalytic circles, there also were personal and cultural hostilities: between Melanie Klein and Anna Freud, between Melanie Klein and her daughter, Melitta Schmideberg, and between newly arrived Viennese refugees and those already acclimatized or native to the United Kingdom. The Controversies, then, hold tensions within analytic experience, not only from the sides of the child and the adult but also between analysts trying to establish the authority of their respective theories and training techniques. Together the Controversies were a confrontation within the very fault lines of psychoanalytic technique and theory, and also with the possibility that for both contexts, a certain pessimism might be admitted. And yet, with so much at stake, one might still venture to view these encounters as ambivalent, because these discussions moved between the extremes of conserving and innovating affective logic, both for those analyzed by Freud's first circle—Freud, Abraham, Ferenczi, and Sachs—and for those analyzed by Anna Freud and Melanie Klein.

The Controversies erupted in the middle years of Melanie Klein's and Anna Freud's respective development.[4] Klein was sixty years old, had been a practicing child analyst for about twenty-three years, and had lived in London for about sixteen years. She had emigrated there from Berlin in 1926 and was sponsored by Ernest Jones, the founder of the British Psychoanalytical Society. Freud was forty-seven and had been practicing child analysis since about 1922. She too had been sponsored by Jones but had been in London for just four years, having fled Vienna with the Freud family in 1938.[5] By the time of the Controversies, both women had produced influential publications that shaped the very questions that child analysts would ask. Each had followers of her own approach: people who had been analyzed either by her or by Freud's first circle. If all of these details suggest rather established camps, it also was the case that at the time of the Controversies neither were their respective theories completed. But their doubts, when expressed, were jotted in the margins of their papers or confessed privately in letters to supporters. Both women found themselves acting—at least publicly—as if their respective ideas were without argument, and as if their approaches could settle the very dilemmas—both theoretical and practical—that institutionalization brings to child analysis and psychoanalysis brings to the design of the objects of theory.

Documentation of these Controversies is extensive. Originally it included theoretical papers, minutes of meetings, memos, commentaries, personal reminiscences, and correspondence. Less formal are the letter exchanges, something very special to and controversial within the history of psychoanalysis. Sigmund Freud's vast archival correspondence inaugurated the discovery of key concepts, discarded speculations, and tried to dismantle the transference.[6] Letters began new disputes, carried old grudges, publicized secrets, acknowledged misjudgments, noted daily life and its tragedies, and so enacted traumatic breakdowns. Many who have traced the history of the Controversies begin not with the theoretical papers but with a series of letters that Freud and Jones exchanged in 1927. Lyndsey Stonebridge's and John Phillips's (1998) introduction to writings on Melanie Klein also begins with the Freud–Jones exchange, suggesting the dramatic problem that the letters only hint at: controversies in general and the work of Melanie Klein in particular take psychoanalysis "to the limits of what is imaginable about psychic life" (3). If we bring Anna Freud to this limit, we can add as well the problem of how education can be imaged and what then might count as evidence for it. Where then does the possibility of education emerge, and where does it reach its limit?

The British Psychoanalytical Society's Controversial Discussions debated a key tension that educational institutions know well: whether its internal workings could tolerate its own scientific differences, made largely by the difficulties its theory, practice, and training posed for all sides. If the different sides demanded something impossible of one another, it was only because psychoanalysis demands so much from its participants. And the topic that haunts the participants, in ways that continue to visit, concerns how psychoanalysis that argues both for the creative force of psychical reality and for its destructive potential can think from the directions, timing, evidence, force, and goals of education for both adults and children. For anyone interested in the promise and perils of education, a large question that these Controversies leave us with is: *What then is education that it should give us such trouble?*

There were hopeful hints, at least in the beginning, that analysts who encountered difficulty each day in their practice would be able to work through, with their colleagues, analytic principles for the larger good of psychoanalysis. Initially, Anna Freud felt that analysts should be able to solve their disputes: "If we should be able to solve our own personal problems and those of our patients I cannot see why we should not be able to solve the Society's problems" (cited in Grosskurth 1986,

298). Her feelings presupposed that the analysts themselves were not bringing unresolved conflict to the debates. Analyst Sylvia Payne, in a letter to Melanie Klein, dated March 16, 1942, articulated the stakes differently:

> I feel it essential to start with that we should not expect full agreement, but that we should even be able to tolerate doubt and uncertainty without relapsing into hopelessness and despair and the conviction that the disagreeing party is personally hostile. (cited in Grosskurth 1986, 295)

Payne may well have been referencing the problem of how to conduct oneself reasonably during the unreason of war, for there we need our enemies, and the measure of friends is their loyalty. But she also may have wanted to convey something difficult about accepting doubt and uncertainty.

The borders of the hostility can be placed somewhere between the expectations for what should happen and the sad unravelling of attention. With each Controversial Discussion the stuff of hostility grew larger, aggravated by the trading of rumors, accusations, recriminations, acrimony, personal attacks, name calling, and even public humiliation. These debates were taken personally, for part of the stakes involved the only personal tools that analysts have: interpretation, subjectivity, and a willingness to acknowledge the indiscretions of the unconscious, all of which are intimate, bound by neither the rules of consciousness nor civility. The pessimism that such affects carry was not strange to the analysts themselves, and everyone knew that the course of the development of psychoanalysis was made by its internecine conflict. After all, the story of psychoanalysis is filled with the leitmotif of Oedipal rivalry, primal hordes, and monumental betrayals, what Steiner (1995a) calls, in his introduction to the *Freud–Jones Correspondence,* "a veritable deluge of transference and counter-transference" (xxv). Neither Payne's cautionary tact nor Anna Freud's wish for cure could be realized. And Melanie Klein also would comment sadly, in the early part of the Society's discussions, "I think we must face the fact that the situation in the Society is incurable" (cited in Grosskurth 1986, 305).

In this chapter, I consider how these Controversies became—and have continued to be—controversial, not just to recount a history of child analysis but also to raise questions of our own contemporary education. As we will see, a painfully bitter dispute concerns the authority of education as a process in and an outcome of relations between adult and child, adults and adults, and adults and the institutional setting. This complex called into question the querulous relation of theory to practice. The Controversies offer us an occasion to consider education from its beginning, so to say, with the problem of how the human comes to distinguish between reality and phantasy, and then, how we figure the adequacy of education's claims to know this difference.[7] My return to the Freud–Klein Controversies holds in tension a genealogy of a few psycho-analytic concepts disputed in the Controversial Discussions, consider-ation of contemporary educational problems read through the dynamics of the Controversies, and speculations on the psychical dynamics at work in education, then and now. To read the numerous accounts of the Freud–Klein Controversies is to recognize the troubled and ambivalent development of psychoanalysis and bring to education the question of why it is so difficult to tolerate different views of practice, particularly views that center on a certain pessimism toward the educational project. Like psychoanalysis, education is a theory of conflict and is marked, consequently, by the very processes that it attempts to understand, namely, the vicissitudes of love, hate, and ambivalence in learning and in not learning, and the susceptibility of humans both to the breakdowns and reparations of knowledge and authority. Finally, when we view education from the prism of the Controversies, we can consider how education affects its own imaginary and why education breaks down when its topic turns to pedagogy.

These Freud–Klein Controversies are one of the most documented touchstones in the development of child psychoanalysis, not because of their historical interest but for the types of questions that they offer today. First, the Controversies leave us with precocious questions: Where does education come from? What is the status of aggression and negativ-ity in psychical life? What is the relation between external and internal events and between phantasy and reality? And crucial to my own argu-ment in this chapter, what can education even mean? Second, the Con-troversies return to the question of what psychoanalytic knowledge is—how it is made, justified, argued over, and experienced from the transfer-ence—concerns we would do well to bring to our own educational knowl-edge. These are questions that call attention to the status and boundaries of epistemology and ontology in learning and teaching. Jacqueline Rose (1993) puts the dilemma boldly: "[I]f knowledge borders on fantasy, fantasy is always in part fantasy about (the borders of) knowledge." She goes on to revise old questions relevant to any endeavor: "Where does the possibility of knowledge come from? Can we conceive of a limit point where it ceases to be?" (174). In conceiving of such a limit, say in thinking that knowledge and phantasy are no longer binary oppositions, what else can happen to educational knowledge and our desire to know and be known?

The force of these traumatic conflicts in terms of the Controversial Discussions is reminiscent of earlier events, suggesting the uncanny time of trauma, what Sigmund Freud termed *Nachträglichkeit*,[8] a psychical temporality that is recursive in its structure and delayed in its knowable effect. When Ernest Jones founded the British Psychoanalytical Society in 1919, its first problem was one of membership. In her history of the Controversial Discussions, Pearl King (1991) poses the founding problem of the Society as one of education: "Who were appropriate people to be members of a psychoanalytic society and what basic theories should they hold?"(11). These pedagogical questions open the problem of how a profession legitimizes itself, justifies its internal authority, and lends continuity to itself over time. But if settled too quickly, membership requirements assume that individuals come to a profession already formed and foreclose the very problem of where theory comes from and the way education undergoes its own vicissitudes despite the theories held.

By 1927, the debates over technique and theory in child analysis between Melanie Klein and Anna Freud had already heated up and were argued over in the Freud–Jones correspondence (Paskauskas, 1995).[9] In a vitriolic exchange of letters beginning in the spring of 1927, Ernest Jones wrote to Sigmund Freud about Melanie Klein's pioneering work with children. Klein had just immigrated to London from Berlin a year earlier and was welcomed into the British Psychoanalytical Society. While Jones knew of the rivalry between Anna Freud and Melanie Klein, in a letter to Freud he attempted to defend Klein's work, telling Freud that Anna Freud's work with children was immature and stemmed from an incomplete analysis or, in Jones's words, "imperfectly analyzed resistances" (Paskauskas 1995, 617). This comment brought out Freud's wrath, since he had analyzed his daughter himself.[10] Freud's first response was measured and distanced; he would rather see science settle disputes over the veracity of knowledge, but he also was chagrined over the way disputes within psychoanalysis were reduced to the analysis of the analyst's personal flaws:

> When two analysts have differing opinions on some point, one may be fully justified, in ever so many cases, in assuming

that the mistaken view of one of them stems from his having been insufficiently analysed, and he therefore allows himself to be influenced by his complexes to the detriment of science. But in practical polemics such an argument is not permissible, for it is at the disposal of each party, and does not reveal on whose side the error lies. We are generally agreed to renounce arguments of this sort, and, in the case of differences of opinion, to leave resolutions to advancements in empirical knowledge. (Paskauskas 1995, 619)

Jones breaks this rule again, and in his next letter he insists that his observations were not about public disputes but were "private and personal" (1995, 620). A few letters later, Freud recounts one of the first paper fights between Anna Freud and Melanie Klein. He worries that his daughter's work is not being published in London because of Klein's influence. His anger is directed at Jones's earlier insistence that Anna Freud's work suffers from her "incomplete analysis." Leaving the third person, Freud breaks his own rule when he writes to Jones on September 23, 1927:

In London you are organizing a regular campaign against Anna's child analysis, accusing her of not having been analysed deeply enough, a reproach that you repeat in a letter to me. I had to point out to you that such a criticism is just as dangerous as it is impermissible. Is anyone actually analysed enough? I can assure you that Anna has been analysed longer and more thoroughly than, for example, you yourself. (1995, 624)

Steiner's (1995a) view of this exchange reaches the heart of the dispute, not in terms of who is analyzed best—as if this question did not also require analysis—but in terms of the difficult knowledge of psychoanalysis itself.

One can grasp almost physically the impossibility of distinguishing clearly, or rather distinguishing absolutely, between the mixture of epistemological, personal, and emotional elements in play in the defense of certain principles in the field of psychoanalysis. It is as if the unconscious as an object of research were taking its revenge, making its presence felt as the subject, impossible to control with any assurance. (xxxix)

And without any assurance on how psychical processes are enacted in research, since indeed the concept of the unconscious breaks open the wishes to assure, how then can knowledge advance without being vengeful? We might rework this observation for education as well: defenses of educational practices are a strange combination of epistemology, desire, and affective investments in being known and in knowing others. But precisely because of these elements, education cannot be mastered, and its effects are neither predicted nor controlled. And here begins the trouble.

The Freud–Jones correspondence tells a story of terminable and interminable education, of the gap between knowledge and its realization, and of the stormy relation between adult analysis and child analysis. These tensions are acute in the professional training of educators, where theories and practices take on urgent formulations and demands and where failure in education wavers between blaming educators and blaming students or their families, a dynamic reminiscent of the Freud–Jones argument. How can we separate the structure and edifices of education from the knowledge we make of those structures? How can we characterize the break between knowledge and understanding? What experiences come to count as learning, and how do they measure up as development? How are the stage and the staging of education both influenced by participants' unconscious phantasies and susceptible to kernels of historical truth? The Controversies' argument over the differences between adult and child analysis offers this question to education: What are the differences between professional education and children's education? When does education begin, and like analysis itself, can it ever be complete?

EDUCATIONAL ISSUES

The psychoanalytic theories of Melanie Klein and Anna Freud were derived from their work with children, their attempts to listen to the children's symptoms, their innovations and conservation of Freud's thought, and perhaps just as significantly, their own self-analyses. At times, their respective writings seem to trail each other; both wrote about school phobias, reading difficulties, children who bully others or are subject to being attacked, children who lose things, including their intellectual curiosity, problems of precocity and sexuality, and physical expressions of anxiety, such as stuttering, tics, night terrors, and tantrums. They heard, in the strange utterances of their young analysands, unconscious emotional dramas. Throughout their long careers, they would wrestle with all sorts of ordinary symptoms that were not, during their time, thought to affect children. Moreover, the significance of affective states—for example, feelings of unhappiness, suffering, depression, and of being unwanted and unloved—is only communicated indirectly and only approached intersubjectively. And precisely because their objects of research are so elusive—made up from dreams, play, drawings, fantasy, inchoate longings, and even through transference and counter-transference, and arguments with their young analysands—both women worked extremely hard to establish the relevancy of their interpretive claims.

What made these labors of child analysis so difficult was that the affective experiences these analysts explored belong, as we will see, not just to the children; each analyst wrestled with these very human dilemmas in her own life and confronted these affects yet again when trying to convince others of her theory's authority. Thus from the beginning of Klein's and Anna Freud's research and practice, the boundaries between objective and subjective knowledge were permeable and made even more so by the trade in accusations over whose theory was more loyal to that of Sigmund Freud and, further, whether either theory preordained the very symptoms that its practice of interpretation addressed. This second difficulty, a common criticism in education as well, also issued from the disparities between what Klein and Anna Freud each claimed for the child. Most important, this concerned their different sense of the poesies of psychical life and of how the tasks we must accept to become human affect and agonize the work of education.

While both women began with an acknowledgment of the utter dependency of the immature human as structuring conditions of psychical life, and so carried over to relations with others and carried within the beginnings of thinking itself, their research strategies and the consequences of analytic technique each of them drew from this dependency diverged. The psychoanalytic problem is how to make sense of the vicissitudes and future of this helplessness. Klein, for example, felt that the primal distress made from not knowing, what Freud called *Hilflosigkeit*, enraged and frustrated the infant to such an extent that anxiety and aggression marked every moment of normal development.[11] This primal helplessness contained a kernel of negativity and aggression that marked the limit of influence and so too the potential for gratitude and poignant thinking. Anna Freud did not attribute such formative aggression or sadism to the infant and felt instead that the ego, with the aid of its mechanisms of defense and the love from actual parents, was adept at learning to sublimate instinctual conflict and acknowledge the demands of external reality.

Indeed, when it came to the life of the child, Anna Freud argued that the child was most influenced by the external world. This insistence on locating influence speaks a profound difference in the way each understood the conditions of external reality and internal phantasies to mean for a child's capacity to tolerate anxiety and frustration and then to make something creative from this difficult mix-up. Their views of how a child was influenced shaped their thinking on the analyst's approach. For Anna Freud, the analyst must win over the child and be prepared to open some possibilities through confidence building, while foreclosing others by rational persuasion and assuming the position of authority. Melanie Klein felt the child was already under the sway of bellicose internal reality; the analyst's work was to occupy these tensions, through interpretation to the child, without the promise of betterment and without an appeal to authority.

On the question of where anxiety comes from, their understanding of the gap between knowledge and its realization led their clinical use of interpretation to diverge significantly. Melanie Klein believed that, like the adult, the child could benefit from deep interpretations; Anna Freud felt that the child in analysis would benefit more from the analyst's position as a sort of role model, what she called an "ego ideal." While Anna Freud did not eschew the importance of phantasies for the life of the child, she also maintained, through her theories of the ego's defense mechanisms, that there were three sources of anxiety: the object, the instinct, and the superego. For Klein, anxiety was constitutional and had only one source: the death drive, and so a fear of annihilation.

Melanie Klein's clinical work with very young children and infants laid the foundation for theories of object relations and for her difficult claim that phantasies structure knowledge of both the inside world, by introjection, and by the outside world, by projection. Her insistence on the absolute primacy of phantasies takes us to a very difficult understanding of interiority and knowledge. In bracketing the consideration of outside processes, Klein was able to think about how instinctual terror and defenses against these drives come too early for the human, even as these processes set the conditions for further development. Not knowing was, for Klein, another way to consider phantasy. Phantasy is there, Klein believed, from the beginning of life. In the words of Juliet Mitchell (1998), it

> emanates from within and imagines what is without, it offers an unconscious commentary on instinctual life and links feelings to objects and creates a new amalgam: the world of

imagination. Through its ability to phantasize, the baby tests out, primitively "thinks" about it, its experiences of inside and outside. External reality can gradually affect and modify the crude hypothesis phantasy sets up. Phantasy is both the activity and its products. (23)

This "commentary" is inchoate, preverbal, and fragmentary. It represents the baby's premature attempt to master bodily anxiety, an anxiety that, in Klein's view, is crude, terrifying, aggressive, and subject to turning back against the subject. And yet phantasies, however negative and paranoid, also are the necessary precursors of identification and symbolization, because the baby, from the beginning, equates her or his bodily anxiety with objects in the world. Through the infant's projection of her or his bodily sensations into that first other, a reality that Klein (1930a) called "unreal reality" (221), identification and symbolism emerge. The scenario is painful, for these meanings also must be defended against and, eventually, mourned. Psychical reality is the difficult beginning of cognition, and so cognition, for Klein, cannot escape a certain anxiety, a terrific sense of frustration that she would call "the epistemophilic instinct," or the sadistic drive to know.[12]

Anna Freud would center on problems of normal development, and so she was one of the early proponents of the School of Ego Psychology. She believed that development is gradual, in which the ego moves slowly from being the pleasure ego to becoming the ego of reality.[13] Her understanding of this shift is an interpretation of Sigmund Freud's (1933) famous trajectory of psychical development: "where id was, there ego shall be" (80). Indeed, Anna Freud (1936) insisted that the analyst could only approach psychical reality through an appeal to the ego's potential reasonableness and then an analysis of its defenses. Her interest was in the ego's function of reality testing, and she argued that what it tests is not so much the relation between phantasies and reality but the adequacy of its perceptions, actions, and judgments in the world. There the ego must learn to negotiate relations among reality, the authority of others, and its own morals. If what the ego can notice is tied to instinctual conflict, made from conflict between pleasure and un-pleasure, it had the gift to sublimate these tensions. The superego, for Anna Freud, would be marked by this dilemma of having to choose. And from this choice it would emerge not from archaic phantasies of terror and persecution, as Klein claimed it represented, but from the singular combination of love and authority that actual parents or caregivers bestow upon the baby.

Before, during, and after the Controversial Discussions, Melanie Klein and Anna Freud would argue—with those in their field and in lectures to both the general public and to educators—over the etiology of anxiety, defense, and sublimation.[14] They would privilege different causes of suffering, because their theories attempted to approximate the material from which psychic experiences and interiority are made: endogenous or exogenous, nature or nurture, biology or culture, reality or phantasy? These are arguments over the conditions of being, indeed, over what it is that conditions being prior to its entrance into language and culture, and then, once the human enters into the world, how the world affects being, how being imagines the world as it is becoming a part of the world. Their theories question how education can be imagined, because each analyst was concerned with what makes curiosity in the first place, how curiosity loses its wonder and, further, how teachers who were not analysts might conceptualize the psychical work of learning and interpret this work to their students and themselves.

For Klein, the capacity to symbolize begins in anxiety, essentially made from phantasies, and this stages how the baby uses and tolerates knowledge. There is always an excess to curiosity, for this curiosity also is frustration, at least in Klein's view, and so covers the wish not to know, the earliest stirrings of our passion for ignorance. For Klein, the line between terror and learning is never absolute. For Anna Freud, the ego's interest in noticing the world also emerges from an instinctual conflict, yet this conflict represents a precursor to the work of reality testing and sublimation. The uses and tolerances of knowledge are measures of ego development, made from environmental support and the ego's growing capacity to distinguish between real angst and internal conflict, and between projection and reality testing. Thus Anna Freud argued that educative measures should be joined with child analysis, for education could offer the child strategies of reality testing and, through the analyst's solicitation of the child's help, encourage the child to develop an interest in being needed, helping others, and sublimating aggression. But what happens when education itself is experienced as aggressive and overly demanding?

This may have been Klein's question. She felt there was not much difference between adult analysis and child analysis, at least not in terms of the central rule of analysis: free association. Then came interpretation of the transference. The analyst must allow for the analysand's uninhibited expressions of rage, hatred, and terror. Indeed, Klein offers a powerful documentation of these painful outbursts in her case studies of children. Free association was, for Klein, both contrary to the goals of education and, as we will see, the material from which she paved her royal road to the phantasies. The psychoanalysis must depart from education, because there can be no loyalty to the demands of reality and logic or to the feelings of the analyst. Allowing anything to come to mind, free association renders knowledge and phantasies indistinguishable, a collapse that, for Klein, carries pedagogical value into irrelevancy. This indiscretion was precisely where interpretation emerged and where disputes of Klein's views were affixed. But thorny questions can then be raised. In entering the terms of the child's phantasy, was Klein enlarging her own? Or how, as Kristeva (2001b) asks, can one distinguish between "the use of the imaginary in the cure, on the one hand, and the consideration of an objective and knowable reality on the other?" (175). This is the controversy, then and now.

In a sense that perhaps even she could not admit, Melanie Klein was right about the antagonism of education and free association. When it came to discussions about the education of analysts, neither side would permit the free association of ideas and schools of thought. While each side argued passionately over theories of learning and whether pedagogy would be of use in the analysis of children, when the debates turned to the education of analysts and their training, no comparable argument ensued. It was as though adults had somehow outgrown the nature of their being in terms of learning; the analysts' preoccupation with the child's capacity to be addressed by education was a defense against acknowledging, in their own learning, a failure of influence. Education for adults was reduced to a certain loyalty toward carrying forward a school of thought. There was plenty of discussion over the nature of the analytic relation, the goals, timing, and activities in child analysis, and the nature of psychoanalytic knowledge. But what was lost, when it came to the education of adults, was the problem of where the adult's imagination might come from and the question of how theory emerges from the strangely singular encounter of the analytic session, meandering through the transference and counter-transference.

These problems of imagination and theory are intractable, because in professional training it is difficult to pry apart the learning of ideas from the learning of authority, a dilemma of conflict that constitutes the indelible signature of the transference. There are always tensions in trying to learn how to practice, proving one's competence in spite of having to learn, and generalizing the unique encounter to other situations that defy prediction. If we may as well view these practices under the sign of growing up, this volatile combination of anticipation and retrospection for adults places at odds two sorts of authority: the authority of ideas and the authority of the learner. How is authority made from the transference, and what happens then to authority in this relation? If institutional design cannot acknowledge this paradox, then the transference becomes catastrophic (Safouan 2000). But secondly, institutional disavowal of the conflict that inaugurates thinking about practice in the first place also plays out intimately in an individual's education. Then the problem is, why is it so difficult to acknowledge the tensions and conflict in one's own education? Is professional education somehow reminiscent of earlier episodes of learning authority?

These are painful questions, given the analytic history of each of the protagonists: Anna Freud was analyzed, as a child and as a young adult, by her father, and Melanie Klein analyzed her own children. So any criticism of their respective work was personal. Psychoanalysis, it seems, cannot be disentangled from its own family romance, another story of education. After all, Sigmund Freud (1914b) did not call the baby "His Majesty the Baby" for nothing, and in his essay, "On Narcissism," he observed the parent's overvaluation of the baby as saying something about the parent: "Parental love, which is so moving and at bottom so childish, is nothing but the parents' narcissism born again, which transformed into object-love, unmistakably reveals its former nature" (91). Evaluating narcissism is difficult enough, let alone leaving it behind. Arguments over technique may wield such force, because they return us to that first education that is barely memorable: having to be raised and then raising others. But just as significantly, something can be learned from this resistance to the diversity of technique, for in psychoanalysis its practices depend upon the practitioner's practical and theoretical understanding of how its theories can say something about her or his unconscious wishes for the self and the other. In other words, psychoanalytic objects of research, such as neuroses, psychoses, anxieties, resistance, affects, and defenses, also fashion the interiority of the researcher (Steiner 1985).[15] And yet, admitting a rather democratic notion of suffering was hardly possible. If psychoanalytic theory brings learning and suffering into intimate relations, perhaps this can account for why we do take our practices personally.

The difficulty of determining once and for all the difference between adults and children in terms of the time of learning is repeated in the dissonant, uneasy place of education within psychoanalytic thought. Sometimes education refers to child rearing, sometimes it refers to didactic inculcation of rigid morality, and sometimes it marks the larger culture's disavowal of conflict and the difficulties of life. At other times, education is compared to authoritarianism, and then it was thought to be a source of repression. Anna Freud defined education as all types of interference, suggesting that, as a relation, education must emerge from mutual conflict. In the early history of child analysis, a more positive sense of education linked the exchange of ignorance for knowledge to becoming enlightened, placing education close to the Kantian *Aufklärung*,[16] or reasonable knowledge, that can be put into service for the dual purpose of curing ignorance and repression and for becoming reflective. As for the positive purpose, it encourages a rather vicious tautology: education causes repression and is the cure for repression. Or perhaps it resides somewhere between repression and desire. If this definition of education forecloses the question of where repression comes from by placing it solely in social processes and ignoring psychical demands, there is still the problem of why we are so susceptible to social processes and to repression. As for the second meaning of education, the work of becoming reflective raises precisely the problem of what might count as cure: consciousness cannot guarantee its own transparency, because reason cannot escape its own psychical dynamics, its own passion for ignorance, or its own unconscious dream work, made from such dynamics as distortion, repression, deferral, substitution, condensation, turning into its opposite, and so on.

These difficulties keep education in the Freudian category of "the impossible professions," discussed in chapter 1. Here, a double impossibility is admitted. There remains the problem of why knowledge is resisted and how it is that phantasies exert more persuasive power and pressure over judgment than does reality. The other impossibility is directed to the work of educating: those who practice as educators must struggle with the inherent difficulty of trying to persuade individuals to change the ways they think, believe, and work. This places the educator's efforts fairly close to that of the cajoling or punishing parent and its authority. But dependency on an outside authority cloaks a greater dilemma: teachers are not their students' parents even though in education as in the family, relations of authority are caught in transferential dynamics of desire: desire for learning, learning for love, and wanting to be, and to have the authority that knowledge bestows. If education is reminiscent of family romance, part of the difficulty is trying to figure the relations between being influenced and being compliant and between dependency and autonomy. How do others become entangled in these events of the self?

Along with this seemingly pessimistic view, Freud also put great faith in the possibility that knowledge can help individuals construct insight, support thoughtfulness, work though neurosis, and prepare the way for love of ideas. It is a possibility that leans upon the question of how insight into the self is made and how others are involved there. Learning from knowledge of psychical reality was, for Klein, the condition of even coming to know outside reality. It is a knowledge that must be made retrospectively, that might allow individuals to suffer differently and, over the course of their lives, to ask themselves to create ever-new answers to the interminable life question of what happiness and unhappiness can mean. And while it seems as though Freud would like to have education in these two contradictory ways, as both resistance and insight, Pontalis (1981) argues that there is no contradiction in such an approach: "One must indeed encourage parents and educators not to lie to children, not to answer with 'childish sayings,' in other words with myths concocted by adults for children, but one must not expect such knowledge to replace the unconscious" (96). Somewhere between the tenderness of comforting and the distancing of disillusioning, knowledge of the self and other is made.

Does this ambivalence over the uses of knowledge and over that which resists its use animate the analyst's education as well? Pontalis's (1981) discussion of the stakes of learning to become an analyst suggests that the ambivalence has more to do with the very processes that psychoanalytic theory tries to clarify than with its actual knowledge: "Psychoanalytic theory harbours the very mechanisms which bring it to light: resistance, repression, distortion, displacement, repetition, etc."(106). Psychoanalytic theory also is made from the very psychical processes that it attempts to describe. So the problem is to try to understand this expressive drama and the interpretations one can make from it. This work constitutes the interminable analytic education.

Psychoanalytic training is organized as apprenticeship and is made from two different kinds of knowledge that are assumed to be at odds: practical and theoretical. The actual experience of being analyzed is a significant part of one's analytic education, not only because it distinguishes the analyst from those who practice what Sigmund Freud (1910) called, when he founded the International Psychoanalytic Association, "wild analysis." In conceptualizing how one learns from the practices of psychoanalysis, and the becoming of an analyst, Freud places a contradiction at the heart of this education, making sure that the analysis respects the gap between knowing about psychoanalysis and being analyzed, between intellectualization and becoming oneself. In Eigen's (1997) more contemporary view, "Psychoanalytic experience is not the same as knowing about it. Patient and analyst are faced with the problem of passing from the wish to 'know thyself, accept thyself, be thyself' to becoming the reality such words suggest. There is a gap between knowing about x and being x" (213). And in some sense education as a method should not and indeed cannot fill that gap. The field of education takes a different view: there shall be a meeting of theory and practice, and it shall be experienced as one learns to teach and as one teaches others. From an analytic vantage, the very conflict that inaugurates knowledge—that is, the difference of theory and practice—is foreclosed in the idealized coupling of theory and practice and the wish for a practice without conflict.

Experiencing an analysis was already a prerequisite for the work of analyzing others, but at the time of the Controversies, the meaning of the analysis for education threatened to break apart under the weight of the question of whether this training analysis should be aligned with a particular school of thought.[17] This was a deeply personal issue, because one's own analysis is the heart of one's practice, and any outside criticism is a delicate matter. But also, education for the analyst has two warring dimensions: theoretical knowledge of the unconscious and subjective or idiomatic knowledge of the self through one's own analysis. For these dimensions to be meaningful rather than simply placed into a hierarchy of value, they must, by nature, be thought of and encountered as being at odds. This would be a productive tension if it could allow for a different sort of listening practice, capable of reading, as Freud (1913) puts it, "between the lines of [the analysand's] complaint and the story of his illness" (140). The Controversies was a vehement argument over what complaints might signify to the analysands and where the place of education might figure: within the nature of the complaint or somewhere in the story of illness?

The meaning of education within child analysis carries another resonance, because the young analysands are still involved in and dependent on their actual schooling and the authority of their families. This was Anna Freud's position when she asked about the timing of education: what is retrospective knowledge if education, for the child, was still unfolding? Psychoanalytic pedagogy, for example, was thought to be a remedy for education that did not have psychological significance. And yet, if education was part of the difficulty that children brought to analysis, and indeed, both Klein and Anna Freud attributed intellectual inhibition to traditional education, then what new tensions might occur in analysis for both parties if the analyst depended on educative measures?

The Controversies over education invoked a sort of splitting between, on the one side, good education from bad education and, on the other side, bad education from worse education. This gradient is not so easily communicated because of a necessary entanglement of morality with autonomy and of knowledge with desire. Some of the difficulty emerges because education is never, at least in analytic terms, solely a rational affair, and thus it cannot secure itself through rational persuasion or better planning. Indeed, these very methods are not beyond anxiety or its defense. How does one distinguish absolutely rational education from irrational education? Other difficulties cohered in the education of analysts. If education vacillates between the wishes of the adult and the desires of the child, if the knowledge promised can neither meet the demand to know nor satisfy belief, then how does one consider the directionality of influence and susceptibility?

At times, the Controversies tried to foreclose the dilemmas that education represents, because the debates acted out something agonizing about the frontiers of education itself: education is made and broken somewhere between reality and phantasy. One part of the debate intensified the question of whether educative goals should or even could become the key that unlocks the analysis of children. Another part occupied the education of analysts, but there education was reduced to its most rigid: didactic training. The literal questions of how to think about the differences between child and adult analysis returned to the education of the analyst: what can theoretical conflict mean in the analyst's education?

In her paper on technique submitted to the Society during the Controversies, Marjorie Brierley (1991, 619) wrote about "the spur of therapeutic anxiety." She tried to help others acknowledge how the analyst may feel toward the radical uncertainty that is also psychoanalytic practice. There is, Brierley tried to convey, a resistance to one's own feelings of helplessness in the analytic setting and also in how the Discussions progressed. And perhaps there also was a plea to notice what Schafer (1994, 361) called "the inherent ambiguity" of psychoanalytic work. What, then, can it mean to acknowledge psychoanalytic views, not from certainties but from vulnerabilities, the questions that cannot be answered?

There is a certain irony, for while some of the arguments had to do with which psychical and social conflicts children experienced, when it came to adult education, part of the desire was to eliminate conflict from the adult's experience. But there were also the psychical processes these Controversies animated. It seems as if the insistence upon practices were a defense against how working with others affects the self. Thus education had to be diminished. Whereas the tensions of education were stressed in the first instance of child analysis, when it came to the training of analysts, education was reduced to an answer to the question of which theory and which practice shall dominate training. Both sides did grapple with how education influences not just the learner but also the imperatives of the teacher and the analyst. However, while education in child analysis was admitted as a danger (as both inhibition and sublimation), when it came to the education of the analysts, the danger lost its constitutive power—or so it can seem when the status of conflict, doubt, and uncertainty is removed from education.

While raising crucial issues on the status of theory and practice, the Controversies are unique in that these two areas were intimately tied to the large question of how an institution is affected by its own school of thought and by the nature of its disputes. The British Psychoanalytical Society confronted the problem of whether its internal workings could tolerate its own scientific differences, and just as crucially, the difficulties offered by its theory, practice, and training.[18] Within issues of how members were to conduct themselves during the Discussions lies a theoretical question: how can an institution survive its own discontentment, internal contradictions, and its desires for continuity and creativity? Arguments between analysts also were animated by epistemological tensions made from the uneven relations in theory, practice, and research, the elusiveness of theory to observation, and then the question of how theoretical claims could be justified through interpretation and its capacity for generalization. The Controversies intensified the very question of knowledge and its limits in its arguments not just over how appeals to knowledge could be made, communicated, and distinguished as significant but also in terms of our double susceptibility to knowledge and to our own unconscious urges.

THE DREAM AND THE CHILD

Let us use the Controversies today to open one of the key fault lines within psychoanalysis and, more generally, within the practices of the human professions. Our issue is with the status of the relation between theory and practice and whether, for example, one must lead to the other. Freud tried to allow for the gap between observable phenomena and theoretical constructs because we are more than the sum of our appearances. Indeed, psychoanalytic inquiry must reside in that aporia, otherwise it could not claim any of its central categories: psychical reality, the unconscious, and the interpretation of dreams. Moreover, psychical life is not the same as conscious or observable life, and this difference must be maintained if any theory of the force of affect, ego defense mechanisms, anxiety, and phantasy is to be thought. But we are left with the question of what knowledge can mean if this radical instability is acknowledged.

The problem of knowledge and where it comes from is a key dilemma in child development, whose theory claims a causal relation between task and experience and between mind and body.[19] Psychoanalysis seems to complicate these relations because of its insistence both upon the unconscious and that sexuality begins at the beginning of life, rendering development uneven, painful, and subject to regression. Sexuality does, after all, change the quality of this choice between the dream and the child. Indeed, if sexuality is viewed as the origin of curiosity, and so as the very grounds of cognition, then new questions can be raised, such as: "Are there relationships, causative or simply parallel, between the psychomotor perceptual-cognitive states in the child's development and those of its psychosexual and emotional evolution?" (Petot 1991, 96). That is, how can we think of the child as split subject? If we subscribe to stage theory as the basis of learning theory, what might it mean to take seriously, as Klein does, that psychological knowledge comes before knowledge of physicality? Or, to follow Anna Freud's view, what do we do with the idea that awareness of outside authority comes before and constitutes knowledge of internal authority?

The Controversies confronted a constitutive problem in any practice: how that mix-up of desire, dream, perception, and the unconscious also affects our theories. How can one know these dynamics, and can ephemeral matter such as the unconscious become the basis of theoretical knowledge and generalization? Where do interpretations come from, and how do they become persuasive and useful? When Gregorio Kohon (1999a) asked André Green for his views on the status of knowledge in psychoanalysis, Green put the choice psychoanalysis confronts as one between the dream and the child. "The 'child' represents all this developmental point of view, the misunderstandings created by baby observation and what not. The 'dream' is the true paradigm of psychoanalysis . . . the dream develops outside consciousness. . . . There's the diminution of censorship, and therefore the emergence of desire" (50). If the foundation of psychoanalytic knowledge cannot be built upon consciousness and empiricism (if it is possible to imagine the unconscious as a resource for theory), then how does the dream-work become a paradigm for knowledge?

It is not only the child who dreams but the dream of the child, indeed, the child as dream that interferes with the question of knowledge in education. Can educators face the same sort of choice, between the empirical child made from the science of observation, behaviorism, and experimental and cognitive psychology and the libidinal child who dreams yet still desires knowledge? The field's dominant tendency is to choose the empirical child over the dream, the child the adult can know and control. But in so doing, education has reduced the child to a trope of developmental stages, cognitive needs, multiple intelligence, and behavioral objectives. And these wishes defend against a primary anxiety of adults: what if the dream of learning is other to the structures of education? And yet if we return to the question of the dream as a strange model for education, if educators are to choose the child who dreams, what Pontalis (1981, 95) would call, as he thought about the work of Melanie Klein, "the question child," then education might come to reside in that very intersubjective place between the borders of knowledge and phantasy and, as Klein did, test its own knowledge against that of the child and so affect the adult. Knowledge would be exchanged, but the question of the unconscious use could never be secured. The inaugural contradiction that Freud places at the heart of the psychoanalyst's education—that theory and practice will be at odds—would thus become a metaphor for any relation in education.

CHILD ANALYSIS BEFORE THE CONTROVERSIES

Child analysis has always had its controversies, and not just from those outside looking in who continue to express a strange combination of horror and incredulity toward psychoanalytic claims about childhood conflict, sexual researching, and infantile sexuality. The claims made in the name of the child were startling: children suffered, had a complex inner world, and were susceptible to their own libidinal and aggressive drives. And while this outside incredulity was not surprising—after all, psychoanalysts expect resistance—psychoanalytic communities also were ambivalent about the directions, influence, and training of child analysts. The actual child presented a significant challenge to one of the goals of adult analysis: reconstruction of the repressed past in terms of its present repetitions. How could the child reconstruct the past before it could even be established? Just how archaic is psychical conflict? Was the child even capable of free association? Was the child capable of a transferential relation with the analyst when the child's actual authority figures—the parents—were still central in the child's life? And yet, the child also presented a possibility for the curative power of psychoanalysis: that the early working through of neurosis might allow for a better and more insightful adulthood. A further question can be raised: can prevention ever come early?

From its inception, child psychoanalysis was caught in two debates. One concerned the nature of the child. How would the child's psychical life be depicted and understood? What kind of research allows for this sort of knowledge? The other debate concerned the question of lay analysis. Would the young field of psychoanalysis be taken seriously by the public if its practitioners were not from the medical profession? Historically, child analysis was a central avenue into the psychoanalytic profession for women, and this meant that the defense of lay analysis was caught somewhere between the qualifications of women and of the child. Sigmund Freud's (1926c) defense of lay analysis addressed three problems: he argued for the child's ability to benefit from analysis; he placed a kernel of the adult's symptoms in the child; and he separated the medical profession from psychoanalysis. In doing so, Freud suggested three axes of resistance to lay analysis: theoretical, professional, and psychical. To defend the practice of child analysis, he made a subtle argument for the destiny of neurosis which, he claimed, is not bound by chronology or even by external events of great magnitude. Children, like adults, are subject to their own inner conflicts and develop symptoms to protect the neurosis.

Freud's defense of lay analysis is a curious document, in that he wrote it as a dialogue, or argument, with an imaginary "impartial person." The impartial person worries whether children should go into analysis: "What? You have had small children in analysis? Children of less than six years? . . . And is it not most risky for the children?" (1926c, 214). Freud tries to assure the impartial person that educative measures are central.

> [Children] give unambiguous information on problems which remain unsolved in the analyses of adults; and they thus protect the analyst from errors that might have momentous consequences for him. One surprises the factors that lead to the formation of a neurosis while they are actually at work and one cannot mistake them. In the interest of the child, it is true, analytic influence must be combined with educational measures. (1926c, 215)

Child analysis seemed to offer the hope of theoretical progress to the larger field of psychoanalysis as well. The openness of the child could clarify the technique. We might say that child analysis mirrored the promise of what the child might represent in terms of future potential: child analysis promised something prophylactic, a new vantage from which to understand what Serge Lebovici (1998, xiii) calls, in his introduction to one of the first published histories of child psychoanalysis, "the process of subjectivation" as it unfolds.[20] And in suggesting the possibility of understanding how the human becomes human, child analysis also was viewed, at least initially by those inside, as a means of verifying the adult's constructions of childhood in the analytic setting. Given the child's proximity to education—to parents, institutions, and symbolization—child psychoanalysis was haunted, from its inception, by the symptoms of education. While there may be a hint of social engineering—a faith in the analyst's capacity to prevent neurosis from having a future—Freud would leave it to others to decide what, specifically, might constitute freeing or nonrepressive educational measures. It was this space that the Controversies would try to close.

Hermine Hug-Hellmuth is credited with sketching out the foundations of child analysis. She was the third female member and the first Gentile accepted into the Vienna Psychoanalytic Society in 1913. She also was the first child analyst to be recognized by Freud. Her biography is notorious, partly because of a scandal surrounding her own publishing, around 1922, of an adolescent's diary that she edited. The diary's sophisticated observations led to considerable debate as to whether it was authored by a young girl or fabricated by Hug-Hellmuth. But also, mystery surrounds Hug-Hellmuth because of the sudden violent ending of her life, and because she did not wish her work to be posthumously published. In 1924, at age fifty-three, Hug-Hellmuth was robbed and murdered by her nephew, a child she had raised since the death of her sister. She had analyzed her nephew, and before her death she understood that she could not help him. In 1925, Siegfried Bernfeld wrote her obituary for the *International Journal of Psychoanalysis*: "In a will made a few days before her death, she expressed a desire that no account of her life and work should appear, even in psychoanalytic publications" (cited in MacLean and Rappen 1991, 42–43). Almost sixty years would pass before her previously published work could be translated, compiled, and edited into a single volume.[21]

Hug-Hellmuth's 1920 paper, "On the Technique of Child-Analysis," urges analysts to distinguish child analysis from its adult counterpart.[22] In

Hug-Hellmuth's view, the analyst must be the child's advocate; she must work to "break the ice" and establish rapport by asking for the child's help. The analyst also is to construct the content of play, supplying the child with scenarios that will form the basis of the child's talk. These scenarios are to address the child's conscious perceptions, and the analyst must be cautious in offering interpretations. Mainly, the analyst is to reassure the child of her or his goodness, thus linking self-esteem and confidence building to the problem of undoing neurosis. Two years after Freud's (1926c) call for child analysis to have an educative value, Hug-Hellmuth (1991) defined the nature of that value: "The curative and educative work of analysis does not consist only in freeing the young creature from his sufferings, it must also furnish him with moral and aesthetic values" (138). Here is where child analysis is put in the developmental service of *Aufklärung.* And while, at least in the beginning, Melanie Klein adhered to this view on education, her own son's analytic education suggested that educative measures were not sufficient for the prevention of neurosis and intellectual inhibition, because the child resisted enlightenment. Indeed, the scary idea that Klein would try to confront is that educative measures suffer from these very symptoms; again, something within education itself can make us nervous.

How did Melanie Klein come to leave behind her early faith in educative measures and shift her practice from analytic education to psychoanalysis? The same year that Hug-Hellmuth gave her paper on the techniques of child analysis, Klein's own technique began to question the dominant suppositions of Hug-Hellmuth and Anna Freud. For them, anxiety develops from external circumstances; guilt and moral anxiety occur late in the child's development, because Oedipal anxieties are a later development. This meant that psychoanalysis must be closely allied with didactic education, opening some choices for the child but foreclosing others. Originally, like Anna Freud, Melanie Klein held a strong belief in the curative process of knowledge for character development and for liberating intellectual inhibitions. Klein's (1921) first case study, reported to the Budapest Society in 1919 and which served as her admittance into the Society, describes her progress with her own child Erich's psychoanalytic education. In it she claimed that in answering Erich's questions honestly and by urging him to give up his religious illusions and superstitious explanations of sex by offering him accurate knowledge, he would be able to free his intellectual inhibitions. By the time Klein (1921) published this case, she added a second part on repression. There she admitted that Erich remained unsatisfied with his mother's rational explanations and, in the face of rational knowledge, continued to prefer not just his phantasies but his wishes for another family. His symptoms of running away from home, even at a very early age, were not broken by rational information. Simply put, Erich refused to believe his mother and then stopped asking questions.

Petot's (1990) study of Melanie Klein's early theories insists upon the psychoanalytic problem:

> [O]n the first occasion the approach to the unconscious was only a means toward a project of elitist pedagogy in the context of an ideology very near to that of the *Aufklärung*, the rationalist philosophy of enlightenment, critical spirit, free thought, and the rejection of authority and religion. In Melanie Klein's real practice, this ideology served as the rationalization of a narcissistic approach to Erich. (33)

Just as Melanie Klein asked Erich to leave his illusions behind, she herself would have to change not just her philosophical hopes for the power of rationality to liberate inhibitions but also the cultural desires that rendered her approach ideological in its faith in the curative efforts of knowledge. Significantly, Klein's narcissism also was at stake: first as a mother who wishes for omnipotence over her child's development, then as a teacher who wishes to master the mysteries of how the child learns, and finally as an analyst who wishes to solve suffering through interpretation. And yet, as Likierman (2001) points out, this understanding of the desire for education is not only a story of narcissism. Klein's attention to Erich's intellectual inhibitions also was tied to her own struggle to be recognized as a thinker and to free herself from her history of intellectual constraint. In this way, Klein's shift from psychoanalytic education to psychoanalysis also is a working through, a mourning, of what is lost when education, ostensibly, is found. How strange then that a case study that leads her away from educating her son would return her to a confrontation with her own education—not enlightenment, but the unconscious nature of existence as such.

A comment offered by Anton von Freund after her paper, which Klein originally dismissed, slowly affected her rethinking and her own self-analysis.[23] He suggested that her work with Erich was not yet, in its interventions, psychoanalytic. While Klein's initial rule was only to answer Erich's direct questions and provide him with specific bits of information, von Freund argued that a true psychoanalytic education would "take into account 'unconscious questions' and reply to them" (Petot 1990, 28–29). He also offered practical advice: Klein must distinguish her parental relations from the analytic ones and set up formal times for analysis. It was in taking up the more difficult insistence of von Freund that Klein would distinguish herself from her peers. To reply to unconscious questions, Klein had to encounter and analyze Erich's phantasies, and this shift in the psychoanalytic object, from the child's conscious occupations to his unconscious anxiety, meant a dramatic change in her understanding of the child, the nature of knowledge, and psychoanalytic cure. In the case of the child, Klein would come to believe that phantasies inaugurate development. In the case of the psychoanalytic encounter, Klein would leave her desire to mold the child's character and so abandon educational goals for the uncertainties of free association. And finally, as for knowledge, it would no longer be on the side of enlightenment: in this redrawing, epistemology emerges in the wake of anxiety and phantasies. Petot's (1990) summary of Klein's new position still startles:

> The child's good social adaptation and success at school cannot be the goals for the child analyst; they are at most secondary . . . "normality" cannot be stated in terms of objective criteria, but in terms of liberty, fluidity, and variety in the creation of fantasies . . . no reference to external criteria can be acceptable in psychoanalysis. . . . The first lesson of Erich's education may be stated in the following terms: the objectives of the analysis of children can be defined only in psychoanalytic terms. (44)

Psychoanalytic cure meant the freeing of phantasy, not rationality. Normality now involves the right to elaborate psychical reality. Even Anna Freud (1936) would come to know this tension when she noted one of the ego's mechanisms of defense as intellectualization. But what Klein's change signified was a radical reconsideration of normality and knowledge through the making of psychoanalytic knowledge. And because Klein felt that education could not support this reconsideration, it became irrelevant.

While Klein narrated many of these changes to her technique in her 1921 paper, "Development of a Child," it would take years for her to consider the consequences of that great turning away from psychoanalytic education. When Klein (1955) reflected upon the history of her technique, she also would register her own shock:

This new approach soon confronted me with serious problems. The anxieties I encountered when analysing this first
case were very acute, and although I was strengthened in the
belief that I was working on the right lines by observing the
alleviation of anxiety again and again produced by my interpretations, I was at times perturbed by the intensity of the
fresh anxieties which were being brought into the open. (123)

Interpreting the child's phantasies was in itself painful for the analyst, for
where would the boundary be that would separate the child's anxiety
from the adult's anxiety, if education could not secure this limit? This
difficulty, for Klein, inaugurated her lifetime insistence upon analyzing
unconscious anxiety and aggressive impulses, interpreting the transference, and offering deep interpretations (Petot 1990, 136).

Nor was only education set aside. Klein felt that neither rapport nor
appeals to external reality could be of any use in the analytic session. Nor
would the influence of either external conditions or the analysts' nurturing
qualities obstruct disquietude of interpretation. Klein had thus moved from
the question of how the world influences the child's development to a
consideration of how the child encounters and creates by phantasy the
internal world of object relations. With this move, she threw away any
appeal to the impartial person that Freud (1926c) created in his defense of
lay analysis and raised a significant dilemma for our theories of knowledge:
what are the boundaries and limits of education? The problem is that Klein
posited an education that comes before education, and she called it "phantasies." Klein's approach has allowed child analysis to begin in an original
aporia located in "the appearance of objective knowledge or savoir-faire and
its translation into the sphere of object relations; in short between simple
knowing and realization. It is this gap which is filled by the working
through process" (Petot 1991, 123). This is the same fault line in knowledge that Freud placed at the heart of psychoanalytic training and learning.
Learning is a working through.

What can it mean to allow in the heart of subjectivity a division
between knowledge and its realization? What resistance is encountered?
Classically there is a huge opposition between what Freud saw as the
reality principle, or the demands of law and culture, and the pleasure
principle, or the libidinal demands for satisfaction without consequence.
Initially the child experiences this breach before knowledge occurs. Phantasies are both the resistance and the company that are far more persuasive than any appeal to leave them behind. This is the Freudian space of

the Oedipus complex. Admission into human society and object relations has a severe cost; knowledge and realization are not the results of development, nor even cognitive processes. But Klein would define the problem of learning to become an individual as one of freeing phantasies, not abandoning them. Anna Freud, however, saw the work of the human in more adaptive terms, for while a human is subject to flights of fantasy and to wishful thinking, all signals of instinctual conflict, she believed that the trauma of the Oedipal conflict could be resolved with an acceptance of reality. Only for Klein would this cost mark education: while education has not thought the force of its internal phantasies, its own epistemophilic instinct nonetheless sutures its edifices and design. If education wants to be on the side of cognition, Klein seems to suggest, it will need to ignore all that comes before cognition and then make cognition a painful, fragile experience.

In 1926, Freud contributed to the thirteenth edition of the *Encyclopaedia Britannica* the first entry on psychoanalysis. In reviewing its key theories, again Freud dated sexuality at the beginning of life, defining it as instinct and as noncoincidental to genital development. Because for Freud sexuality is tied to primary narcissism and not, at least in the beginning, to object relations, the child realizes physicality before any knowledge. Klein turned this view on its head with the counterintuitive claim that phantasies, as psychological knowledge, precede awareness of physicality. These speculations regarding what sort of knowledge comes first are situated in the realm of the fantastic—the realm within which the child herself or himself has a very particular and difficult bit of work to do as she or he enters the Oedipal complex. She or he must make some sense of sexuality through the other, from within the confines of the family's libidinal relations and from the push of her or his own drives. Freud posed this work as conflictive:

> The most important conflict with which a small child is faced is his relation to his parents, the *"Oedipus complex"*; it is in attempting to grapple with this problem that those destined to suffer from a neurosis habitually come to grief. The reactions against the instinctual demands of the Oedipus complex are the source of the most precious and socially important achievements of the human mind. . . . The super-ego, too, the moral agency which dominates the ego, has its origin in the process of overcoming the Oedipus complex. (1926b, 268, emphasis in original)

Freud's direct statement gives no hint that by 1927 the status and timing of the Oedipus complex and the poiesis of superego and moral development would be the focus of debates between Anna Freud and Melanie Klein. Did the Oedipus complex refer to actual child/parent relations, the cultural working out of the incest taboo, or to the child's phantasies about the primal scene and parental love? If these were the child's phantasies, how did they emerge? Which analytic technique would be most useful in listening to the child's inner world and so to the child's unasked questions?

Anna Freud's 1927 lectures on technique in child analysis and her critique of Melanie Klein's early theories continued to put education in the service of psychoanalysis.[24] The response from British child analysts allied with Klein was negative. Indeed, it was this negativity that drew Freud's anger into his correspondence with Jones. That year, what added fuel to the fire was a paper by Joan Riviere that took Klein's views to their absolute and terrifying limit. Riviere's (1991) essay, "Symposium on Child Analysis (1927)," was extremely critical of Anna Freud's claim that there is indeed a significant difference between adult and child analysis.[25] Anna Freud assumed that the difference emerged from the child's dependency and immaturity. For Riviere, when it came to the question of phantasies—and for her that was the only question—and their analysis, actual chronology mattered little and if, she reasoned, chronology meant nothing, what then could development mean? Riviere sided with the analysis of psychical reality and ended her critique with the rigid polemical insistence that psychoanalysis must only address the child's unconscious phantasies: "[Analysis] is not concerned with the real world, nor with the child's or the adult's adaptation to the real world, nor with sickness or health, nor virtue or vice. It is solely concerned with the imaginings of the childish mind, the phantasied pleasures and the dreaded retributions" (1991, 87). And yet what does it mean to throw the world out of the analytic setting?

Anna Freud eschewed neither phantasies nor the interpretation of child dreams, but she nested her interpretations within the child's actual reality. In opposition to Klein, she felt that phantasies kept the child back, while a love for the world outside would become the resource for the child's freedom. She was most concerned with the conditions under which psychoanalysis occurred, and so she felt that the analytic ground had prerequisites. Before the child could listen, the analyst must support the child's capacity to develop her or his own confidence in the world and so, it followed, confidence in the analyst. Only this trust lets the ego risk and make its pleasures in finding a world. In Anna Freud's early lectures on child analysis, she went to great lengths to justify her insistence that child analysis has a specific pedagogical purpose, and that the analyst must demonstrate her or his alliance to the child by being supportive and useful, by gaining the child's trust through the making of a strong bond with the child, even if this work meant delaying analytic interpretation. But she also tried to distinguish good education from bad education, telling teachers in her 1930 lectures, "As a method of therapy, the analysis of children endeavours to repair the injuries which have been inflicted upon the child during the process of education" (1930, 129).

Strong disagreement over how analytic insight could be made from psychoanalytic technique was part of the burgeoning conflict between Anna Freud and Melanie Klein. While both analysts utilized play in the analytic setting, their views on how to interpret play, or the symbolic reach of the child's relation to objects, varied significantly. What analytic scenes are being enacted in the analytic session? And how does the transference work in child analysis? Anna Freud seemed reticent to affix the child's play solely to its psychical reality, or to use the transference as the basis of interpretation. She argued that the child is not yet ready to reenact new editions of prior love relations, because the prior relations are not yet past! Indeed, for Anna Freud, the transference is a developmental achievement, because the child is still in a state of dependency upon the parents, not just in terms of having her or his daily physical needs met but also in requiring the parents' actual presence in the working out of morality. This means that the superego develops gradually, which led to Anna Freud's insistence that to support its development, the analyst must offer herself or himself as an ego ideal and as an object of authority. In Anna Freud's (1926) words, the work of the analyst "combines in his own person two difficult and diametrically opposed functions: He has to analyse and educate, that is to say, in the same breath he must allow and forbid, loosen and bind again" (65).

Melanie Klein first presented her response to Anna Freud at the British Psychoanalytical Society in May 1927, just one year after she had first arrived in London. But rather than begin with Anna Freud's text, she returned to that first case study in child analysis, reported by Sigmund Freud in 1909, "Analysis of a Phobia in a Five-Year-Old Boy." Klein congratulates Freud for his courageous efforts in bringing psychoanalytic method to the inner world of the child, and for his understanding that the child's symptoms had meaning and could therefore be altered. The "Little Hans" case study, however, is a rather curious example, partly because Freud saw the child only once, and so the case actually is based upon Little Hans's father's report to Freud and Freud's advice to the father on helping Hans give up his horse phobia.[26] The case study he wrote does give a charming picture of childhood precociousness and adult exasperation in trying to meet the child's knowledge. Klein's use of this case also is curious, because Freud hardly comments upon technique, and he is on the side of psychoanalytic education.[27] Klein, however, sees this case—and not Anna Freud's work—as the foundation of child analysis; in Klein's reading, it justifies her view on the necessity of analyzing the child's Oedipal complex. Klein also saw the case as supporting her insistence on relating sexuality and curiosity to the drive to know, and so to the need to make conscious unconscious anxiety by the analysis of phantasies.

Herein lies the crux of Klein's argument with Anna Freud: for Melanie Klein, the analysis of unconscious anxiety must and can be readily encountered as the basis of analytic work. The analyst must offer neither praise nor blame, but only interpretations. As for interpreting the symbolic reach of child play, because the child is so closely allied with unconscious wishes, play—itself a symbolic representation—is not only comparable to free association but allows anxiety content to be readily observed. There is no prerequisite for analysis, because for Klein, when it comes to the unconscious, there is no difference between adults and children. In her critique of Anna Freud's *Introduction to Techniques of Child Analysis*,[28] Klein (1927) pinpoints their difference directly: "I believe then that a radical difference between our attitudes to anxiety and a sense of guilt in children is this: that Anna Freud makes use of these feelings to attach the child to herself, while I from the outset enlist them in the service of the analytic work" (145). Enlisting anxiety, however, also leads to a very different analytic position: the analyst can no longer be an advocate and must be detached. Klein admitted this as a painful insistence: "Analysis is not in itself a gentle method: it cannot spare the patient *any suffering*, and this applies equally to children" (emphasis in original, 144).[29]

As if to answer some of these criticisms, Anna Freud (1928) published "The Theory of Child Analysis." Klein is only mentioned once, as someone who works with play technique in the analysis of small children. Like Hug-Hellmuth, Anna Freud emphasizes that the child cannot construct her or his history, because the troubles brought to the analytic setting are utterly current and grounded in conflicts with reality. This difference is used to support Anna Freud's view that the child's superego is neither archaic nor structured by sadistic phantasies. Rather, it is still being built, so to speak, and the materials for its construction are the child's actual relations of love and authority with the real parents. In Anna Freud's view, education must be an intimate experience in the analytic session, for unlike the adult analysand, whose superego is very difficult to transform without reconstructing childhood and infantile anxieties, the child is overly susceptible to the adult's influence and authority precisely because the superego is developing and thus registering the history of these libidinal relations. Anna Freud (1928) also minimizes Klein's insistence that education is separate from child analysis by poking at an anxiety she attributed to Klein: "I do not see why we should be so frightened of this word [education], or regard such a combination of two attitudes as a disparagement of analysis" (163). Indeed, taking education into account allows the analyst to understand the external conditions and events that also affect internal distress.

Klein did see something very frightening about the wish to educate, because she tied it to a superego that is violent, sadistic, and severe, and she claimed that the epistemophilic instinct, or the drive to know, is the outcome of this primal sadism. For Klein (1927), the role of the analyst is not to help strengthen this psychical agency but rather to encounter it:

> If the analyst, even only temporarily, becomes the representative of the educative agencies, if he assumes the role of the super-ego, at that point he blocks the way of the instinctual impulses to Cs [Consciousness]: he becomes the representative of the repressive facilities. . . . [Psychoanalysis] must enable [the analyst] to be really willing *only to analyse* and not wish to mould and direct the minds of his patients. (167, emphasis in original)

This is a position that Melanie Klein would maintain throughout her long career. Her research would begin, however, with a question that, as Pontalis (1981) points out, both touches the heart of education and causes its aberrations: "What holds the child back?" (96). The origin of intellectual inhibition was Klein's question in her work with her son Erich. Pontalis suggests that her research into this question makes all the difference to the techniques of child analysis: "The technical debate opposing Melanie Klein to Anna Freud reflects the confrontation of two ethics: for Anna Freud, in the end, it was a question of making the child find the adult's alleged autonomy; for Melanie Klein, it was a matter of coming to meet the child's psychic reality and measuring adult knowledge against it, 'in the spirit of free and unprejudiced research' " (ibid.).

If Anna Freud's position was one of *Aufklärung*, of analysis on the side of enlightenment, of hope in the capacity of rationality and reasonableness to overcome primary narcissism, then Klein's position relied on a kernel of madness that she thought structured the very problems that the wish for rationality and education ultimately buried: from one side, pessimism, and from the other side, guarded optimism. The Controversies did not just oppose these two ethics to each other but encountered their tensions. If the question of autonomy within a psychoanalytic society was central, did that mean making an allowance for divergent views or ignoring them? What can adult autonomy mean if adults are subject to their own psychical reality, to the transference, and therefore they too unconsciously enact the very dilemmas made from all that exceeds autonomy, namely, dependency on and vulnerability to others. This is a problem of what it means to meet one's own psychical reality as a test to conscious knowledge. One might say that the Controversies also were about the difficulties of free and unprejudiced research in relation to another difficulty, acknowledging the paradox of being free, and then one might wonder whether this too is a conflict that belongs to education.

PHANTASY AND REALITY, KNOWLEDGE AND REALIZATION

On September 18, 1933, six years after the difficult exchange between Jones and Freud on the future of child analysis, Jones again broached the topic of conflict within analytic societies. Difficult historical events precipitated his remarks: the death of Sandor Ferenczi, of Freud's first circle, a few months before, and then, across Germany, the Nazi burning of Freud's books.[30] The analytic community had begun its dispersal into exile,[31] and the *Anschluss* was imminent. In previous letters to Jones, Freud had expressed his deepening depression over whether psychoanalysis would survive Nazi persecution. Jones, however, perhaps sounding very close to Melanie Klein, felt the biggest problem facing psychoanalysis was internal, or "the tendency toward quarrelling and internal dissension in so many societies" (Paskauskas 1995, 729). He offered Freud three reasons why psychoanalysis had not been successful among analysts:

> First, that so many were originally neurotic and have chosen the career as a method of holding their neurosis at bay. Secondly, that continued work all day in the realm of the unconscious imposes

a strain which only the most balanced natures can sustain. . . . Thirdly, and last not least, is the fact that so very few of them are adequately analysed. (729)

These reasons for the failure of a practice are oddly reminiscent of the ways contemporary educators are blamed for the failure of education. Yes, educators do suffer from the anxieties of their own education. They may even enter the field of education to relive their childhood. Yes, education makes us tired. And yes, our education is inadequate. But these agreements are in the realm of phantasy, and there, no learning occurs, because there is no reality to lose or to find. With this third reason, Jones seems to return to the scene of the crime, accusing Freud of not analyzing his daughter sufficiently.

This strategy is, as André Green (1999b) has suggested, all too common and rather tautological: "The analyst's feelings when confronted with failure can be divided broadly into two categories: paranoia projection ('it's the patient's fault; he was unanalysable . . . ') and depressive self-accusation ('it's the fault of the bad analyst who was badly analysed')" (101). But there is also, in these observations, something true in psychical life: there is paranoia and depression. And this returns us to something more difficult, namely, the limits of analysis itself. Jones's reasons can be read as signalling a central problem that inaugurates both the psychoanalytic dialogue and the educational dialogue: how do practices account for their own limits? What belongs to the subject, and what belongs to the world? What is the relation between the psychical and the social? How does the "inside" get inside? Can the other go there? How does one know the irrational from the rational? And how does one tell the difference between knowledge and its realization? Even if we have good reasons to worry and can acknowledge that the outside world makes us miserable, is that the end of the story? How much of the failure of a project, a theory, or a practice is due to its own internal conflicts, and how much is due to outside conditions? Finally, what if education only emerges from this vast uncertainty?

There is another interpretation as well, a story of interminable education, an utterly human endeavor made from the flaws of perception, projection, resistance to knowledge and, yes, even theory. There is something in education that is radically unknowable and has been named, over the course of this chapter, as the gap between knowledge and its realization, between reality and phantasy, and between resistance and insight. If we believe Jones, then the difficulties of the field can be found within the practitioner's limits and not in the limits of the clients. If we consider Green, then the more difficult question is, how can a profession think within its failures and work through its own defenses against that which it cannot understand?

These questions, at stake in the Freud–Klein Controversies, have been written into the very history of child analysis.[32] They also should occupy education. Somewhere between reality and fantasy, between need and want, between the affect and the idea, and between dependency and autonomy, there can emerge the material from which the subject spins a life. Kristeva's (2001b) study of Klein seems to reside in this gap, what Kristeva sees as the transference relation. But this relation should not solve much, Kristeva goes on to note, because "The model of this perpetually renewed knowledge of reality is nothing less than the transference relationship. By respecting the fantasy and interpreting it, the analyst does not establish the reality to be known or the law to be followed, but gives the ego a chance to constantly create a reality" (238). We might add that both education and psychoanalysis are that chance.

Winnicott was a participant in these Controversies, and during one particularly explosive meeting, he had to remind the participants that bombs were falling outside and that it was time to go to the bomb shelter (Phillips 1988). It is a story that also is now a piece of these Controversies, another return of the question, not so much about whether there were actual bombs but rather of whether reality can be known without phantasy and whether phantasy can be known without reality. Near the end of his life, Winnicott (1988) would write a preface to a book that he did not finish, *Human Nature*. In his introduction, he begins:

> THE TASK is the study of human nature.
> At the moment of starting to write this book I am all too aware of the vastness of such an enterprise. Human nature is almost all we have. (1)

That the theme is without limits, that the theme itself articulates a certain limit, is part of the difficulty of psychoanalysis. If human nature is almost all that we have, is that why we have education?

Freud (1937b) too would acknowledge this aporia in one of his last papers, "Constructions in Analysis." There, Freud does not settle this difficulty with knowledge. Instead, he illustrates the problem even further, drawing from his well-worn metaphor, archaeology, but now with some distinctions between the work of the analyst and the work of the archaeologist:

[P]sychical objects are incomparably more complicated than the excavator's material ones and . . . we have insufficient knowledge of what we may expect to find, since their finer structure contains so much that is still mysterious. But our comparison between the two forms of work can go no further than this; for the main difference between them lies in the fact that for the archaeologist the reconstruction is the aim and end of his endeavours while for analysis the construction is only a preliminary labour. (260)

Regardless of technique, the capacity for the analysand to construct meaning only begins the analytic work. We are back to the place that Eigen (1997) formulated as "a gap between knowing about x and being x," between knowledge and its realization. We also are entering the realm of education, not as completion, or *Aufklärung*, but as preliminary labor.

"Constructions in Analysis" also suggests something of the divide and the bridge between constructions and historical truths, or what Anna Freud and Melanie Klein called "phantasies and reality." Tracing the elegant design of delusions, Freud (1937b) returns to the poetic view of a method in madness by offering the idea that there resides within madness "a fragment of *historical truth*" (267, emphasis in original). Just what precisely this truth might be, or what counts as significant, would be the work of the analyst and the analysand to discover and decide, and this construction would only prepare the common ground for them to begin their work. Perhaps such a construction can help us think about resistance to education and how this resistance also is the ground of education. There is a certain logic in not learning, so that the gap between knowledge and its realization can contain a fragment of historical truth. What complicates this logic is that if fragments of historical truth lie in the gap between knowledge and its realization, the truth of one's experience will always be a question. The Freud–Klein Controversies and our own contemporary debates suggest, however, that the kernel of historical truth is not easily found, especially when it seems to be covered over by institutional denials of the troubles that inaugurate practices. Then the common ground of education seems to collapse from the very weight that constitutes it in the first place, namely, the uncanny play of reality and phantasies and the accompanying positions of alliance and detachment.

What, then, is education that it should give us such trouble? In his rereading of Klein's case study of the adolescent, Richard, carried out in the midst of the Controversies, Adam Phillips (1998a, 107) argues that

Melanie Klein's technique of child analysis offers the question, from where or whom does the unconscious come? Klein did not ask this question herself, but her interpretations are sustained by the view that to understand the force of reality one must go directly to the inner world of phantasy, a world that is in profound disagreement over what becomes of reality when it must pass through object relations, a world that must be encountered before it can be believed or even known. And yet the articulation of unconscious phantasy cannot be direct, because there are always two questions: To what does play refer? And, then, how much play should interpretation enjoy? From a Kleinian stance, we can ask the same of education: From where, or whom, does education come? Is it from the desire to know, something already there, or is this desire somehow taken from the other? Is this desire for education on the side of phantasy or reality? And how can we choose at all?

Anna Freud's unasked question comes from a different direction: From where, and whom, does authority come? How can we know if we are taking the side of the child, and when do we leave behind our own insistences and allow for a gap between our knowledge and the child's realization? What happens to education if it is understood to constitute all forms of interference? These questions are sustained by her view that to understand the force of phantasy and how an individual can suffer, one must call the ego back to the world of education. That new knowledge can help the ego live better and, moving close to Kleinian theory after the Controversies, parts of this call must urge reparation, not just for the world but for the ego's relation to knowledge as well. Anna Freud knew that education, even in its most gentle moves, could still be a blow to narcissism, to a desire the ego also requires for its confidence in venturing into the world. What Anna Freud is asking is that education work to repair its own harm. But what she also would understand, and this is an understanding that she shared with Klein, is that such a repair can only occur after something breaks. Today we might speculate about "this something" that breaks as residing in phantasies and in reality, but as also inaugurating the chance of theory and practice. This was and is the trouble of education, then and now. Perhaps that something, its fragments of historical truth and its kernel of madness, is what make education, for both children and adults, so difficult, so subject to aggression, and yet always promising for reparation. These destructive stakes gamble with what Freud called "working through," and with what we might come to risk as a controversial theory of learning.

Chapter Three

Why Return to Anna Freud?

Teaching about psychoanalysis in the university turns learning on its head; after all, so much belief about the nature of learning and teaching and what counts as its evidence must be held in suspense and so too must the teacher's usual appeals to the student's rationality, preparedness, and willingness. Moreover, however intellectually assured the teacher may be in this topic, her or his own learning also should be surprised. Sigmund Freud (1919) wrote a short paper on this very topic outlining a few problems, from the perspective of both the university and psychoanalysis. In Freud's view, it would be to the benefit of the university more than to the field of psychoanalysis if some of its theories were to be taught there; psychoanalysis would be beneficial to those studying medicine and psychiatry but also interesting to those studying the humanities and social sciences. The method of teaching, Freud advises, would have to be didactic, through lectures and discussion. And learning more about psychoanalysis would have to come from experiencing an analysis. Freud then concluded by suggesting a modest yet utterly complicated goal: "[I]t would be enough if he learns something *about* psychoanalysis and something *from* it" (173, emphasis in original). One might characterize a certain paradox of pedagogy as the meeting of modesty with complexity. That is, before one can decide whether the knowledge offered is relevant, useful, and even profound, one has to encounter the knowledge.

With this encounter in mind, I bring a small psychoanalytic text to my teacher education course. Perhaps anxieties flourish when psychoanalysis enters the teacher education course, for there, those who are learning to teach feel terrific pressures to learn a great deal about how other people learn. And yet to suggest that education can make one nervous, that it has psychical consequences, and that not only will one's students refuse to learn but so too teachers will defend themselves against new knowledge—to suggest all of this and still try to learn something about and from psychoanalysis is quite a pedagogical feat. This chapter narrates my pedagogical misadventures made from asking my undergraduate education students to read and discuss Anna Freud's (1930) "Four Lectures on Psychoanalysis for Teachers and Parents."

The Anna Freud readers meet in this chapter has left behind the vituperative qualities that marked debates over education during the Freud–Klein Controversies. Then the paradox of child analysis revolved around the problem of whether education had any role at all. During the Controversies, education was depicted as heavy-handed, manipulation, inviting neurosis, and moralistic, indeed, as a rigid reality principle. Anna Freud thought that educational attempts could be otherwise, even as she offered in her "Four Lectures," stringent critiques of compulsory education. For her, the relation between the analyst and the young analysand was like a delicate education, and the work of the analyst was to offer to the child what might best be called "a helping hand." That meant at times foreclosing some possibilities, and at other times pulling back and allowing the symptom its ingenious expression. Yet for this to even occur, a great deal is required from the one who lends a helping hand. Simply put, one must be willing to have her or his hand bitten.

Adam Phillips's (1998a) summary of Klein's argument with Anna Freud draws us back to the psychoanalytic stakes of that early debate:

> [B]y exploiting the child's positive transference, by encouraging the child's identification with the analyst [Anna Freud] was merely "teaching" the child instinct control, not reaching, as Klein was, the depths of the child's personality. For . . . Klein . . . the teacher—after the seducer—is the analyst's negative ideal. (108)

Phillips's description may be heavy-handed, but he touches upon a few of the teacher's raw nerves: immediate gratification may inhibit the slow work of learning, the teacher may wish to teach control, but the actuality of teaching belongs to another realm, and while the teacher may seduce the student into an encounter with knowledge, for that encounter to be meaningful, the teacher also must bow out. In addition, there is another set of questions, namely, how does the teacher work toward inviting the students' interest in material that at first glance is not acceptable to them? And then, what psychological significance on the nature of teaching can be made from this educational imbroglio?

In this chapter, I play with the image of the teacher as the analyst's photographic negative and imagine pedagogy as symbolizing something of the arguments made with both knowledge and ignorance. My understanding is influenced by Winnicott's (1996) discussion of the pleasures and dangers of first learning about psychology in educational settings. He offers two stages in learning. Students might learn some content. Then they ask, "Yes, but is it true, is it real, how do we know?" (13). In this second act, Winnicott warns that the knowledge can be made true if it can survive the destructive qualities of this question. But also, something new is asked of the teacher, particularly if she or he can accept additional advice from Winnicott: "Psychology does not try to teach you what to do when [someone] needs your help. It can do a lot, however, toward enabling you to be more sure of yourself, to understand what is going on, to grow on experiences, to see where mistakes might have been made, to prevent distress and disasters" (15).

If part of the teacher's work is "merely teaching," or better, in Gardner's (1994, 128) discussion of trying to teach, learning the necessity of the teacher as "being a bit off," that is, not knowing precisely what is going on yet still persisting in her or his attempts, is there anything particular in that effort we can use to compose new pedagogical relations? In returning to how Anna Freud worked and spoke retrospectively about her practice—after all, in this chapter we meet an older Anna Freud— can we learn something about the teacher who may come to be less interested in instructing others and more cautious about the need to have others identify with her or him? If we lose the interest in telling students what they should learn, what else might happen in our classrooms? Suppose then that the teacher tries to encounter the otherness of the student, not by knowing something about the depths of her or his personality but rather through acknowledging how the student's work of thinking influences her or his own?

Such occupations were not where I began when I introduced my undergraduate students to the writing of Anna Freud. Indeed, my preoccupations were with offering some time to explore the vicissitudes of psychical reality and to consider sexuality as touching the urge to learn. These hopes were the occasion for meaning to break down. I was not prepared for the hostility that a majority of my students felt toward Anna Freud's little book. I also was not prepared to be stopped by the hostility. Many students who first encountered Anna Freud needed desperately to fight with her ideas before they had any idea with what Anna Freud seemed to be fighting, or indeed, with what they themselves were fighting in fighting with her. To make sense of what worried these students, and what worried me, my work became setting aside the teacher's wish that the lovely knowledge proffered could just be accepted enthusiastically. This chapter narrates the twists and turns of our various fights, not so much with Anna Freud, although she was used ruthlessly as a transitional object. Indeed, into her theories, students did project both their own worries over trying to know the other in pedagogical exchange and their frustrations with a theory meant to unsettle cherished assumptions about what it means to learn, and not to learn at all. If at first glance their incredulity, made from worries over the invisible reach of psychoanalytic theory, seemed to protect gigantic and passionately held misconceptions that were reminiscent of the workings of phantasy, then the work of considering pedagogy as conditioned upon having second thoughts opened our curiosity toward trying to learn from these psychic events. My learning to tolerate the awkwardness of learning—indeed, its performativity— both for the students and for myself was our pedagogical dilemma. To understand what can happen when curiosity, in whatever form, is given its allowance means revising an old question that Pontalis (1981, 95) asked, which he considered the beginning of Melanie Klein's research: "What holds the child back?" What holds the teacher back?

That there is an unconscious need to defend oneself against the making of insight is the other side of Felman's (1987) interest in what she called, along with Lacan, "the passion for ignorance." At times, we do try to conduct our teaching as if learning will be no problem for the learner, and if problems emerge, they are somehow viewed as obstacles to the wish for learning to be no problem. What is missed is an element of destruction and aggression that is also a necessary part of trying to learn (Winnicott 1990a). Yet we also can admit that ideas, words, and books arouse anxiety in the learner and then notice that the learner has methods for defending herself or himself against knowledge. In the context of teacher education, I have often wondered whether the expectations and anticipations one brings to teacher education work as a defense against accepting ideas that insist upon the complexities and uncertainties of teaching and learning. Comments such as "It is nice in theory but not in the real world," or "I don't have the time to think slowly," or "I can't see how such an idea can be implemented" may well represent unfinished symptoms that defend against the more difficult question of what happens when our pedagogy is caught somewhere between ignorance and knowledge, between not knowing what to do but still having to act, and between not seeing and seeing too much.

Teacher educators are not immune from such defenses; they may regularly dismiss texts and ideas that seem abstract or too theoretical or controversial for their students. While such decisions may seem justified by pointing out the need for practicality, convenience, or adherence to program design, psychoanalytic views suggest more is at stake in teaching than what one imagines as institutional mandates and students' supposed needs. Indeed, Anna Freud has some very interesting theories to help us think about the ways we do defend against reality and phantasy; her early work on the ego and its mechanisms of defense offers some important speculations on the precarious work of learning to live. The problem, however, was that studying defense mechanisms could not occur without animating their very enactment; arguments made by my students to dismiss Anna Freud were symptomatic of the defenses that she so elegantly elaborates. While the ego's defense mechanisms work to ward off the perception of danger, they cannot, in and of themselves, answer the great questions also invoked: From where does danger emanate, and what is the nature of that danger for me?[1]

The history of the concept of the ego's mechanisms of defense suggests something about the process of revision that psychoanalytic ideas undergo. The ideas that would become Anna Freud's (1936) book, *The Ego and the Mechanisms of Defense*, were first presented to the Vienna Psychoanalytic Society in 1935. One year later, the papers became a book, and she presented the German issue to her father, Sigmund Freud, for his eightieth birthday (Young-Bruehl 1988). It would not be translated into English until the conclusion of World War II. At that time, Anna Freud was not yet fluent in English and so could not check the accuracy of the translation. Years later, she would joke about the problem of translation: "We always used to say that the most satisfactory translations are the Japanese, as we can't check them" (Sandler, with Anna Freud 1985, 294). In 1966, Anna Freud revised the text, although the crucial questions she raised, namely, how the ego defends itself against inside and outside pressures, and how this defense returns to shape the ego, remained central. The story of this book traverses Anna Freud's long career as a child analyst and as one of the people who brought psychoanalysis a bit closer to understanding practices in education. But this relation, however didactic it can appear from her lectures, essentially was ambivalent, because the subtext of these lectures raised two interminable questions for teachers: What are you doing when you try to teach? Who do you imagine you are teaching?

When Anna Freud consented to reexamine her early work on the ego at age seventy-six and conducted the interview in English with Joseph Sandler (1985) and other colleagues, this return allowed for a lively and contentious conversation. The book that resulted from these talks, *The Analysis of Defense: The Ego and the Mechanisms of Defense Revisited,* was published after her death. It is organized in interview format, and each chapter corresponds to a chapter in the revised version of the *Ego* text. For those who know the work of Anna Freud, it may come as no surprise that her earliest commitments as a thinker and defender of her methods are elaborated on in the late interviews. Many of her strategies suggest new directions for education, for example, her interest in taking the side of the child, the symptom, and the conflict; her insistence upon simplicity; her respect for the creativity and troubles of psychical life; her pleasures in finding humor in and compassion for losing and being lost; her belief in the creative power of sublimation; and her stubbornness for holding onto her own ideas, even when the ideas are no longer popular, easy to accept, or feel outmoded. For contemporary readers of Anna Freud, there may be too much with which to argue. It is, however, for the sake of argument and for occasions to speculate upon and interpret educational scenes not often considered central to teaching that I regularly introduce a few of Anna Freud's (1930) lectures to my undergraduate students who are engaged in learning to teach. Not surprisingly, the introduction is rather awkward; their interpretations are made from a volatile combination of hostility and incredulity, and therefore they carry psychoanalytic qualities of affect such as negation, resistence, denial, undoing, and splitting, all of which are put into the service of the ego's strategies of defense.

Anna Freud's view of the ego and its mechanism of defense may well stem from her work in educational contexts. Her definition of education as constituting all forms of interference and as "a never-ending battle" anticipates the very need for the ego to defend itself (1930, 101). The work of the bodily ego—perception, observation, projection, hallucination, and reality testing—means that the ego ventures into the world, even as its outward explorations suggest something of its internal pressures. In this protracted conflict, the ego prepares itself to meet other egos. But the anticipation is anxiety, and it is structured from worries over what might happen before an event is experienced. The time of anxiety can only be articulated in the grammatical tense of the future perfect, where both present and future actions yet to be accomplished are already completed. Anna Freud called this anticipation and protection against what is perceived as danger a "mechanism of defense." Despite its warlike suggestion, we might approach the ego's work as ambivalent, as caught somewhere between the passionate desire for both knowledge and ignorance. A mechanism of defense attempts to mediate the ambivalence, but its attitude is precocious in that it relates and equates the psychical to the social, even as it tries to protect and resolve, at least at the level of phantasy, anticipations that threaten to undo our observations, coherence, and standing in the world. To even encounter these speculations, one must begin with the psychoanalytic assumptions that perception is an emotional experience, that one projects psychological qualities into the world, and that consciousness is an exception. These are difficult leaps of faith, not just because we hope our perceptions of the world proceed from the qualities of things already in the world; they also are difficult because to refuse these assumptions is to conjure up psychoanalytic resistance, itself a condensation of ego defenses.[2]

The students in my classes do not, at first, see the relevance of the reading assignment or what use that psychoanalytic insight might hold for the study of their own lives. These complaints are two sides of the same coin. They insist that Anna Freud is old-fashioned, that children are too young to be affected by their inner world, and that looking too deeply into one's own life can only cause grief. These responses, however, seem to be more about their anxieties of what such knowledge will do to them, a reverse of the more typical complaint of how to apply knowledge. Like many who are learning to teach in both university classes and in school settings, the students seem desperate to prove their competency, to be seen as worthy of the profession of teaching, and to be liked and admired by their own students. Caught in the constraints that they meet and make, both in schools and in universities, the students are suspicious of any knowledge that bothers their wishes for certainty and control, even as many also can admit their discomfort at feeling controlled by others and the pleasure that they make from the experience of doubt. And while at some level these newly arrived teachers would like to take the time to explore ideas and meet experiences that are not their own, they quickly forget that exploring ideas and meeting the views of others also means getting lost in thoughts, losing their place, surprising their old knowledge, allowing new knowledge its capacity to survive their attacks, and transforming these accidents into pleasurable learning. Anna Freud's lectures can remind students of the difficulties and pleasures in learning. And yet, appreciating something difficult about pleasure also means thinking about sexuality in terms of moving sexuality closer to phantasy than to reality.

I find myself lecturing on Anna Freud's lectures, perhaps because I have both the hope that new ideas can influence old worries and the wish that something I say might animate their weary interest. I admit to wanting to correct misperceptions but know that these misperceptions also are libidinal; that is, a great deal of their phantasies about psychoanalysis sustains deep investments in their wish for an education without conflict, an ego that is mastery, and a knowledge unencumbered by intersubjectivity. The strategies I employ to rethink these wishes—both mine and theirs—belong to Anna Freud.[3] Perhaps her greatest strategy was respecting the anxiety ideas raise and in inviting her audiences to think more deeply, "to see whether your knowledge has gone deep enough and wide enough" (Sandler 1992, 12–13). In her "Four Lectures on Psychoanalysis for Teachers and Parents," and indeed in much of her work for popular audiences, for example, in *The Harvard Lectures* (Sandler 1992), where she spoke with education undergraduates, Anna Freud admits that what she has to offer may cause a bit of discomfort and surprise. She also maintains that these first affects can be useful for thinking about the great questions invoked through learning and teaching, questions that may never be answered but, when asked, open new considerations of the status, timing, and uses of psychical obstacles in and for the work of teaching and learning.

UNFINISHED SYMPTOMS

When we are first confronted with new ideas, the earliest flutters of learning are made from fear. Inhibition, or a wish to stop an activity that is felt as distress, is one configuration anxiety might press into shape. Anna Freud's (Sandler, with Freud 1985) view of the inhibition allows us to look for ambivalence as well:

> I think an inhibition is really meant to be an unfinished symptom because there is the movement forward of the wish, and then there is the counterforce against it. That is inhibition. I think the characteristic of the inhibition is that the wish is kept alive, and very often remains conscious. (217)

If an inhibition is an "unfinished symptom," the learner's response to the new material will try to finish up the symptom. I witnessed this dynamic the first day my class tried to discuss Anna Freud's (1930) lectures for teachers and parents. I tried to take their questions seriously, particularly those that seemed to ward off engagement or dialogue. This capacity to tolerate the detours of learning, perceiving, and interpreting the unfinished symptom without mobilizing one's own defenses may be one of the most demanding experiences for any teacher. Anna Freud suggests this often when she encourages teachers to study what students—and what they themselves—dismiss, throw away, ignore, lose, and forget. And yet this discarded content also carries with it a kernel of revenge—it threatens to return angrily to bother the one who is discarding it.

Anna Freud's lectures often are met with the students' hostile dismissal. They deny that the lectures have any relevance to modern education. Some of the reasons for this awkward meeting are interesting, while others are predictable. The interesting awkwardness has to do with when the students try to step inside (as opposed to step upon) the logic of Anna Freud's lectures. The predictable reasons have to do with students' preconceptions of psychoanalysis and their schooled disagreements with what they imagine Sigmund Freud said and did. I note these disagreements as schooled, although it would be more accurate to say that the disagreements come from a rather wishful secondhand knowledge of Freud's work. However, there is more at stake in their dismissals, and it has to do with the startling reach of psychoanalytic insight and then the uncertainties made because education cannot only proceed by mastery and will. According to psychoanalytic views, we always mean something more than what we consciously intend, and exploring the unconscious dimensions of our desires means confronting truths about ourselves that are very difficult to admit. Also, there is the nagging question of what education means if the teacher is neither in control of her or his pedagogical reach nor the students' responses. These tensions cannot be taught, although the teacher can witness their performance.

Most students are surprised to learn that Sigmund Freud's papers comprise twenty-four volumes, that over the course of his writing he revised and argued a great deal with himself as well as with others, and that by the end of his life, he considered the limits of psychoanalysis in relation to the difficult question of learning from suffering. When I lecture on Anna Freud's life work, the students are surprised to learn that Erik Erickson was her student and analysand,[4] that she wrote guidelines for child custody cases and coined the phrase "in the best interest of the child," that she never went to university but did graduate from normal school, that her arrest by the Gestapo in Vienna in 1938 led to the Freud family's decision to flee Vienna, and that she was a teacher for elementary-age children. However these details work to humanize the figure of Anna Freud, they do not immediately help students become open to her writings.

I ask students, as they read the Lectures, to compose a question for Anna Freud. I read their questions as little clues of resistance, as precursors of defense, as longings, and as unfinished symptoms of learning. Their questions run from the ridiculous to the sublime. Some students begin quite literally and probably are asking me as well when they wonder if lectures are good models for education. A majority of the students create great difficulty from Anna Freud's insistence that sexuality begins at the beginning of life, and that sexual development proceeds through stages conspicuously named oral, anal, and genital. Sometimes they read this progression too literally, and other times, they seem shocked that the baby feels bodily pleasure before she or he understands. Many students are incredulous about the Oedipus complex, penis envy, castration, and all of the strange and estranging concepts that somehow articulate the fear of loss and of losing love, of primal helplessness, as well as unintended work of refinding lost objects in reality and phantasy. These students are sure that if children are curious about their own sexuality or the sexuality of others, it can only be a sign of sexual abuse.

Students' questions do reflect a stunning literalness that seems to foreclose any interpretative work and deflect their own worries, their fear of the uncontrollable emotions that suddenly break out in classrooms, and their wishes for a magical pedagogy that performs what Anna Freud called "rescue fantasies." The problem with insisting upon the literal as a measure of reality is that the kernel of phantasy at stake in thinking returns to harass the very reality our thoughts try to secure. One student collapsed reality and phantasy when she wrote: "When you refer to boys and sons always being jealous of their fathers because they got to sleep with their mothers etc. . . . how could we change this?" In my reading of the question, the problem is with the last anxious clause and the view that teachers should take conflict away from the student or somehow prevent its occupancy. But also, something happens to language in this question, and it is difficult to figure out the nature of the worry or even what teachers must change.

Under the title "A slightly rhetorical question for Anna Freud, resulting from a bit of skepticism," another student asks: "Anna, are you suggesting that parents should allow children to continue putting excreta in their mouths in order not to force them to suppress their every desire?" This student is aware of the conflict between instinctual freedom and social constraint but does not trust the possibility that the child herself or himself can resolve this dilemma and still manage to find some suitable pleasure. So the conflict returns as scandalous—as if Anna Freud is asking this student to eat excrement—and then as provoking the adult's need to draw some sort of line. Indeed, when it comes to drawing lines, some students are quite suspicious of Anna Freud's notion of developmental lines and their constancy of pressures. Another student asks: "What happens if one doesn't even 'hit' the points on these paths?" Perhaps the student is worrying, as with the first question, about whether teachers are responsible for the proper alignment of their students. The phrasing of this question is curious; it suggests the wish that one must strike quickly, indeed, "hit" development before the oral, anal, and genital stages can hit back. Another question tries to suggest a problem with how anti-racist education is ignored: "Anna, you speak of the anal, the oral, and the genital. But what about race?" This question, however, feels too garbled for any answer. Perhaps this individual also is wondering, are the anal, the oral, and the genital all that there is for the body?

It may seem curious to read many of the above questions as a sort of return to the Freud–Klein Controversies. After all, the students did not know of this event. But they did know something of the dilemmas of trying to teach, and their questions were a condensation of worries and profound inquiries into the object relations of pedagogy. Certainly the students' questions shadow many of the debates on the teacher's position, whether, for example, the teacher should be detached, strict, permissive, or serve as a role model. Should the teacher, indeed, can the teacher identify with the child's or the adolescent's inner conflicts? And when would the teacher know that this is what she or he is doing? Can the teacher "merely teach," despite the crowded inner world of everyone involved? What can the status of knowledge be in the face of phantasy? What does it mean to face phantasy? And also, what does it mean to meet the autonomy of the other without trying to shape it? Finally, there is the pesky question of when education begins.

Other students become preoccupied with Anna Freud's criticisms of educational methods. "If," writes a student, "education is harmful, should we get rid of it?" Another student worries about the uncertainty of knowledge in relation to her identity as a science teacher. Her question is actually in the form of defending the rights of knowledge to answer: "As a science teacher, I am fully aware that room for error must be permitted, but how does one teach math, science, physical laws, the periodic table . . . with uncertainty? This is factual information. Uncertainty cannot exist." Here, error and uncertainty are collapsed, and facts are used to ward off the intimate problem of not knowing, even from certainty. There also is another hint of worry if the last statement is read as negation, which is to say, if in reading the question, we take away the "no." If uncertainty can be made from certainty, how can one know either one? Where does uncertainty reside? In the knowledge exchanged? In the claims advanced by knowledge? In the encounter with the knowledge or with the person teaching? Does knowledge make errors, or is the error what makes knowledge? These worries over how to stabilize knowledge are transformed into a different question, now displaced onto a phantom student.

Some students worry about conformity but do not consider how conformity works in the service of knowledge claims. One person wondered, "Without an element of conformity in the classroom, how can a teacher teach?" In this question, it is difficult to determine whose conformity is at stake, the teacher's or the student's. Another student seems torn in wondering if "encouraging conformity and encouraging individuality can be implemented in the classroom simultaneously." Here, there is that ambivalence made from "merely teaching," and the uncomfortable sense that teachers do require something of their students, however politely they might ask, and their students also know this and are not so easily urged by appeals to conformity or individuality.

At times, a question expresses quite clearly the hostile feelings of the questioner: "Anna, how does it feel to have a pig for a father?" I found this question painful to read and difficult to accept. Indeed, my feelings were hurt, and I debated whether to even let this student know how her question had affected me. This is the teacher's dilemma: should she use her feelings as a means for the student to identify with her? And if the student is unconvinced that the teacher's feelings matter to the teacher, what can happen next? Hoping that the student would care about my response, I did pull her aside to acknowledge my hurt feelings. I also reminded the student that Anna Freud loved her father and did not see her father as an animal. Finally, I asked the student what she wanted from this question, and she admitted what she did not want: to learn something from Anna Freud. I did invite her to try another question when she felt she could do justice to her curiosity. Still other students worry about how to recognize psychical dynamics that Anna Freud describes. Writes another student: "How are we to know when these defense mechanisms are taking place?"

A few students take inhibition from another vantage. For example, one student wrote: "Is the knowledge that comes from learning a burden? Would Anna Freud see learning as a risk-taking activity, and is there a cost involved?" Another offers the following worry: "How can the teacher learn to control and be aware of his or her own conflicts prior to teaching?" Both questions seemed to be in dialogue with one of my early claims to the class: we learn before we understand, and mistakes can be read as unfinished symptoms of learning. These questioners try to make sense of the idea that there can be no education without some sort of anxiety. And yet, while many students acknowledge that anxiety is a central experience in their education, one student asks, "How can anxiety be so great for learning when many people dread this so?" This question reaches into the limits of anxiety and perhaps the student's own worry that while anxiety might provoke learning, it also can become a persecuting object. How can anxiety work in both directions and still be considered anxiety?

Finally, many students are quite puzzled about Anna Freud's definition of education as all types of interference and her desire to limit education. Writes one student: "Is all interference bad?" A few students see interpretation itself as interference. "Is it possible that some things need not be analyzed and taken at face value?" In this question, there is a wish for meaning to be literal but also a worry that meaning cannot be faced. How can we face meaning if all we have is interpretation? Other students assert that only bad education is interference, and that learning should proceed without internal or external conflict. Their wish for a conflict-free education, made from an absolute splitting of good and bad, is not yet seen either as a defense against the vast uncertainty of teaching or as a rescue fantasy. On the other hand, many students become pre-occupied with rescue fantasies in education, particularly the teacher's rescue fantasy. These students find that such a concept helps them move a little slower when they desire to save a child. Some read their educational rescue fantasies as their desire to save old versions of the self by finding a suitable proxy. One student reported the strange tense of time invoked by the grammar of rescue fantasy, "as if in saving the child I am saving myself from what has already happened to me as a child."

Some students do change not just their view of Anna Freud but their capacity to make some relevance from her writing. For these students, Anna Freud's writing reminds them, and then they remind me, that there are other scenes of education, that internal conflicts are as important to the learner as those conflicts found on the outside, and that we might take the point of view of the discarded content. Indeed, from Anna Freud's perspective, internal conflicts help us notice the outside conflicts in the world. But this means that the testing of reality will always be faulty, since this very work is invoked from a position of anxiety. For other students, however, the making of relevance is a rather ambivalent affair, and while some of their questions hold the tension made from the wish to both attach and to ignore Anna Freud's ideas, other questions carry a silent warning to the teacher that cannot be persuaded through any analysis of negation: this idea will not be tolerated.

"WORDS AROUSE ANXIETY"

Teacher education does have a history of acknowledging, both consciously and unconsciously, that learning to teach and teaching alike are times of great anxiety. The tension, however, is in how anxiety is conceptualized and where it attaches. While earlier discussions place anxiety in the problem of beginnings and beginners, recent discussions of anxiety in the pedagogical exchange conjugate anxiety in learning within both larger crises in our world and with what Winnicott (1992a) calls "fear of breakdown," a fear that anticipates a shattering of experience before that experience can even be made. Comparable to the structure of deferred action, fear of breakdown suggests that what was not yet experienced in the past did in fact occur, and that symptoms of its missing details exert pressure on how the present can be encountered.[5] Anxiety in this recent literature becomes more relational, even as it is still tied to the workings of defense mechanisms.

Willard Waller (1961), in the first published account of the sociology of teaching, asks the question, "What does teaching do to teachers?" Waller was interested in the pressures the teacher feels, the popular image of teaching that the teacher confronts and lives, and the institutional demands for certainty that teachers negotiate. Years later, I began my study, *Practice Makes Practice: A Critical Study of Learning to Teach* (1991), with Waller's question but addressed it to those just entering the profession of teaching. What does learning to teach do to student teachers? At that time, I was interested in bringing together the history made from the student's institutional biography of learning with the history of teacher education and seeing, in this meeting, a series of cultural myths that defended against feelings of helplessness, uncertainty, and dependency in teaching and learning.[6] While learning to teach is a time when great anxiety is difficult to distinguish from great wishes to overcome the first awkward attempts in teaching others, I noticed that anxiety, no matter how long a teacher has been practicing, does not go away. It does become more refined in its disguise, more socially accepted, more intellectualized. Like anyone else, teachers learn to place their anxiety alongside the problems and tensions that, while not necessarily the cause of the discomfort, seem to justify the unease.

The worries and anxieties many teachers have noticed also are addressed in psychoanalytic writing. Gardner (1994) captures the teacher's anxious efforts at the fault lines of inattentiveness. Trying to teach too much, what Gardner calls "the furor to teach" (8), may actually be a defense against the fear of missing the student and, in this loss, not being able to settle one's methods and, more intimately, one's reason for being. In his view, all that teachers can do is teach in "remarkable ignorance" (viii). It is not that teachers do not know something. Surely they do. But what remains in the realm of ignorance is not just what learners do with the knowledge proffered but which knowledge of what circumstance becomes interesting to the learner. If we can remark upon our ignorance, we might then begin to question what happens when we acknowledge that our knowledge is made not from solutions but from our capacity to face dilemmas, uncertainty, and unexpected replies to our work. Perhaps the most difficult tension is that while teachers cannot know their teaching, they can become curious about their learning. To revise the question "how do I teach?" to the question "what is learning for me now?" means that the qualities of one's present responses to events, ideas, and other people must become central to one's thinking about dilemmas of teaching. However, when teachers notice dilemmas in their furor to teach, they also might push aside questions that herald doubt and their own curiosity.

Arthur Jersild (1955) makes this point throughout his study of anomie and commitment in teaching and ties anxiety to the very structure of educational thought. He maintains that: "the history of education . . . is in part a history of [people's] efforts to evade or to face anxiety" (27). Maxine Greene (1973) considers how teachers can cope with educational research when so much of it is contradictory. Whom does the teacher believe in the history of education? Greene offers us an ethical question: "What does the known demand of me as a teacher? Each day of [the teacher's] life, he or she has to choose" (152). And yet, choosing the known often is the very place that anxiety resides. Roger

Simon (1992) also looks to the question of educational thought when he considers his students' "fear of theory" (79). New knowledge is first felt as bothersome, indeed, as persecuting what one already knows. And when students consider the theoretical, they often view theory as a dismissal of real experience, a profound idealization, or a useless fantasy. To render theory and practice dichotomous—to split theory and practice as one does with the separation of good and bad—however can work as a defense against not knowing. If the theory is viewed as "not working," and usually learning a theory begins by breaking it before it has a chance to break the learner, then the problems that one confronts can somehow be attributed to the fault of theory. Simon examines symptoms of this fear and finds them in the students' worry over confronting new language and then dismissing it as jargon, in the insistence that the theories met feel as if the old views are diminished and, more generally, in the anxiety made when students confront or feel forced to confront "the disruptive character" of language itself (84). Simon (1995) also will relate anxiety to fear of the other's alterity and to the transferential qualities of teaching and learning, where what belongs to the teacher and what belongs to the student are momentarily indistinguishable. What becomes disruptive is the meeting of the students' and professor's desires, the structure of Eros.[7] Yet these emotional ties, Simon (2000) also will remind, limit the capacity to try to understand historical events that are not easily identified with or even assimilated by one's prior experience.

Anxiety also is there when one does not know what to do with knowledge one wants. In one of the most astounding discussions of teaching as crisis, Shoshana Felman (1992) analyzes her university seminar on testimonial literature and video and her surprise that the students enacted the very breakdowns that resided in the testimonies they encountered. She describes the students' responses as "something like an *anxiety of fragmentation*" (49, emphasis in original); the students, upon viewing two videotaped Holocaust testimonies, felt disconnected from their own present, lost in worries over how to speak about their witnessing, and separated from those who did not experience the seminar. While silent in the seminar, they could not stop talking in the corridors. They had broken the frame of Felman's seminar, just as the testimonies break the frame of understanding. Felman discussed her students' distress with her colleague, Dori Laub. They agreed that "what was called for was for me to resume authority as the teacher of the class and bring the students back into significance" (50). And for Felman, calling students to make their own significance from the anxiety of fragmentation meant inviting them to testify to their experiences of breakdown with the seminar readings and videos. The authority Felman assumed was made from her insistence that what the students had to say, even if she asked them before they were ready to say it, was significant. "Each great subject," Felman writes, "has a turning point contained within, and that turning point has to be met. The question for the teacher is, then, on the one hand, how to access, how *not to foreclose* the crisis, and, on the other hand, how to *contain it*, how much crisis can the class sustain" (56, emphasis in original). The paradox is that one cannot predict the amount of crisis a class can contain until the crisis becomes too much. But neither can one predict what will become a crisis, and so we must return to the question of anxiety in learning.

If, as Anna Freud (Sandler, with Freud 1985) reminds, "words arouse anxiety," exactly what is anxiety? In psychoanalytic views, anxiety is the special way for the ego to anticipate what might happen next. Worries tell a story about worrying, and anxiety is the ego's way of both worrying about potential danger and defending against the perception of the danger. Adam Phillips (1993) suggests that worries are "our most intimate inventions" (50). Because they are so intimate and dear, however, Phillips also maintains, "It is, of course, easy to forget that worries are imaginative creations, small epics of personal failure and anticipated catastrophe" (50). Anna Freud offers a way to think about the journeys of neurosis, or what she calls *the Neurosenbildung*: there is an arousal of danger, an anxiety, a defense, a compromise formation, and finally a symptom (Sandler, with Freud 1985, 275). For Anna Freud, there are three sites of potential danger in which anxiety is made: anxiety can emanate from the id or from unconscious content; it can come from not being able to meet the demands of the superego; and it can come from the world and thus be *Realangst*, or justified fear.

Given the complexity of anxiety, rational persuasions are not helpful in determining where anxiety attaches. One can make anxiety from anything, and in education, the smallest detail or the tiniest word can provoke the ego's defenses. Returning to the students' responses to Anna Freud's lectures, they often fixate on one word that causes something to be upset. The word suggests a dynamic relation between the thing and that to which it refers, and this relation can plunge one into the murky spaces of free association, slips of the tongue, and sexual innuendo. It is not the word but the force of the affect that the word comes to represent that upsets students. For example, one student worried about the Oedipal complex and could not accept the view that his students transferred old conflicts and desires made from libidinal relations with parents onto the figure of the teacher. The Oedipal complex became a literal experience and therefore could not be a phantasy or even serve as a metaphor about worries over knowledge, ignorance, love, and loss. That Eros irrupts in the most surprising ways was too much to think. It is difficult to determine whether the student was upset about the transference or sexuality, given that both signal demands for loving and being loved. But the worry also can be read as not so much about this student's students but with the self. Should the teacher be a beloved object? What if the teacher fell in love with the student? How does the teacher respond to the student's affect, if the teacher cannot control the vicissitudes of her or his own affect? The worry was over the affective bonds teachers and students do make with one another, and with knowledge as well. In discarding the terms Anna Freud offered, the student could deflect the more painful question, from where does the danger of love emanate? Even these speculations may not get at the complexity of this student's view, nor illumine the conflicts the anxiety tries to ward off. One meets the heart of this complexity in Anna Freud's short vignette, "The Robber Story."

"ROBBER COME"

When I came across this story (Sandler, with Freud 1985), I was struck by the question Anna Freud asked a distraught child, and how this question played with the problem of identification with the analyst. In retelling the story to my class, I left out Anna Freud's question to the child and asked the class to think, after hearing the child's worries, of a question they could ask:

> I once described a little boy patient of mine who had terrible anxiety attacks when he was in bed at night because he was sure a robber was hidden behind the curtains. He was sure that as soon as he moved at all in his bed or, worse still, as soon as he got out of bed to fetch something, or to reach for a glass of water, the robber would pounce on him and destroy him. One felt quite sorry for the child. (207)

Before the students heard Anna Freud's response to the child, they offered interesting questions: "What does the robber want?" "Why does the robber come?" "What could you do to fool the robber?" "Where does the robber hide?" When I asked the class what these questions might have in common, one student quipped, "We took the side of the child." Perhaps it might be more accurate to consider that the class took the side of the phantasy, trying to persuade the conflict to go away. But the students also seemed willing to enter what they imagined as a piece of the child's logic and to consider what the child was worried about when the child worried about robbers coming. They felt that if they somehow understood what the robber signified to the child, then they would be able, perhaps, to talk the robber out of the child. And yet, in attempting to figure out how the robber was used by the child, their answers still seemed stuck in the educationalist view that the child wanted the attention of the adults, did not want to go to bed when the adults told him to, and made up a story to disguise his stubbornness. They had not yet entered the child's logic but the adult's logic made from their dilemma with the child. And curiously, in the sorts of questions they raised, the students' identifications seemed closest to the work of the robber, perhaps a wish to rob the child of his robber.

After the short discussion, I offered them Anna Freud's response to the child: "But I remember I asked him once in the hour, 'What do you do if the robber doesn't come out?' and he said: 'Then I say: robber come'" (Sandler, with Freud 1985, 207). The class laughed in delight, for while they did want their own answers to address the logic of the child, they forgot that logical questions can also mask more important ones. For Anna Freud, the question was what the child actually wanted for himself. Whereas the class wanted to take the robber out of the child, Anna Freud saw the robber and the child as the same. She offered a way to bring the robber closer to the child and suggested, with her question, that the child needed the robber in order to make and disclaim excitement and sexuality, for each night the boy was masturbating and did not want to get caught. The robber was helpful, for it allowed the boy to both make his pleasure and continue it, even as he worried it would be stolen from him. Seeking thrills and creating suitable objects upon which to project such thrills is a part of the work of our phantasies. Another part is that our phantasies also can contain anticipated punishments for having them in the first place. Calling the robber was ingenious. Whereas logical questions attempt to correct the symptom, questions that can address the unconscious desire take residence in the symptom, perhaps disrupting the symptom until it can no longer be used. If the symptom does not come, it must be called!

And yet, there are many tensions in this story, for if our desires must be projected, the question of projection, for Anna Freud, raised new sorts of difficulties.[8] In conversations with Joseph Sandler (Sandler, with Freud, 1985), Anna Freud tries to distinguish our capacity to externalize and put something of ourselves in the world from our capacity to project. In Anna Freud's theory, projection is only possible when the self recognizes its own boundaries and the boundaries of another. She quips to Sandler, perhaps playing on Sigmund Freud's view that the ego is not master of its house: "If you haven't built the house, you can't throw somebody out of it" (238). But once the house begins to be built, to continue the metaphor, what is perceived as "trash," or as unwanted material, must be put outside. This is the beginning of projection, where the unwanted parts of the self are projected onto others. However, not just any other will do. It is no accident that the boy projected his excitement onto the figure of the robber, for the child is stealing pleasure and then makes the robber come to steal away yet also to preserve the very pleasure that the boy makes! This brings us to Anna Freud's view of the steps of projection: while the unwanted material is projected elsewhere, once it is outside it comes back, quite aggressively, toward the self. Projection is a to-and-fro-movement; the boy's excitement is cast out but then returns as persecution. The robber, it seems, has multiple uses in this boy's psychic drama: as allaying guilt over sexual excitement, as a punishing force, as some kin to the superego, and as stealing a possession that is already marred by ambivalence. His unconscious sentence might go something like this: "Because I am stealing forbidden pleasure, someone must steal it from me so that I do not get caught but rather warn others there is a thief." While for Anna Freud projection is one of the ego's defense mechanisms, the mechanism helps protect against anxiety but not against that which poses as an attack. Thus the boy needs the robber to double his pleasure: the pleasure of projection and the pleasure of having to flee the danger. However, this interpretation of the boy's use of the robber did not give many in the class as much pleasure as trying to suggest a question to ask the child. Indeed, many refused to believe the story of the robber had anything to do with sexuality, and it was as though the robber returned to ruin the experience all over again.

By the end of our discussion we could, however, begin to wonder how our questions and demands may suggest something about what each of us wants for ourselves. This is not the same as the old debate about teacher-directed questions and the very painful experience of students having to go fish for the teacher's baited answer, although in this familiar scenario, it often is the case that the teacher takes a great deal of pleasure when the student confirms the answer that the teacher expected, and when the teacher can refuse the student's unanticipated answer. This pleasure, made from confirming one's own authority and the students' compliance to the teacher's knowledge, often is denied in the name of preparing students to do well on their tests and school assignments. Indeed, we could ask the teacher who is worried about the students' mistakes, "What if the mistakes do not come?" Like the child who responded, "come robber," the teacher's pedagogy might actually be calling the mistakes to come. And then, of course, the return of the mistakes seems to persecute the teacher, even though the teacher may unconsciously thrive on being needed or on being caught in not knowing what to do. This insight, that the desire to correct mistakes might be a symptom of the teacher's own unresolved conflicts, also can be felt as a dismissal of the real angst of the teacher when, at times, needed mistakes are interpreted as disrupting the teacher's desire for competency. The story of the robber reminds us that residing in any mistake and in its interpretation is a history of desire and relationality, of aggression and hostility, and so, of the strangely erotic mix-up of reality and phantasy.

"HOLIDAY FROM THE EGO"

During the time Anna Freud was preparing for the publication of her book, *The Ego and the Mechanisms of Defense* (1936), there was a popular German novel, *Holidays from the Ego*. She remembered this novel when she was asked by Sandler (Sandler, with Freud 1985) if the ego must always protect itself and feel dread. This question is reminiscent of the one a student raised earlier: "How can anxiety be so great for learning when people dread this so?" Anna Freud's response is worth the educator's consideration, for while the ego is the seat of anxiety, its work is not just limited to warding off danger.

> There is sometimes a feeling of relaxation, of comfort, when the ego can let go and let the id take over, as for example at the beginning of sleep. I remember at the time there was a novel in German that attracted quite a lot of attention. It was called *Holidays from the Ego*. It had nothing to do with psychoanalysis, but described a kind of sanatorium where people went to have a holiday from the ego. It was a very comforting place, because the discarding of the secondary process, and whatever comes into the ego from the side of the superego, as well as all the other demands for delay, were, well, on holiday.

So one can look at [the ego] from two sides. (Sandler, with Freud 1985, 280–81)

Perhaps the common holiday occurs during daydreaming, and yet this little break is not often tolerated in school, for daydreams seem to be beside the point, or perhaps a way to escape the point. Students' daydreams, in education, seem for the teacher like an obstacle, not a holiday. When I ask my students if they can describe daydreams, their early descriptions are fraught with anxiety, for they seem to worry about their own students' capacity to stop paying attention and to drift far away from the teacher's efforts. This phantasy student makes teachers lonely. Curiously, they do not begin with a discussion of their own daydreams, their own wishful thoughts. And yet, all of the students admit that during my class, they must drift to another place, even if just momentarily, in order to relax with or ignore the force of an interpretation. If I admit that these little escapes can make me lonely, then we can engage the question of how the student's need for privacy in the classroom is difficult for the teacher.

Can the teacher's ego take a holiday? And where would it go? These questions are useful if teachers are to begin speculating on the specific moves that they might take when encountering what they imagine as the logic, worries, and desires of another. Such moves may well shadow the development of a symptom, but a symptom that says something about the problem of understanding and the fear of being misunderstood. If we learn before we can understand, much of the enterprise of education offers the ego-gratifying view that we must understand before we can learn. And this makes it very difficult for the teacher's ego to go on holiday.

A QUESTION OF BEST INTERESTS

Many of my students are quite surprised when they learn that Anna Freud coined the phrase "In the best interests of the child." While the wording is familiar, it is not often the case that my students bring something of this uncertain measure to their pedagogical practices. Initially, it does feel like one more demand upon the teacher. And wondering about the best interests of the child clashes with the other demands teachers try to balance: their own, the curriculum, the community, the school culture, the provincial policy, the grade, the standardized test, and the supervisory relation. With such inside and outside conflicts, the best interests are not easily discernable. How can one know the best interests of a child, and are the interests continuous, stable, and predictable? When Anna Freud brought this phrase to divorce law and child custody, she was surely aware of the internecine battles over the child, of how the child becomes an object of parental gratification, and of how an upbringing is often defined in its most normative, adaptative quest. But she pushed aside such battles when she centered on the needs for the child to have a loving environment. Because this measure is so fragile, Anna Freud tried to suggest something of the child's vulnerability, and this acknowledgment led her to make a plea for what Elizabeth Young-Bruehl (1988) describes as "professional modesty, which means a plea for self-knowledge and a constant recognition that the science of child development is not a panacea" (418). Significantly, the very measure that Anna Freud offers can be used to consider the limits of our professional knowledge.

Anna Freud's (1930) last lecture to parents and teachers focuses on the uneasy relations between education and psychoanalysis. Near the end of the lecture, she returns to the difficulties of interpreting the best interests of the child. One boy gave Anna Freud a fragment of a book that he planned to write with the title, "The Wrong Things Grown-up People Do." Essentially this young author berates adults for all of the orders they give him, for not believing that he has any judgment of his own, and for inhibiting his desires. "Now suppose," Anna Freud writes, "that these notes were found in a school and taken to the principal" (132). A conservative principal might read these notes as being rebellious of authority and seek to punish the child. The modern educator "might have the highest hopes for this child's future, and would see in him a future leader and liberator of the masses" (132). But Anna Freud argues that both views are wishful mistakes. She interprets these fragments as a statement of worry and fear, "that he needed neither admiration nor harshness and restrictions, but only—by some means or other—an abatement of his fears" (133). It is not the case that this child has nothing to complain about, but his complaints about the outside world also resemble the inner conflict—the anxieties within—that pushes him to meet, with his own threats, what causes him fear. If educators are to take the side of this child, they will have to move slowly and modestly, challenging their own self-knowledge, their dreams for the child, and their capacity to overidentify or underidentify with the child's symptoms. The problem is how one comes to distinguish the difference between anxiety and criticism, when our capacity to be critical is founded upon our capacity to be touched both by danger and our uncertainty over where the danger comes. In many ways, this was the dynamic at stake as students engaged with Anna Freud. Their criticism emanated from the dangers and pleasures of uncertainty. This leads me to think that if the students are to read Anna Freud, they must be able to collapse anxiety and criticism to even begin to sort them out. This, of course, means anguish for the teacher as well, and a willingness to question one's own title, "The Wrong Things Grown-up Teachers Do."

When my students encounter this little author's fragment of a story, their responses do enact the range that Anna Freud also suggests. Sometimes a student can identify with the note sent to the principal and feel ashamed, as if he or she was caught again. Those who feel themselves victims of educational method take the rebellious side. Those who feel worried about not being listened to, or about being sent to the principal, identify with either the child who feels smothered by adult prohibitions, or the side of education that meets rebellion as a threat to its own integrity and answers with harshness. The third choice Anna Freud offers, however, does seem to allow breathing room, time to wonder what else is at work in the story, what anxieties work within, and what happens when the world that is inside meets the world that is outside.

"IT WILL BE ENOUGH..."

Sigmund Freud's (1919) modest goal for teaching psychoanalysis in the universities brings together two aspects of learning—learning about psychoanalysis and learning from psychoanalysis. Both seem necessary to one another, and perhaps this relation is part of what one can learn, provided that some emotional significance can be made from the work of learning. At her best, Anna Freud's work can be used to remind us of the vulnerability of being educated and having to educate others. Of course, this is more than merely teaching. If we can turn to the interminability of education, of constantly having to choose sides, even though one cannot consider all of the sides, and of having to work without understanding the effects of one's efforts, then we can think differently about the ethics of educational practice in relation to the teacher's inner world. We might also refind some pleasure in our respective beginnings. And in this awkward first attempt, mistakes can be seen as unfinished symptoms, as fragile compromises that hold and perhaps can be used to repair broken meanings. If we must call the mistake before it calls us, we must still try to figure something of this strange address.

In psychoanalysis there is the conviction that, however long it may take, the ego can learn something from the mechanisms of defense that it employs to participate in and at times obscure the force of the world. To notice that the teacher's ego must defend itself against the students' refusal to learn and that, at times, one form that this defense can take is in "the furor to teach"—to fill the students' silent spaces with the teacher's knowledge—might allow the teacher to investigate the conflictive qualities of her or his own pedagogical response and what it means to ask a question and not receive the answer expected. Curiosity toward these dynamics might allow for a different sort of patience that comes with the view that each of us learns before we can understand, and that in this deferred time of learning, we are susceptible to misunderstanding, to fixing too quickly, to forgetting that anticipation and the efforts made there are just the fragile beginning, and to asserting the tense of future perfect as if worries do seal fate. And so, while it may be too harsh to demand that the ego take a holiday, occasionally it might take a day off.

Like my students, I pick and choose ideas from Anna Freud. Some of her theories do seem antiquated, dropped from psychoanalytic inquiry, or made modest in emphasis. At times her capacity to take the side of suffering seems to eschew what she also understood as *Realangst*, or the actuality of danger in the world, which chokes the creative capacity of the inside world. At other times, one can begin to appreciate the difficulty of siding with discarded content and the pleasure of trying to take flight, which also is part of what inhibits and invokes pedagogy. If some of what Anna Freud has to say over her eight volumes may seem rigid and even authoritarian at times, her allegiance to the project of psychoanalysis, her father's legacy, and the demands of adaptation and sublimation allows education to look differently at itself, to make room for the ambivalence that also is a part of learning. And while often, in her lectures, Anna Freud acknowledges that she is oversimplifying, omitting contradictory details, and merely touching upon dilemmas, these admissions also are those of the teacher and the student. We must pick and choose something from knowledge, but in this strange experience, we also are obligated to ask whether the choices serve the interests of the symptom, and then, what such choices can mean for the self. This, I think, is what Anna Freud can teach and why, in her consideration of the small epics of growing up and growing old, in her insistence upon the relevance of even the tiniest details as invoking responses to big events, we might bring her back to contemporary education, not as a projection but as an unfinished project.

CHAPTER FOUR

"THOUGHTS AWAITING THINKERS": GROUP PSYCHOLOGY AND EDUCATIONAL LIFE

At the close of World War II, D. W. Winnicott (1994) addressed politicians and administrators, inviting them to consider the unconscious. It was a strange invitation, audacious really, because he knew something about the psychical difficulties of doing just that. Maybe Winnicott meant them to inquire into relations between the psychosis of war and the more ordinary neurosis made in institutional life. Perhaps he wanted to shake their confidence in the pervasive wish that policy makers were rather like curators in a museum when he writes: "The unconscious may be a nuisance for those who like everything tidy and simple, but it cannot be left out of account by planners and thinkers" (113). Another effort to bring thinking and the unconscious a bit closer became more pointed: "In human affairs, thinking is but a snare and a delusion unless the unconscious is taken into account" (1990d, 169). How is it possible to take the unconscious into account when it can only be known through the indirection of its symptoms and then the gamble of interpretation, and when its very qualities are other to the conventions of logic? And what, then, does one take into account when one takes into account the human affair of the unconscious?[1]

97

There is something asocial, even antisocial, about the unconscious, and this makes Winnicott's invitation to think about the unconscious uncanny, because he is addressing what is there but is still missing: forces that fundamentally influence—by its symptom—the emotional qualities exchanged within the scene of group deliberations. Sigmund Freud's (1916) description of a symptom is that exchange: "The construction of a symptom is a substitute for something else that did not happen" (280). The symptom is a placeholder, made from that volatile combination of wishes and fears that belongs to individuals. These asocial qualities are brought to groups and serve to substitute for thought, even as the symptom also composes group psychology by marking what is missing, what could have happened but did not. Yet it is difficult to grasp our unconscious susceptibility to others, particularly if we are trying to understand something as elusive as a missed experience. The difficulty is twofold: one part belongs to the contradiction between what happens to each of us in the world and how our perception of the emotional qualities of our events may or may not be in tune with either those of others or the event itself. How can we know an experience that has been missed? The other difficulty is trying to communicate to others something of this dissonance that is not yet apparent, ready for thinking or, paradoxically, even actually experienced.[2] Both difficulties, as we will see later in this chapter, belong to the psychical design of the transference, communicating, however awkwardly or lovingly, our susceptibility both to the other's vulnerability and to our own. Group psychology is the nature of that communication.

There is, in educational life, something paradoxical about how the unconscious can actually be considered, particularly because—to return to Winnicott's earlier warning—the needs for tidiness and simplicity, so tied to dreams of mastery, prediction, management, and control, are all idealizations that defend against the loneliness of institutional life. Psychoanalytically speaking, these very needs are the imaginary sites where meaning breaks down, loses its object, and even reverses its intentions. We know that educational life prides itself on its deliberateness and its capacity to proliferate measurable outcomes. At the level of group organization, there also is the institutional hope for people to somehow learn to work with one another. But agreement on the meanings of practices, in the case of the group, seems to lag behind and even ignore how practices are mandated, where they come from and, more significantly, how they are interpreted. Indeed, the tension is that the institutional ethos of systematicity, or the belief that a system of operation can be transparent unto itself, forecloses any thought of the unconscious and, hence, the work of interpretation itself. Alan Bass (1998) locates the disclaimed tension: "Wherever one finds systematicity, one can, from a psychoanalytic point of view, ask the question of what unbearable piece of reality is being defended against by means of the system" (426). For Bass and for many of the analysts discussed throughout this chapter, interpreting group life is the analysis of defense, where the defense is a defense against thinking. Indeed the group's capacity to think is delayed by the group's processes of splitting its understanding of itself and the world into us and them and therefore sustaining its own moral outrage, exclusionary practices, and so its capacity to be influenced.[3] One split off thought denies the group's aggressive qualities. Another fragment of group disorientation is externalized and projected, where the group defends its own solutions by setting outside of itself the volatile combination of uncertainty, circumstantial events, and doubts that compose its knowledge.

In this chapter, I explore the difficulties and work of thinking within group psychology, a curious direction, for a great deal of the writing on group psychology suggests that the last thing individuals do when they join together is think.[4] And yet, if group psychology is to become a kind of after-education, an occasion for individuals to think through the ways they are influenced and influence others, then groups must be willing to begin thinking from a constitutive vulnerability, crafted from vulnerable states of dependency and the social scaffolding that welcome the learning of autonomy as a relation.

My consideration of the problem of learning and not learning from group experience and group psychodynamics draws upon psychoanalytic discussions of group psychology, with particular attention to the elegiac writings of analyst Wilfred Bion, known for his pioneering work with leaderless groups and his many discussions on both the difficulties and the possibilities that result from trying to persuade groups to study their tensions, breakdowns, and affective inarticulateness (Symington and Symington 1996). He also is known for acknowledging how group psychology infuses the capacity to make theory, and so is affected by its object. Perhaps it is not so surprising that many of his theories emerged from his own experiences as an officer during the First World War and from his later work with soldiers suffering from war trauma.[5] For in these settings, group psychology emerges from helplessness and loss and may become caught in unconscious repetitions of its own traumatic symptoms. Indeed, much of the literature in group psychology begins with the effort of trying to understand group psychology from its most extreme conditions: war, hostility, social trauma, and profound social breakdowns, and these aggressive events return to the group to structure unconsciously their very capacity for language, theory, thinking, and intersubjectivity.

Wilfred Bion is relevant to a discussion on educational life, for two additional reasons. He offers important challenges to the ways in which learning from experience is idealized in education by arguing that idealization is made from its underside, "a lack of faith" in knowledge (1994a, 89). That is, if idealization is a form of splitting, it allows for the exaggerated confidence that knowledge can both transcend contradiction and immunize itself from all that it cannot understand. Idealization is a defense against experience and the accompanying anxiety that interpretation might ruin the goodness of knowledge. The phantasy is that both knowledge and the one who knows will not survive the doubts that also are knowledge. Bion groups this anxiety under the sign of experience and so lends difficulty to the work of thinking thoughts; he argues that thinking is a process of claiming the adventure of emotional significance, even if this journey leaves one uncertain and vulnerable. Thus for Bion, thinking is not equated to intellectualization, a cognition devoid of phantasy, or an assumption of the mind/body split. Instead, it is tied to and embroiled in language. The difficulty of thinking thoughts prepares how language is used within groups: whether the group uses language as a form of action that precludes awareness of the interpretive work that allows meaning to be meaningful, or whether the group can think of language as a form of thought and therefore as requiring thinkers who interpret. Another difficulty is linked to the basic assumptions that unconsciously bind the group and foreclose its capacity to acknowledge its resistance to ideas and change. The problem of thinking with others involves the move from action to thought and from self-deception to analytic love. This trajectory is explored further in chapter 5 but gains its theoretical force from Bion's association with Melanie Klein, who dramatized theoretically the problem of splitting and idealization and so, of envy and gratitude in our earliest object relations.

The second reason Bion is significant to educational life is summed up best in Mary Jacobus's (1998) consideration of Bion's contribution to the school of British Object Relations: "In particular [Bion] gives contemporary post–Kleinian analysis its distinctive focus on (not) learning, (non) meaning, and (un) knowing, with an accompanying emphasis on the destruction of the links that make thought possible, as well as on the importance of being able to learn from experience and being able to bear not knowing" (99). Thinking begins with the dilemmas of "being able to bear not knowing." It is a working through. Yet as Jacobus points out, being unable to bear not knowing is distressing and destructive to the very capacities that allow groups their potential to interpret, think, and tolerate that which cannot be mastered but remains the basis for the epistemology of educational life. Bion characterizes what is missing in the psychical qualities of this unclaimed experience when he speculates that prior to thinking, there are still thoughts.

This brings me to this chapter's title—"Thoughts Awaiting Thinkers"—a phrase of Bion's made to convey the illusive and phantasied qualities of thought animated when groups of people join together.[6] Bion's (1993) notion of "thoughts" is comparable to a terrible preconception: "I shall limit the term "thought" to the mating of a preconception with a frustration" (111). The group meets a new idea that frustrates what it knows and so sends the new idea away. At first glance, its reasons seem justified: the idea is not practical, no one understands it, there is no time, it is not pure, it might cause distress in others, and so on. Its expulsion of a new idea, however, is just the beginning of the drama: exiled ideas return, as if only to persecute the group, to threaten its precarious unity, and to represent its own failure to tolerate the unknown. These are the paranoid thoughts that frustrate and so appear as if without a thinker. Thinking, for Bion, is the "apparatus to cope with thoughts. . . . It will be noted that this differs from any theory of thought as a product of thinking, in that thinking is a development forced on the psyche by the pressure of thoughts and not the other way around" (ibid.). This is the curious design I use to explore group experiences of destruction and reparation. I will suggest that our capacity to think thoughts is made through the self's identification with the group's capacity to think. From this identification, or more simply, from these emotional ties, the group imagines and enacts a theory and a psychical economy of authority and knowledge.

While it often is impossible to distinguish between the terms of authority and knowledge, I use "authority" to convey a series of libidinal relations and pressures between individuals and that presents a question of susceptibility. Authority circulates during times when one looks to others for sustenance and response, when one must look away and ignore the leader's demands, and when group members make faith in their own capacities for knowledge. Perhaps these vicissitudes are best expressed by Parthenope Bion Talamo's (1997) discussion of Bion's (1997b) *War Memoirs*. We learn how Bion's ambivalence toward the group structured his theories and led to "the recurring theme that underlies the Diary of the individual who is both part of his group, in tune with it, and against his group, at war with it and with himself, which in later psychoanalytic writings is carried over to illustrate the mental workings of the individual and his internal group" (311–12). Authority is both an effect of group psychology and is created through its libidinal ties. Consequently, authority is sutured by fragments of ambivalence. It is both inside and outside and so allows for individual distinction and social bonds. It may also appear as a thought without thinkers. In this view authority is neither a power that presses down upon others nor an individual possession one acquires or bestows. Rather, and perhaps paradoxically, authority allows for knowledge to be made between people, but only if both knowledge and authority can be doubted.

My discussion of "knowledge," what Bion calls "K," is meant to convey the qualities, significance, and uses of conceptual relations that the group can make between its affects and its ideas and thus includes a knowledge of phantasy. At times, the group affects seem to take cover in or cover over the very ideas that the group encounters. Without the capacity to think through the ways in which affect and ideas become attached to or dissolved by experiences, events, and objects in the world, group psychology is subject to serious regressions, or what Bion calls "Minus K," a concept that I introduced in chapter 1.[7] The leader in the group is implicated here. From the vantage of psychoanalytic views of group psychology, just as thoughts make the thinker, it is the group that makes the leader, and the leader is a symbolic measure of the knowledge that a group can tolerate. The creation of a leader also is the playground for anxieties, aggression, and Eros. Following Bion's (1994b) claim that "loss of individual distinctiveness applies to the leader of the group as much to anyone else" (177), much of this chapter explores how the utter difficulty of making individual distinction, and worries over its loss, invokes the thoughts that await thinkers. Indeed, thinkers are a metaphor for after-education.

Finally, one of Bion's many contributions particularly relevant to this chapter is his view on the difficulties of mental activity, or thinking within groups. The idea that individuals construct group dynamics without being aware of the nature of their contribution or their responsibility, that they can unconsciously enact what Bion called "basic assumptions,"[8] made from emotional states of the group, allows new thoughts on the problems of thinking, knowledge, language, and authority in educational contexts. Indeed, as a precondition for thinking within the group, the group's capacity to tolerate frustration must be made from encountering new ideas rather than shoring up old defenses.

Every group, then, has a story to tell about itself, but the story wavers between illusion and disillusion. Paul Hoggett (1998) puts the narrative tension boldly: "The story the group tells about itself is designed not only to mislead others, but also to mislead the group itself. It is a self-deception. When dissent breaks out, the new ideas threaten to inaugurate what Bion likens to a process of catastrophic change in which the group fears that it might fall apart" (20). The paradox is that while groups must change in order to meet new conditions and create ideas for their revitalization and well-being, fear of change is a symptom that defends against the capacity to recognize social relations sustained through a self-deception. Hoggett argues further that the group's affect, its fear of falling apart, also substitutes for new ideas. This defense is quite complex; new ideas are perceived as persecuting objects, the group must then defend itself against feeling attacked, and all of this makes it difficult for the group to distinguish the difference between new ideas and old anxieties, between the loss of distinctiveness and the loss of love.

CROWDS AND GROUPS

If at first glance affective states seem to reside within individuals, the research on group psychology suggests something more dynamic and relational. While the group often seems to have more tolerance for experiences of monotony than for change, for rendering impersonal and anonymous its capacity for attack, and for projecting its emotional states outside of its own workings, these paranoid defenses can be worked through, provided that the group begins to develop language as a method of thinking and responsibility as opposed to a mode of action and defense. And yet the field of education seems to focus on the importance of leaders and their various qualities, indicators of ineffective and dysfunctional organizational cultures, taxonomies of knowledge, and operational procedures that a leader might adapt in advance to help organizations work more effectively. These very indicators foreclose the group's capacity to think and tolerate development.

This managerial orientation to education was not always the case. There is a minor history of research that acknowledges institutional life as being made from unconscious affects and conscious struggles over the status of ideas, knowledge, and authority in group psychology (Appel 1996). One assumption is that when groups of people are brought together for larger purposes than the ones they bring to the institution, when group psychology meets individual psychology, more is at stake than adherence to the rules and routines of institutions, the capacity of members to follow its leaders, and the ways policy can work as a social safety net to anticipate the fragilities and breakdowns of institutional life. Indeed, earlier discussions on the problem of thinking in group life suggest that two related experiences often are conflated: when individuals attempt to influence the group without themselves becoming influenced, and when their anxieties over changing become enmeshed in group emotions.

As early as 1899, William James's (1983) published lectures, *Talks to Teachers on Psychology,* warned against overlooking the complexities of institutional life and the accompanying refusal to see realities that are not one's own:

> Hands off: neither the whole of truth, nor the whole of good, is revealed to any single observer, although each observer gains a partial superiority of insight from the particular position in which he stands. Even prisons and sick-rooms have their special revelations. It is enough to ask of each of us that he should be faithful to his own opportunities . . . without presuming to regulate the rest of the vast field. (149)

These presumptions are symptoms of group psychology. There is the wish for no difference, even as one imposes her or his particularity onto the whole as if it could summarize the truth.

The mix-up of perception with regulation also occupied Waller (1961) in his ominous chapter, "Crowd and Mob Psychology in the School." Crowds, Waller suggests, are more frequent than mobs, and what characterizes the crowd are its qualities of vacillating attention, its susceptibility to its own excitement, and its loss of critical faculties. Crowds also seem to take on their own personality: they can be hostile, aggressive, receptive, or loving. Waller's observations are drawn from his understanding of the characteristics of classes in schools and the common view of teachers that some classes seem easier to handle than others. While he suggests that teachers never forget times when the crowd that is the class suddenly becomes almost like a mob, he also considers the teacher's capacity to provoke the class into a mob. This latter scene is not easily recalled by a teacher, because it also is tied to the teacher's own unconscious demands and to what James understands— to return to his warning—as the partiality and then the idealization of the observer's perception.

Many analysts and researchers who have worked with groups discuss how difficult it is for the group to acknowledge, let alone learn from,
its collective emotional life (Anzieu 1984; Bion 1994a, 1994b; Kernberg
1998; Knoblock and Goldstein 1971; Volkan 1994). While Bion (1994a)
frames the emotional qualities of resistance within psychoanalytic groups
most directly, his observations are relevant to ordinary experiences in
educational institutions.

> In every group it will be common at some time or another to
> find patients complaining that treatment is long; that they
> always forget what happened in the previous group meeting;
> that they do not seem to have learnt anything; and that they
> do not see, not only what the interpretations have to do with
> their case, but what the emotional experiences to which I am
> trying to draw attention can matter to them. They also show,
> as in psycho-analysis, that they do not have much belief in
> their capacity to learn from experience—"What we learn from
> history is that we do not learn from history." Now all of this,
> and more like it, really boils down to the hatred of the process
> of development. . . . There is a hatred of having to learn by
> experience at all, and lack of faith in the worth of such kind
> of learning. (88–89)

Growth and development are painful experiences, even if change is desired.
Groups may well be caught within this ambivalence but, rather than confront feelings of being torn, it is more typical to tear apart or disclaim an
interpretation meant to help the group notice its apathy and defenses
against having to learn. Bion is asserting something quite distressing: hatred of development is indeed a part of learning. Tolerating frustrations
made within the group means confronting the group's wish that it can
magically change without learning from its own efforts, even if these efforts
are those of evasion and destruction. But, also, the group must develop its
own capacities to recognize the subtle qualities of the hatred of development and encounter its own difficulties in thinking its thoughts. To tolerate development means that the group must come to find knowledge
worthy. That is, the knowledge the group makes must be able to survive
the group's hatred. And finding that knowledge is worthy means allowing
for both its subjective and unknown qualities.

Bion's (1994a) description of his work with groups is filled with his
frustrations and doubts. He wonders if his own theories are worthy but

he also puzzles over the group's refusals of his interpretations. They believe interpretations can only reflect Bion's own feelings, that his interpretations are only subjective and thus cannot reflect the group's reality. Bion, however, feels the group has not yet made a reality, because it refuses both its subjectivity and his own. This double refusal of subjectivity is, for Bion, a symptom of the hatred of development and so, a hatred of the social. We have reached the other side of James's warning: if partiality is a quality of perception, it is also the means to evade the grounds of its own narrowness. Notably, Bion claims that his emotional experience of the group is the basis of his interpretation. Indeed, the problem is that the group, in fact, affects Bion:

> I began to wonder whether the group approach to problems is really worthwhile when it affords so much opportunity for apathy and obstruction about which one can do nothing. In spite of the effort that is being made, I cannot see that the conversation is anything but a waste of time. I wish I could think of some illuminating interpretations, but the material is so poor that there is nothing I can pick up at all. Various people in the group are beginning to look at me in a hopeless sort of way. (47)

Second thoughts with a tongue-in-cheek quality allow Bion to continue his work: "[I]f a group affords splendid opportunities for evasion and denial, it should also afford equally splendid opportunities for observation of the way in which these evasions and denials are effected" (49–50). The splendid conflict can move from a preoccupation with obstacles to an interpretation of preoccupations as obstacles, and from these interpretations to a consideration of how evasion and denial are used and confronted. Denial and evasion of any interpretation still mean something: what is evaded is the individuality of its members or, as Bion puts it, "the group's failure to afford the individual full life" (54). Affording a full life would mean that the subjective nature of interpretations is not the ground for their rejection. Indeed, for meaning to become meaningful, it must survive its subjective qualities, including the hatred of development.

A NOTE ON RESISTANCE TO GROUP PSYCHOLOGY

If the group has difficulty accepting thoughts on how to think of its psychological experiences, if evasion and denial are part of what happens to the group when confronted with its mentality, then this evasion seems to repeat itself at the level of research in education. That is, a case can be made for the ways research forecloses the significance of emotional life in organizational culture. That cultural life compels, through its insistence on group membership and distinction, an acting out of psychical conflict is barely acknowledged. Sarason's (1982) now classic study of the difficulties of institutional change, and his worry over how it is that the more things change, the more they remain the same, seems to have become part of the public imaginary that looks with great suspicion on both the promises of educational innovations and the idea that education also can effect its own imaginary. Much earlier, analyst Siegfried Bernfeld (1971), Anna Freud's and Sigmund Freud's colleague, offered a similar observation on the ambivalent views of a public caught between "a tolerance for the ideas of education [and] a resolute and cold disbelief in its programs, means, and promises" (3). We saw this dynamic at work in the Freud–Klein Controversies, discussed in chapter 2.

While Bernfeld describes the problem of group psychology in authoritarian forms of educational design, Sarason eschews both its extremities and the possibility of depth psychology as being helpful in the analysis of school culture. Sarason argues that using a psychology of the individual to consider the organizational dynamics of educational change is useless. While it may be easy to see an individual's personality, Sarason reasons that it is difficult to see what antecedes personality, namely, the social structure and organizational features of schooling. But is this really the case? Narrowing down of psychology to the subjective, as Bion argues, does not settle much, precisely because social structure is a human artifact and, therefore, the problem is subjective: How are individuals affected by and how do they lend their affect to features of schooling? We can reverse Sarason's argument as well: How might a reconsideration of social structure and organizational features lend insight into the individual's relations with others? Our issue can now move closer to what Bion observes as the hatred of development. In psychoanalytic terms, neither group psychology nor individual psychology are separate experiences. Development is always social. Group psychology begins at the beginning of life, where the infant learns in extreme helplessness and dependency to elaborate her or his life with others. Group psychology, then, invokes the very conditions for becoming an individual, and part of becoming an individual means worrying about the loss of distinction, the worthiness of one's subjective insistences, and the uncertain meanings of dependency beyond childhood.

Educational studies of a group psychology center on the question of the relation between the individual and the group, highlighting the making and undoing of emotional ties in institutional settings. For example, Jersild (1955) and Knoblock and Goldstein (1971) focus on affective states of loneliness, anxiety, and hostility in the work of teaching, suggesting that while individually experienced, the investigation of these affective states as statements of need may lend insight into group experiences. In one of the classic educational studies on group dynamics, Schmuck and Schmuck (1983) offer a succinct history of its rise and fall. While their overview does not include the postwar research of Adorno and others (1950) on the authoritarian personality, the psychology of prejudice, and their psychological instrument that attempts to measure individuals' susceptibility or proclivity to fascistic institutional structures and the appeals of fascistic leaders,[9] Schmuck and Schmuck do raise comparable issues, such as alienation in groups, social intolerance, the fragility of democracy, and "group think," or the ways individuals seem to lose their critical faculties when following crowds. Their history of the field also takes seriously John Dewey's call for classrooms to be little experiments in the making of democracy that can tolerate disagreement, new knowledge, and conflict. North American postwar group dynamic theories began as a response to the problem of how democracy can work in institutional life, and how "each generation must learn democracy anew" (Schmuck and Schmuck 1983, 3). Notably, they connect the making of democratic life to freedom of inquiry and to a reconsideration of the grounds of subjective experience in education.[10]

To return to an earlier history in educational thought, where the quality of emotional life matters, is to be struck by both the excitement made from joining an educational critique with educational innovation and the insistence that educators' relations with self and others should become social research. As well, one can notice a time in educational experience where the complexity of understanding individual and group experience was influenced by psychoanalytic theory. From this research came the experiments of the late 1960s and early 1970s in encounter movements, free schools and public alternative education, new and innovative School of Education programs, and humanistic orientations to education. These experiments were, to a large extent, pedagogical responses to student protest movement demands to join social responsibility with personally relevant education. They drew their intellectual justifications from such diverse practitioners as Carl Rogers, Ivan Illich, Maxine Greene, Sylvia Aston-Warner, and Paulo Freire, and from political

movements of national liberation, civil rights, and social protest. All of
these thinkers considered what education has to do with the making of
freedom, responsibility, and social imagination. Their consideration of
the obligations that these experiences demand emerged from serious critiques of authoritarianism, conformity, passivity, and compliance in education.[11] By the early 1980s, the popularity of group psychology receded,
along with reduced governmental funding of public education during the
Reagan administration, and the return of managerial models in education, such as measurement and behavioral objectives, the individuation of
accountability in educational life, the rise of standardized testing, the
Back to Basics movement, and zero-tolerance discipline policies.

As we enter the twenty-first century, programs for accountability,
testing, and zero tolerance have all but foreclosed creative orientations to
group psychology in educational life and any possibility of education
being more than a problem of systematicity.[12] Ironically, these very institutional responses may be an effect of group psychology in education,
even as they render group psychology more evasive and more aggressive.
This is because such initiatives are based on the idealization of knowledge, the eschewal of doubting authority, and the expulsion of not knowing, not learning, and meaninglessness. The absolute splitting of learning
into measures of success and failure may actually deprive knowledge of
any authority, if part of what allows for the acceptance of authority is a
measure of ambivalence and doubt. It is almost as though these initiatives
repeat a hatred of development by ignoring the problems that all groups
face: not learning, meaninglessness, and apathy toward new ideas. And
yet to consider these initiatives as an effect of group psychology in education means that hatred of development and the phenomenon of thoughts
awaiting thinkers is not just a problem for individuals but an aggressive
psychical dynamic that is repeated at the level of institutional design and
social policy.

In 1965, Winnicott (1990c) again addressed those who make social
policy. If the title of his talk, "The Price of Disregarding Psychoanalytic
Research," tries to tell the whole story in miniature, his reason psychoanalysis is disregarded seems utterly commonsensical: "A major consideration must be that the public generally must not be expected to be
interested in unconscious motivation" (174). On one level, who can
blame anyone for not wanting to know about a kernel of negativity?
After all, confronting the unconscious means de-idealizing the self,
accepting one's constitutive vulnerability, and noticing the fragility of
consciousness. But Winnicott also insists that in the exchange made from

disinterest, something important is missed: "We pay the price of just staying as we are, playthings of economics and of politics and of fate" (175). Indeed, not changing may well be as difficult as changing, and contemporary work that draws upon psychoanalytic insight suggests as much. If resistance to knowing is a significant dynamic in public life,[13] there also is the possibility of using analytic insight to move beyond repetitive conflicts, with one provision: we must witness the unconscious.

WHAT IS GROUP PSYCHOLOGY?

Sigmund Freud inaugurated the psychoanalytic study of groups in his 1921 paper, "Group Psychology and the Analysis of the Ego," with the claim that ego psychology can be the basis of group analysis. Perhaps more interestingly, his paper insists that it is difficult to decide, finally, what belongs to the individual and what belongs to the group. This latter problem is, of course, the ego's problem of distinction and belonging, and so it harkens back to the original debt of psychical design: the place of the other. In a community of egos, these wavering psychical boundaries also are experienced as a problem for the group. Freud acknowledges this doubling in the paper's opening:

> It is true that individual psychology is concerned with the individual man and explores the paths by which he seeks to find satisfaction for his instinctual impulses; but only rarely and under certain exceptional conditions is individual psychology in a position to disregard the relations of this individual to others. In the individual's mental life someone else is invariably involved, as a model, as an object, as a helper, as an opponent; and so from the very first individual psychology, in this extended but entirely justifiable sense of the words, is at the same time social psychology as well. (1921, 69)

There is group psychology when people in groups or crowds make some larger purpose, and also when forces of susceptibility to others, or the capacity of a group to influence individuals through relations of the transference, work to transform, through unconscious enactment, psychical reality. Because people are susceptible to each other, Freud suggests that it is more difficult to think in a group than to think alone. Part of the difficulty is that the restraint or repression one might not notice when alone is given free play when with others. Anxiety is contagious, and new worries can be made in groups. Another difficulty with thinking in groups is that groups tend to think in literal extremes, in exaggerations, and through an absolute splitting of good and bad, inside and outside. This is particularly the case when groups feel that they must defend themselves against change and new ideas. Then, internal doubt and ambivalence cannot become a part of the group experience, although the individuals within the group may well be subject to these psychic events. Fundamentally, for Freud (1921), the group is conservative, "demanding illusions" (80), sometimes interested in changing outside events, but more typically resistant to internal change and subject to the "compulsion to do the same as others" (84).

How does one explain the susceptibility of the individual to the group? And what does this susceptibility or dependency do to the ego? Freud rejects theories of hypnosis to explain the problem of why individuals seem to give up something of themselves for group membership.[14] He turns instead to the problem of emotional ties, investigating two kinds—object love and identification. Both forms affect ego organization or, perhaps more accurately, are the ego. Much later, object relations analysts would revise Freud's view on identifications and stress their dyadic nature. For example, Kernberg (1998) maintains that "identification occurs not with an object but with a relation between self and object" (46). The wish for a relation is not without hostilities, because object relations emerge from a kernel of aggression carried by projective identifications, phantasies invoked by the anxiety of influence, susceptibility, and the fear that one's idealizations will be ruined by others.

In the experiences of group membership, Freud argues, individuals appear to give up the more obdurate parts of their individuality for the sake of being loved by the group, for the sake of libidinal ties. Here is where the fear of loss of love becomes the loss of distinction. Some of what configures this emotional tie is identification with the group's leader and the group's libidinal ties to the authority. When individuals identify with another, they do so generally because something desirable about the other returns to the self. Parts of the other, in identification, are incorporated into the ego, which then alter the ego's view of both the world and the self. But because identifications also are such an early form of emotional ties, there is an ambivalence between being like the other and having the other. Whereas one position incurs ego ideals directed at the self, the other position moves to object love, directed to the other. Freud's model for this developmental line is drawn from a child's relation to her or his parents; the first love relation and the first relation with authority occur simultaneously and are made in extreme dependency and infantile helplessness. Freud does not separate love and authority. Indeed, at first they are experienced as the same. This confusion of being and having, of love and authority, suggests one reason emotional ties also can work against the capacity to think, even as they also are the grounds of phantasy and thought.

Whereas Freud focuses on libidinal ties as the basis for group psychology, Kernberg (1998) suggests that prior to the libidinal tie is the capacity to regress. Everyone has the capacity to regress, and, in group psychology, regression is a defense against the loss of identity in groups. The potential to regress affects personal identity, for in regression one can exhibit crude aggression and hostile defenses. Kernberg argues that aggression, not Eros, is the beginning of group psychology. In his reformulation, both leaders and members regress "along two axes: dependency, narcissism, primitive hedonism, psychopathy; and moralism, paranoid-prosecutory control, sadism, violence" (47). In Kernberg's view, both libidinality and aggression are always features of group psychology. Libidinal ties may be a means to sublimate aggression; aggression, however, is a symptom of not being able to tolerate the dual experience of dependency upon the group and the maintenance of self-autonomy.

To understand something of group psychology, one also must speak of the role of leaders or authority figures. Freud returns to our earliest experiences of authority: the child's place in the family. He suggests that to keep the love of one's parents, the child must repress hostility toward other family members and even learn to identify with those who might displace her or his standing with the parents. Freud (1921) writes:

> So there grows up in this troop of children a communal or group feeling, which is then further developed at school. The first demand made by this reaction-formation is for justice, for equal treatment for all. We all know how loudly and implacably this claim is put forward at school. If one cannot be the favourite oneself, at all events nobody else shall be the favourite. (120)

The children in this example do not suppose that the teacher should be treated like the students, only that no student should have more of the teacher than any other, and that no student should be treated differently than the other. Social feelings for justice and duty began as original hostility or jealousy, but the hostility becomes sublimated and turns into something more socially acceptable, namely, a spirit of equality for those who follow.

While feelings of jealousy and hostility are sublimated, they also return easily in group psychology, particularly if there is traumatic perception or anxiety that equality may not mean being treated the same as everyone else, or when the idea of equality must be subjected to interpretation and revision. Rather than interpret the stakes of equality, groups have a way of making internal hierarchies and divisions, and this informal inequality enlivens the original hostility. There, hostile dynamics return unconsciously and ruin the very institutional policies meant to contain them.

Since Freud's speculation on the question of group psychology in relation to the ego, there have been important revisions and new theoretical views. While still considering questions of how individual narcissism and omnipotent wishes become enacted within the group, new emphases involve studies of the following: the difficulty of a group self-analysis (Anzieu 1984; Bion 1994a, 1994b); the difficulty of national reconciliation and detachment from histories of genocide and fascism (Mitscherlich and Mitscherlich 1975); regression in groups and the ways group psychology predates identification with the leader (Kernberg 1998); the difficulties groups confront when attempting to discuss painful topics, social cruelty, and adequate interventions (Molnos 1990; Simon, Rosenberg, and Eppert 2000); the problem of the need for enemies and alliances in international relations (Volkan 1994); and the effects of brutal dictatorships and social trauma on political opposition (Hollander 1997). Anzieu's (1984) study on the uses of projection and phantasy in groups offers insight into the binding and unbinding of emotional ties. His general observations suggest some of the tensions:

> When human beings are together to work, to play, to defend themselves, to steal, to kill, to believe, to change the world, to be taught or cared for, feelings, desires, fears and anxieties excite or paralyse them. They may experience a common emotion which may give them an impression of unity: conflicting emotions may tear the group apart; several members may withdraw and defend themselves against group emotions that they feel to be threatening, whereas the others, frantically, joyfully, let themselves go; or most members may withdraw when faced with invasive emotion, in which case the group is dull, apathetic, and wordy. (106)

In one of the few contemporary discussions of the uses of psychoanalytic insight in school organization, Maud Mannoni (1970) argues for an analytic position to understand the institutional uses of obstacles, aggression, and resistance: "Psychoanalysis has meaning only if it can be conducted from a position where the analytic spotlight makes it possible to change the language of education" (251). And yet, according to Bion (1994a), something happens to language in groups: its symbolic qualities are lost, and language becomes a symptom of the loss when it is reduced to a mode of action. Perhaps the most stringent example is the policy "zero tolerance," where cause and effect are literally collapsed into crime and punishment. Zero-tolerance policies foreclose the capacity for symbolization and metaphorical knowledge. There is no interpretation that can somehow contain the more distressing features of epistemological crisis. These distinctions are crucial, because without an understanding of the difference between symbolization and the object, the conceptual distinction between reality and phantasy collapses. Then there can be no epistemological crisis, for there is no reality testing. In Hannah Segal's (1997b) view, when symbolization cannot be thought, the symbol no longer *represents* the object; instead, it *becomes* the object. When this occurs, perceptions of the world become more and more literal and aggressive, and the capacity for thinkers to think is attacked. For Bion, a symptom of the group's psychology can be observed when language loses its communicative value and thus diminishes its members' capacity to symbolize frustration, ambivalence, and the breakdown of knowledge.

The loss of the capacity to symbolize can occur when groups are asked to consider new ideas, examine their basic assumptions, or face new conditions and potential members. Absences accrue when policy structures the uses of language through the disavowal of its symbolic qualities. For example, banning name-calling does not allow the group to think about why its members also may insist that name-calling has no meaning to the one who uses disparaging terms. Indeed, the more aggressive language becomes, the less meaning is bestowed upon it, and the more anonymity prevails. When anonymity characterizes the group, there is an increase in anxiety over the loss of individual distinction and an accompanying disparagement of subjectivity. Bion calls this situation "catastrophic change" (Grinberg, Sor, and Tabak de Bianchedi 1993, 76), when hostility and defensive actions foreclose conscious awareness of the actual stakes in accepting a new idea and in tolerating the development that learning from experience demands. If the capacity to tolerate the vicissitudes of symbolization, and if its interpretations allow group psychology its freedom and valiancy, then this freedom, as we shall see, emerges from what is at first felt as the ruins of language.

THREE IDIOMS OF GROUP PSYCHOLOGY

Admittedly, much of the literature in group psychology seems to focus on the "badness" of the group: its regressive potential, its deceptive qualities, and the aggressive features of its libidinal ties. Such negative critiques of groups may offer a further reason this literature is so renounced and, more intimately, so difficult to identify with. After all, while it seems easy to point out the failings of others, reflecting upon one's own responsibility is far more painful. Indeed, this may be why Winnicott (1990c) argued that "the public must not be expected to be interested in unconscious motivation" (174). And yet, given educational views on the importance of learning from one's own mistakes and tolerating the breakdown of meaning necessary to the processes of learning, we are obligated to consider some of the difficulties of learning that each of us encounter when we try to learn from group breakdowns.

Bion (1994b) offers insight into the dilemmas of learning from breakdowns. He suggests an implicit difficulty in learning from experience, indeed, hatred in having to learn, because learning requires a toleration of frustration and uncertainty, a reconsideration of the meanings of past experiences, a reconstruction of prior affective relations to past and present knowledge, and an interest in changing one's relation to and theory of knowledge. Learning from "difficult knowledge" is demanding work, and not learning may be a defense against new knowledge that, upon first encounter, threatens the integrity and ideals of the learner and causes what Bion (1994b) calls "mental indigestion" (8). Ideas can literally make one sick, but they also offer the potential means to understand the obligations that learning requires.

If self-deception is one of the possibilities replayed within groups, another experience can be created: making emotional ties that can work through original hostility and contain the more devastating destruction of regression and violence. This working through of the fear of losing one's distinctiveness, or even the problem of not knowing how to make oneself distinct within a group, suggests the double work of any group: allowing for difference and tolerating new uses of language that open thinkers to using their thoughts. Within this dual work, if a different sense of authority within groups can be made, then the group also may elaborate its capacity to tolerate new knowledge of itself. In the three examples discussed next, I offer a sense of group psychology that exceeds the group's initial negative qualities. Yet, as we will see, the negative may well inaugurate new thinkers.

EXAMPLE ONE: FROM MAKING FIGHTS TO MAKING IDEAS

Perhaps it is not an accident that Richard Rose, director of the Necessary Angel Theatre Company in Toronto, situates one of his defining moments as a director in a schoolyard incident. After all, one can consider schooling as a theatre of the absurd, a place where intention, purpose, desire, and consequence are, more often than not, at odds with one another, where one might choose to notice the irrationality of experience, and where predicaments seem fractured by a fundamental absurdity: the demand to listen to others and to do one's own work. But to see schooling from these angles takes more than a capacity to observe how others observe.

Notice how Rose recounts a schoolyard fight:

> I was beating up a boy . . . He was the class bully. I'm sitting on Joey, and pushing his face in the snow. The fight is going well . . . My anger seems to be superior to his physical ability. In the audience, watching, are twins, Joey's younger brothers. They are crying because their hero is being humiliated. Beside them is a girl from my class, cheering me on. She hates Joey . . .

> I start to notice them watching me, and I find that I am no longer able to push down on Joey. The grass is peeping through the snow . . . I don't seem to be able to hit or push Joey's face into the snow, and watching them watch me, I sense, is quite absurd—only sense, mind you. I get up and walk away. And the girl—Karen, I think her name was—screams at me, calling me a coward. And then it's very quiet. (Taylor 1998, C9)

Thirty years later, Rose reflects upon what he now senses from the fight: "I remember this because the moment I recognized myself watching them watching me . . . I had a sense of the absurd" (C9). Rose thinks against the common school logic that what should stop the fight is one's empathy, that is, the capacity to put oneself in the loser's shoes and thus understand that it must be terrible to be the recipient of the fist's blows. The arbitrariness of his own partial perspective becomes evident when he attends to the absurdity of the fight: the fight becomes meaningless when Rose is forced to consider not only his own participation but also the experiences of the onlooker.

Rose is struck by watching how others watched him, and he brings this perception back upon himself. He also noticed how his actions affected the volatility of the onlookers' affects: the cheering and the jeers. While Rose goes on to speak of this event as one where he began to think of himself as director, as capable of not just putting on a show but of thinking about the structure of experience as requiring symbolization, he can then think that affects are also subject to reversal, and express a strange mix between what one wants to see, what desires come to the fore, and how one wants to be seen. This is more than observation. The capacity to see how the self is being observed by others allows Rose a conceptual distance that the actual fight foreclosed. This attention does not take a leap of faith or a suspension of disbelief as much as the capacity to think beyond your actions, to notice the relational self, and to imagine how others are seeing you.

Is it too obvious to state that people affect each other, and that the reach of affective ties exceeds consciousness? Perhaps, although it also is the case that experiencing and thinking about the reach of the other usually are denied. So while we may be overly susceptible to imagining how we hope others will view us, taking the leap to another view—of how the other perceives the self—is rather difficult. In this first example of small group psychology, our director seems to be affected not so much by his action—after all, the fight is pleasurable—but by his memory of the onlooker and an idea that his actions can invoke responses that allow him to think differently about what he is doing. If part of his childhood wish is to direct others, to orchestrate affect, indeed, to want the affect of others, Rose also came to see that provoking affect, while not the same as controlling it, can offer new ways of thinking about the self in relation to others.

This returns us to our earlier discussion of Waller, in which we noted how the teacher's actions enliven the crowd into a mob. Rose, however, takes a different tack, and his rethinking of the schoolyard fight breaks through the partiality of the observer's perceptions. For Rose, the volatility of the crowd becomes an artifact. There is a difference between the literal fight and what the fight can symbolize. He notices that the group psychology is inaugurated through his action, and this thought becomes more interesting to him than the actual acting out of his aggression. It allows Rose elbow room to experiment with the meanings of his actions and to walk away from the fight with new ideas. We have left the commonly held school-based view on the nature of fighting and on strategies of prevention. There, fights are considered to belong solely to individuals and are not seen to influence group psychology. From this partial view, the individuated solution is either to teach the aggressor empathy for the loser or to banish her or him with zero tolerance. However,

Rose's recollection suggests a different way of thinking about social breakdowns that precipitate aggression.

Rose symbolizes the language of action into a mode of thought; he views the fight as a symptom of the loss of his own individual distinction, and the distinction of the onlookers as well. The onlookers become an audience, subject to emotional regression. This is where the absurdity of the fight may be located: it does not belong to individuals but rather to a theatre of actions. The fighters are viewed as putting on a show, and observing this opens up awareness of the double work of the group: the fight against considering different forms of action as calling forth affects in others, and the capacity to think beyond the push of emotional needs and demands. This event offers the thought that the loss of individual distinction forecloses the capacity of actors to view their own actions from the perspective of the other. Different from empathetic identification, this capacity for the other to look allows for the idea that the self comes into existence only in relation to others. Rose takes this one step farther: he considers the cast capable of group distinction. In recognizing this, he can then reconstruct his memory of the event scene by scene: from the experience of the fight, to the fighting of experience, to the absurdity of the fight and, then, to the thought of consciously structuring a theatre of the absurd.

EXAMPLE TWO: FROM MOB TO CROWD TO GROUP

Jose Saramago's (1997) harrowing novel, *Blindness*, is a strange excursion into mass psychology, the sudden movement from crowd to mob, and the delicacy of crowd to thoughtful group. The novel's title tells the whole story in miniature, but even in the style of his writing, Saramago eschews the usual signposts of reading: paragraph structure is nearly abandoned, quotation marks that normally surround characters' utterances are missing, visual descriptions of the characters substitute for their names, and chapters are untitled. Abandoning these generic conventions, however, seems to heighten the reader's attentiveness to the dual problem of perceiving and thinking with language, and just like the odd assortment of characters, each of whom is suddenly struck blind in the middle of daily life without any explanation and must figure out how to live, so too the reader must learn how to read. This metaphorical lesson—that what is apparent may not serve meaning—is constantly being learned.

Early in the novel, an optometrist sees a few cases of what he called "white blindness." That very evening, he too is stricken with the white plague. Before the eye doctor goes blind, he reads medical texts, hoping to construct a symptomology. But the symptoms of the blindness that he initially encountered defy logical predictions, and the problem is that the symptom cannot see itself as a construction of what is missing. The patients' eyes appear as though they are seeing normally, but those suddenly stricken complain that a milky white substance blocks their vision. Could it be, he wonders, a psychic blindness, a hysterical symptom of modern life? Are the affected somehow refusing to see? These questions are forgotten when the blindness suddenly becomes his own. Instead, he now wonders if such blindness is somehow contagious, and he urges his sighted wife to leave before she is struck blind as well. She refuses to leave and pretends to be blind when the police arrive to confine the couple.

The thought that the blindness is contagious is without a thinker, even as it structures the actions of the hospital doctors, the mayor's office, the health department, and all institutions that purport to serve people. These officials cannot see their actions through the difficulties of those who are blind; indeed, their first anxiety is to contain the problem, lest it effect them, and in a futile effort to save their own sight, they decide to quarantine those who are struck blind in an abandoned hospital for the insane. Inside, a loudspeaker announces the rules of the institution, but soon after a series of chaotic arrivals, it dawns on the rapidly growing number of internees that the rules are useless, and that this language of action has no referent. Outside, police guard the entrance, with orders to shoot any blind escapees. Many are in fact shot. A few inmates attempt to bury the dead, but they lack shovels. Then, one by one, the guards become subject to the mysterious blindness.

Eventually, with the help of the optometrist's wife, who is still pretending to be blind, some groups of inmates burn down the insane asylum and make their way back to the city. Each member becomes necessary to the group's survival, not just in terms of meeting physical needs, though this they do for one another. It is their creation of a libidinal economy that invokes the desire to learn about the other, to contain another's integrity, and to touch the other with words. In this way, Saramago's novel is a model of the talking cure; it is the use of language—the capacity not just to describe what cannot be observed but rather to use language as a mode of thought—that allows words to repair relationships in the world.

Late in the novel, the following exchange is made between the optometrist's wife and another character, after the group understands that there may be no cure for the blindness.

The only miracle we can perform is to go on living, said the woman, to preserve the fragility of life from day to day, as if it were blind and did not know where to go, and perhaps it is like that, perhaps it really does not know, it placed itself in our hands, after giving us intelligence, and this is what we have made of it, You speak as if you too were blind, said the girl with the dark glasses, In a way I am, I am blind with your blindness. (266)

By the novel's conclusion, neither the reader nor the characters can separate who is assisting whom, and Saramago does not give any reason for either the suddenness of the blindness or the fragile grace made between a group of strangers. He does, however, suggest something about the power of language to urge our capacity for thinking with and beyond blindness. Indeed, when language moves from action to thought, and when thought awakens thinkers, group psychology tolerates its own development.

What, then, is it for the group to tolerate its own development? Saramago suggests that the fragility of development must somehow be preserved within the group. Fragility is made from the group's capacity to recognize the dependence of its membership and to use language as a means of returning confidence that the group can survive its blindness, provided that it thinks. However, this fragility cannot be the basis of predicting how these libidinal ties will develop. Prediction cannot help group psychology. Instead, the fragility must be brought into symbolization as a constitutive vulnerability necessary to the ground of language itself. To tolerate development, the group must learn from its own uncertain experiences of development and from the intelligence of fragility. Recognizing fragility is made through language itself, where relations between perceptions and reality testing are worked through. It also is made from yet another source: the fragility of distinction. Becoming distinct requires the recognition of the other's distinctiveness, and this learning reconfigures the group's worries over loss of individual distinction and love into the idea that what allows distinction its possibility is the vulnerability of each individual.

EXAMPLE THREE: "AN EXPERIMENT STAGED BY FATE"

The catastrophic features of Saramago's novel also belong to Anna Freud's (1951) clinical study of six Jewish children.[15] The children arrived at Anna Freud's nursery, the Bulldogs Bank site in England, after being liberated from the internment camp at Terezin in Czechoslovakia.[16] The nursery was led by one of Anna Freud's colleagues, Alice Goldberger, a refugee from Germany.[17] These children were inmates of the Ward for Motherless Children in the camp from the beginning of their lives, spending their first three years interned there. In the spring of 1945, after the camp was liberated, the children were transported to England to live in Anna Freud's War Nurseries. The children's parents were either deported or killed, as were their siblings. Anna Freud's report, based on the extensive notes of Alice Goldberger and her colleagues, offers a brief, traumatic background, daily anecdotes of the children's behavior in her nursery during their first year's stay, and some speculations on the unusual nature of the children's relations to each other. None of the children had experienced life outside of the transit camp or big institutions, and when they came to England, the children spoke a combination of German and Czech. The report documents their learning English and, except for retaining the German word for "no," their gradual acceptance of this second language is tied to their developing desire to converse with people in the new setting and to explore the world.

Anna Freud speculates that the positive feelings of the children, from the beginning of their stay, were reserved solely for the group. The young children refused to be separated from each other, exhibited deep concern if any members were absent, were sensitive to each other's needs and considerate of each member's comfort, and showed no "sibling rivalry." In the beginning, the children's hostility was directed only at adults, but the aggression was impersonal. Miss Freud (1951) comments on the quality of this little group: "When together, the children were a closely knit group of members with equal status, no child assuming leadership for any length of time, but each one exerting a strong influence on others by virtue of individual qualities, particularities, or by the mere fact of belonging" (171). Whereas children not disturbed by such a devastating history vie for the attention of adults, invoking a rivalry between children, in the case of these children, and because adults did not play a role in the group's emotional life, the children did not compete with one another. And yet there were antipathies within friendships, particularly after the children had been living in the nursery for about three months, and all six children began to make relationships with the nursery staff. Miss Freud suggests that the group transferred its emotional ties to the adults; the group's relations with the adults mirrored its feelings.

The nursery setting, with its emphasis on language learning, learning about nature and the outdoors, and the ethic of children's participation in the life of the nursery, provided a context for the children to elaborate their libidinal ties, making new contacts with people and objects through knowledge acquisition, language development, and group trips. In reading Anna Freud's report, one can get a sense of the staff's patience and capacity to tolerate the children's frustrations, regressions, sexual researches, and conflicting, ambivalent demands. This accepting environment seemed to help the children as a group transform from an experiment in fate to an experiment in group living. The children's own development of libidinal ties within the group allowed for their further development. Indeed, this regard for the group allowed the children to survive their extreme early experience in the Terezin camp and, upon liberation, to continue to elaborate their emotional ties. Moreover, the strength of their libidinal ties to each other was not marked by jealousy, envy, or sibling rivalry. In Anna Freud's (1951) words: "They had found an alternative placement for their libido and, on the strength of this, had mastered some of their anxieties and developed social attitudes. That they were able to acquire a new language in the midst of their upheavals bears witness to a basically unharmed contact with their environment" (229). And, in the slow acquisition of the second language, the young children were able to expand their understanding of their own capacity to take pleasure in learning about the world and themselves.

The six children from Terezin suggest a very different view of the group psychology first posited by Sigmund Freud. Original hostility and rivalry were not a part of their identification with each other, and while these children were quite young at the time of the report, Freud's view that family dynamics structure and transform this hostility into group identification is not relevant for these orphaned children who essentially, at a very early age, helped raise one another. Kernberg's view, discussed earlier, that group identification precedes identification with a leader, seems more adequate an account. However, Freud's view that individuals must give up something of the self to join the group and Kernberg's view that this exchange is a source of personal anxieties inducing regression also are inadequate for the group of children that Anna Freud describes. Indeed, the opposite seems to be the case: the children's identification with one another and the formation of the group allowed for their individual survival.

Once rescued from the extreme situation of the Terezin camp, the new environment of the nursery supported the children's capacity for identification with each other and patiently tolerated the children's capacity to extend these emotional ties to new objects, knowledge, and other people. The environment allowed for development in all of its uneven twists and turns. The nursery staff also could tolerate being objects of the children's aggression. This sort of patience is reminiscent of James's (1983) "hands off" policy. The staff's stoicism in the face of projected hostility suggested to the children that adults can survive their hatred without returning it to them through impersonal policy controls, punishments, and the withdrawal of love.

And yet if these are the necessary institutional conditions for the individuals within the group to survive their extreme beginnings, no prediction can be made as to what this experience of group life might mean for adulthood. When journalist Sarah Moskovitz (1983) returned to this nursery thirty-five years later to learn what had become of this little group, she met a diversity of adults: teachers, housewives, business associates, retirees, and one institutionalized individual. Their memories of childhood were marked by profound sadness; even as many recognized the kindness of the staff, they mourned the loss of individual distinction and of having to grow up in an institution. Many were suspicious of psychoanalysis and resented this part of their upbringing. Indeed, Moskovitz's study suggests that there is no direct relation between Anna Freud's observations of the children and how these children experienced their childhood then and later when making sense of their adult lives. That is, there is nothing predictive about group psychology, even as its analysis can open up new understandings toward how the group experiences the presence of itself.

MEETING THINKERS

In the three aforementioned examples, the institutional context of group psychology seems to fall like a shadow upon the group. Whereas in the schoolyard fight, institutional design seems hardly to matter, in Saramago's novel, *Blindness*, authoritarian institutional response invokes the crisis of group life. Anna Freud's discussion of the six children of Terezin suggests two sides of the institution: the capacity of the social to structure its hatred as institutional confinement, social trauma, and death, and its capacity to bring structures of reparation and institutional life closer together. While Anna Freud's report is made from the contradictory extremes of history, we might consider how these extremes also structure the contemporary wishes of institutional demands and the ways that institutions, through policy and structure, contain both destructive and reparative elements.

One of the ironies in this chapter concerns the insistence that thinking can matter in the ways in which groups function psychologically. The irony begins with the hope that, at some level, educational structures are dedicated to thinking and to the importance of knowledge for individual development. And yet the belief in knowledge, at the level of the institution, often takes the form of idealization and systematicity: discussions of knowledge actually signal a loss of faith when they are arranged tightly in the actions of taxonomies, behavioral objectives, measurable outcomes, and instructional goals. In this design, thoughts do not await thinkers, and knowledge is only knowledge of actions. The difficult work of thinkers meeting their thoughts—through symbolization, interpretation, and persuasion—is foreclosed. So too is the capacity for the group to acknowledge the subjective qualities of understanding. Without an apparatus to meet our thoughts, what Bion called, "thinking," only the concrete in knowledge is encountered. What is missed then (and this returns us to Winnicott's insistence on witnessing the unconscious) is the breakdown of knowledge, the shattering of belief, the fracturing of emotional ties, and not learning. These affective states are then relegated to the outside, or projected onto that which disrupts and then this discarded content threatens to return and so ruin the group. Symptoms of meaninglessness, not learning, and apathy toward ideas feel like thoughts awaiting thinkers. These difficult experiences, however, come from the inside and are effects of perceptions of the outside from within the group.

In education, group psychology implicates the very possibility of how knowledge can be used. We might investigate the difficulties that groups have in making and encountering knowledge in ways that allow individuals new experiments in working creatively and ethically with each other. Then we might come to an understanding of how the language of action in educational life may actually induce the group's tendency to regress, to idealize, and to project unwanted yet internally structuring dynamics of love and hate onto others. To learn from these processes without shattering the group and take from this learning a knowledge of new emotional ties is what the phrase "thoughts awaiting thinkers" implies. We are asked to study our own modes of making knowledge from the authority of group psychology. We also are challenged to consider the very grounds of language and Eros in trying to know the self with others. This is the topic of our next chapter, explored through a different problem, theory awaiting the theorist.

CHAPTER FIVE

THEORY KINDERGARTEN

Eve Kosofsky Sedgwick's and Adam Frank's (1995) introduction to the writings of psychologist Silvan Tomkins invites readers back into the transitional space of "theory kindergarten."[1] Not coincidently, the thought of this archaic space can only be proposed by a theory of psychology. And, true to its dissonant spirit, their first use works with the force of something like a swipe. They write: "You don't have to be long out of theory kindergarten to make mincemeat of, let's say a psychology that depends on the separate existence of eight (only sometimes it's nine) distinct affects hardwired into the human biological system" (2). We are returned to our earliest forms of orality, a rather frightening place. Perhaps we must make mincemeat of a psychology that appears to make mincemeat of us. Here then is just the beginning of theory kindergarten: everything is personified, and knowledge is felt either as friend or foe. If theory never leaves kindergarten, neither does kindergarten ever leave theory.

To be wrenched back into theory kindergarten is *unheimlich,* a strange reminder of what is utterly familiar, something we already know but rarely, if ever, can bear to admit. Christopher Bollas (1987) calls this *not quite* experience "an unthought known" (4). He refers not so much to the protective gestures of disavowal, undoing, or to the other ego defenses, but rather to the difficulty of thinking: the ways the ego structures both itself and the object, and how even if the ego understands the known in terms of its conventions, rules, and traditions, for instance, the ego is not yet prepared to encounter its own thoughts. Within the unthought known, there is a sense of inaugural confusion: no distinction can be made between the passion for knowledge and the passion for ignorance. From this confusion affect begins. In trying to account for whether Tomkins can be taken seriously by those who do not normally consider instinctual forces, Sedgwick and Frank offer us not so much a justification for Tomkins, but rather they raise for theory another sort of dilemma: *why not Tomkins?* Their introduction inspires the question of how we reside in theory from the inside out, that is, through a theory of affect. What happens for theory when the problem of psychological significance can exaggerate or foreclose the fault lines of knowledge?

We do know what holds theory back from its own precocious curiosity. One trouble is resistance, not in the sociological sense of escaping power but in the psychological sense of refusing to know, of leaving psychical significance without thought. When theories of affect are refused, so too is the startling and irrational reach of psychical reality through the transference: the fight among and index of affects, ideas, and objects that makes theory such a quarrel that it cannot quite justify its reasons for arguing. The other trouble is within the theorist in theory. It is painful to entertain the possibility that, however one might try to pin down meanings by such stabilizing concepts as ideology, experience, identity, or culture, for instance, one is still not in control of intentions, of the symbolic reach of representation and, of course, the unconscious. It is difficult to imagine theory awaiting the theorist. That one's own knowledge begins in the failure of projection and in the embarrassment of acting out what one hopes to find is such a difficult and painful admission that it is subject to forgetting. Or one might even hold a grudge against the unconscious. Resistance, too, is a sticky affair: deny it and it is proved; accuse someone of it, and you may be characterizing yourself.

These passionate refusals are close to how Sedgwick (1993b, 25) characterizes ignorance: not so much absence of knowledge but its constitutive and organizing modality. No one is immune, which may be why, at least in theory, we try to keep ours under wraps. In this way, theory, through its very anticipation of the object, has the capacity to work as an ego defense, warding off uncertainty and surprise, splitting good and bad objects, and managing to put its anxiety into knowledge while protecting its illusion of omnipotence. Sedgwick offers us a queer theory about theory as she considers that which holds it together and that which makes it fall apart. And in much of her work, it is the contingent figure of a child—

indeed, a "question-child"—that ushers the problem of theory and its work of reparation into language.[2] This story of knowledge and ignorance has strong resonances with the object relations theory of Melanie Klein, who also tests her knowledge against what the child could not say but nonetheless felt, and who used her interpretations as a provocation to say the unsayable. Klein calls this reaction between the urge and the word and between the child and its objects—phantasy—a quality of relating made from the primal distress of anxiety, a painful constellation of fears of annihilation, of not knowing and, yet, of still needing to know. Surely theory is entangled here.

In this chapter I explore more closely the workings of phantasy and theory by a double movement of thought: destruction and reparation. Some of this conflict was explored in chapter 4 with the emphasis on group psychology. Now, we are investigating the crowded world within and so, with the metaphor of theory kindergarten, a precociousness that wavers between "before education" and "after education." I bring two theorists into tension: Eve Kosofsky Sedgwick, known for bringing her literary sensibilities to the metaphor of queer theory, and Melanie Klein, who constructed a theory kindergarten from the language of phantasy. For the writer and the analyst, the figure of the child—a question-child— will be set free to play and to think. In much of what Sedgwick offers us, this double movement of thought—and so, of theory—is crucial to her method of taking the side of the discarded content, repairing the splitting made severe and grotesque through the exclusionary processes of binary operations, and even reconfiguring the psychological significance of our work in theory kindergarten. Klein as well works in this way, although her sense of theory kindergarten, built as a means to figure out her own son, will in fact change how she thinks and take epistemology to the farthest outpost imagined.

The work we do in theory kindergarten, then, vacillates between discarding content and refinding something of its missed significance. It also is a crowded world, populated by difficult figures. For Sedgwick, then, it is sometimes Tomkins, and for me, it is Sedgwick and Klein. If we never leave theory kindergarten, it is not because our inadequate knowledge somehow keeps us prisoners of illusion. Kindergarten, after all, also is a fun fair of experiments, thrilling surprises, misrecognitions, near-missed encounters, spectacular mishearings, and phantasies that lead, in the strangest directions, our games of "let's pretend." This spirit of bravely or even brazenly entering new kinds of symbolization, of allowing phantasy to become more generous and surprising, are its elaborate and illusive stakes. If, in the first instance, we must destroy knowledge before it destroys us, then we also are able to make second thoughts and so allow our thinking to be a resource for its own repair. To imagine all of this requires not so much that we suspend our disbelief, but that we come to believe something incredible about our own suspense.

Like Tomkins, Klein is a difficult figure for theory. *And why not Klein?* She too takes the side of the discarded content and the infant's anxiety; she places in parentheses explanations for misery, such as the outside world, culture, and identity; she begins with the problem of persecutory anxiety and the phantasies that shatter and make object relations; she separates the goals of analysis from education in ways that put to rest the Kantian *Aufklärung* and the idealizations that secure knowledge to the side of enlightenment; she offers a theory of reading that emerges from primal anxiety and thus refuses to draw the line between symbolization and terror; and, she insists upon negativity as being necessary for creativity, reparation, and gratitude. Klein's theory, particularly after 1935, centers on entanglements of love and hate, positing anxiety—indeed, what Kristeva (2001b, 84) has the audacity to call "a phobia of being"—as the beginning of development. And then Klein will find, within this negativity, both potential and inhibition. But these reasons make it very difficult to recuperate Klein for projects of social transformation, particularly if what is meant by this plan is settling the trouble of thinking.[3] In fact, Klein gives us a view of the constitutive difficulty, indeed, the traumas of being and so of learning, by taking us back to our earliest theory kindergarten, reminding us of its forgotten significance, then and now.

Klein also is difficult to work with for another reason, particularly in relation to the writing of Eve Kosofsky Sedgwick and her project of anti-homophobic theory. Klein's theories of sexual difference and her discussions on object choice cannot be of service to an anti-homophobic inquiry, which is, for Sedgwick and me, an ethical obligation.[4] The figure of the homosexual in Klein's work is pathetically unsurprising, a sexual failure who, having fled the laws of heterosexual development, cannot sustain the good object. It is precisely at this point that her theory prohibits its own urge for reparation. There is no reparative urge in the Kleinian sense of the term: the object cannot be seen as whole, the debt to the other cannot be acknowledged, mourning will be interrupted, the goodness of the object will not be tolerated, the confusion of good and bad will persist, and the sense that the ego has the potential to do great damage cannot be acknowledged. If theory cannot face its own psychical reality, its own phantasies of love and hate, indeed its own grief, then the anxiety that inaugurates what Klein calls the "depressive position," itself the grounds for reparation, cannot be encountered and thought.

And yet even this acknowledgment, that theory can be made from or lose the urge for reparation, is indebted to Klein. And so it must be from another vantage—the place where theory fails—that Kleinian thought might contribute to an ethical reading of how affects, as expressions of both aggression and love, can be creatively thought. Many of her concepts do reside in the urge to make reparation and to integrate the psychical dynamics of love and hate by encountering one's loneliness, sadness, and aloneness. Then there is a new development: gratitude made from the capacity to bear guilt. Klein offers us, through her discussions on phantasy, psychical positions in object relations, symbolism, and thinking. Within this complex, Klein places defenses such as splitting, projective identification, hostility, aggression, and confusion. This hostility of fragmentation—what Sedgwick (1990) writes of as the contradictions between universalizing and minoritizing homo/hetero definition—is still prevalent, not just within the judicial, social, and political ethos of our times but also, more intimately, within our own everyday anxieties over what constitutes and shatters the ground of our theory.[5] One could, after all, read our categories of thought as trying to saying something difficult about psychical reality and its relation to how we can imagine the ethics of social bonds. And both Sedgwick and Klein do just that work in their respective explorations of what inhibits the capacity to love and what provokes love to do its work.

Phantasies, for Klein, structure knowledge of both the inside and outside world.[6] Precisely because they are there from the beginning of life, the material is made from a terrible and persecutory anxiety. The baby can neither ask nor answer the adult question—from where does anxiety come? Still, nascent symbolism registers this grief and performs an agonized answer. Klein's (1930a) description of this inarticulate process tries to bridge phantasy with symbolism and, then, with the stirring of reality.

> I pointed out that the object of sadism at its height, and of the desire for knowledge arising simultaneously with sadism, is the mother's body with its phantasied contents. The sadistic phantasies directed against the inside of her body constitute the first and basic relation to the outside world and to reality. . . . As the ego develops, a true relation to reality is gradually established out of this unreal reality. . . . A sufficient

quantity of anxiety is the necessary basis for an abundance of symbol-formation and of phantasy; an adequate capacity on the part of the ego to tolerate anxiety is essential if anxiety is to be satisfactorily worked over. (221)

Phantasies are "unreal reality," the tenebrous means to constitute the beginning of object relations, and so are our proxies made to represent the baby's premature attempt to master bodily anxiety. This anxiety, in Klein's (1946) view, is angry, terrifying, aggressive, and subject to turning back against the self. Klein will come to call this painful constellation "the paranoid-schizoid position," where phantasies of destruction, including the anxiety that the ego will fall into bits, are projected into that first other: the mother's body. All of these bad injuring objects that terrify the inside are banished to the outside. Yet because these also are the "bits" of the infant, identification follows on the heels of expulsion. Then this projected content threatens to return to have its revenge.[7]

Describing primitive unconscious mechanisms and their content brings Klein (1957) to the limits of language and, hence, to the limits of consciousness itself. In a footnote she writes: "All this is felt by the infant in much more primitive ways than language can express. When these pre-verbal emotions and phantasies are revived in the transference situation, they appear as 'memories in feelings,' as I would call them, and are reconstructed and put into words with the help of the analyst" (180). It is almost as though Klein tried to answer that childlike question—why do we have language at all? However negative, and indeed for Klein there is a kernel of negativity—a madness—within psychical life, phantasies are the conditions from which identification and symbolization emerge. From the beginning, the baby equates her or his bodily anxiety with objects in the world. Through the infant's projection of her or his bodily sensations into that first other—the mother's body—the "meanings," or again, what Klein calls "unreal reality," of hate and love are confused.

For Klein, psychical reality makes cognitive processes possible, even if the beginning must be traumatic. Thinking, the capacity to find newer and newer ideas that can be unmoored from the frightening qualities of concrete symbolization, gradually comes into dialogue with phantasy. Klein (1935) views this dialogue as a more complex anxiety—"the depressive position"—where thinking is poignant and qualified by a certain sadness, and where the ambivalence made from both loving and hating the same object devastates neither the ego nor its other. Only then can there be gratitude, a concern for the other as a separate being, as a whole and complex other.[8] And while thinking is never fully able to escape the shadow of this first terror—indeed, the terror itself is the prerequisite for thinking to even emerge—it can come to tolerate, in very creative ways, the anxiety that sets it to work.[9] This is what Klein means by learning, and perhaps what Sedgwick (1997) means by reparative reading.

These very difficult dynamics and the tender patience necessary to work through them are the heart of Sedgwick's (1993a) extraordinarily complex essay, "A Poem Is Being Written." She projects into the primal scene of writing not only the questions of a nine-year-old child, although these questions do test the limits of what we feel in poetry. As well, there is what Kristeva (2001b) calls "a desire that thinks" (43). Thus readers may feel the heart-wrenching work of what else is being written as a poem is being written when theory is being written. Sedgwick (1993a) uses some very Kleinian moves here, warning readers of the minefield of misrecognitions our own desires are apt to set off:

> The lyric poem, known to the child as such by its beat and by a principle of severe economy (the exactitude with which the frame held the figure)—the lyric poem was both the spanked body, my own body or another one like it for me to watch or punish, and at the same time the very spanking, the rhythmic hand whether hard or subtle of authority itself. What child wouldn't be ravenous for dominion in this place? Among the powers to be won was the power to be brazen, to conceal, to savage, to adorn, or to abstract the body of one's own humiliation; or perhaps most wonderful, to *identify with* it, creating with painful love and care, but in a temporality miraculously compressed by the elegancies of language, the distance across which this body in punishment could be endowed with an aura of meaning and attraction—across which, in short, the *compelled* body could be *chosen*. (184, emphasis in original)

Where Sedgwick ends and the poem begins, where the reader ends and the writing takes over, where the language thrills and then stops one cold, and where being accrues and having overwhelms, how finely frayed are these lines? Indeed, it is a delicate work to choose to identify with the side of the discarded content, with the farthest outpost of the symbol's frontier, with the free association, and with the depressive position. We also might observe that these stakes refuse the familiar reversal of hierarchy, for that would animate projective identifications, still dependent upon fragmenting the object relation in order to relieve one's dependence on it. Working through these manic defenses as well is a new question: What holds the reader back? *Surely, what theory would not be ravenous for dominion in this place?*

Sedgwick (1993b) recognizes that in trying to make from the compelled body something chosen, the passion for ignorance must confuse itself with the passion for knowledge. She writes of the difficulties we make while reading: "There are psychological operations of shame, denial, projection around 'ignorance' that make it an especially propulsive category in the individual reader" (25). Ignorance, for Sedgwick, inaugurates not just resistance but also a confusion of its own time: "The energies of ignorance always make an appeal to, and thus require the expulsion of, a *time before*, a moment of developmental time . . . I don't know in trying to summon up an image of these energies whether it will be more effective to evoke in academic readers the time before we became literate or the time before we became expert at interpreting the signs associated with sexuality" (47, emphasis in original). We might wonder, with Sedgwick, how such a distinction can be made, for there is a great deal of mix-up: our learning of expertise is embroiled with our first theoretical attempts to know sexuality, and these first researches occur before we have language.[10] That "time before" is the time of phantasy, but then to return to Melanie Klein, expelling something does not make it go away.

In our academia, can we ready ourselves to observe how the urge to expel ignorance produces rigid knowledge and more of an unthought known? Shall we admit our adeptness at dismissing theories that run contrary not just to prevailing conventions but, more significantly, to who we think and wish we and others might be in and for our theory? Certainly affect threatens the omnipotence to which theory in silence aspires, and these affective tensions can exaggerate the space between what we know and what we want, between what we find and what we create, and between what we hold and what we destroy. Another sort of unthought known also can be observed here: our internal conflicts structure what can be noticed in the world and, then, held in theory. Moreover, theory nests itself in this terrible difference between inner worlds and external reality. This may be why discussing Tomkins is of some use, and Sedgwick's and Frank's introduction returns us to arguments over the status of the subject and whether its qualities are essentially there or socially induced, over the material of human nature and how this stuff fuels and extinguishes emotional life, and over how affects become hallucination, perception, judgment and, yes, even theory. If theory kindergarten returns us to an uncertain involuntary origin, a time before literacy, that begins in that confusing debate between good and bad and love and hate, and that inaugurates our earliest object relations, can our sense of knowledge and our capacity to think from that which resists knowledge, namely, the unthought known, ignorance, and phantasy, ever escape this first terrible task of having to make something from nothing?

Theory kindergarten may serve as a metaphor for object relations. It also is a psychoanalytic commentary on both the "activity and products" (Mitchell 1998, 23) of knowledge in psychical reality. In theory kindergarten we experience the play of phantasy and reality, of self and other, of hide and seek, and of aggression and reparation. This means, among other things, that using knowledge of phantasy is one way selves secure and undo their first projected boundaries.[11] Yet this process is precarious, vulnerable to its own flaws and reversals, dependent not upon possessing the proper knowledge, for at least in psychoanalytic views and also in much of what Sedgwick writes, knowledge must remain a paradox whether it is partial, split, or integrated. Robert Young's (1999) discussion of post–Kleinian thought also considers this dilemma: "One of the illuminating distinctions that post–Kleinian psychoanalysis has given us is that between knowing and knowing about. In psychoanalysis, knowing about something often operates as a defense against knowing it in a deeper, emotional sense" (65). Sedgwick (1993b) begins in the emotional sense of this confusion when she records "the energies of ignorance" as appealing to "a time before." Our earliest uses of knowledge as deflection and substitution, as condensation, idealization, and as wish fulfillment, as the means to ward off and create new anxieties, and as the basis of what must be worked through all become the work of theory, but this also means that our theory is vulnerable to its own flawed dream work.

For these reasons and more, we must return to theory kindergarten, for our work there may remind us of our first use of objects we try to possess and discard, love and hate, diminish and idealize, and split and integrate. Hannah Segal (1997a) suggests this performance stages "the grammar of object relations" that comes to represent the underlying logic of affect (79). Object relations are not just stories of how we use objects but rather of how, through relating with that first other, we begin to inaugurate and structure our very capacity to position ourselves in reality and phantasy and, so, to think about the very work of thinking. From this view, what also goes on in theory kindergarten is akin to what Sedgwick (1997) imagines when she notices a certain precocious young reader who is

> reading for important news about herself, without knowing what form that news will take; with only the patchiest familiarity with its codes; without, even, more than hungrily hypothesizing to what questions this news may proffer an answer. The model of such reading is hardly the state of complacent adequacy... but a much more speculative, superstitious, and methodologically adventurous state where recognitions, pleasures, and discoveries seep in only from the most stretched and ragged edges of one's competence. (3)

If we read for important news about ourselves, how this news becomes thought of as important is, as Sedgwick suggests, just on the precipice of knowing. Here is another room of theory kindergarten built from an old Jewish joke. Let us be reminded of what can happen when we cannot receive important news. A person had spent a long time stranded on a desert island. Finally, rescuers arrived and found the person but also noticed that this person had spent time building three synagogues. The rescuers asked, "But aren't you alone on this island?" "Yes, of course!" the person exclaimed. "So, why are there three synagogues?" "Well," the person responded, pointing to each building in turn: "This one I usually go to, this one I sometimes go to, and this one I would never step foot in." In theory kindergarten, our objects have more than one use: we have theories that we always use, theories that we sometimes use, and theories that we would never step foot in, even though we must use these in order to disclaim them. Sedgwick's work spins this joke differently; she invites us into theories that we might never step foot in, but once there, we may learn something that startles the theories that we always use and the theories that we sometimes use. If we each must build at least three places in order to know where we are, if it takes three theories to make one theory, then the joke may well be on us: Where exactly are we when we make theories that we never step foot in? What makes theory important news? Why do we have theory at all?

THE QUESTION-CHILD'S THEORY

The time before that Sedgwick evokes can take its residence in Klein's theory. On her way to theory kindergarten, when she was just beginning her analytic practice, Klein (1921) tried a psychoanalytic education with her son, Fritz, with the idea of enlightening him in what she called "sexual matters." By answering any of his questions with honesty, she thought that she could help him avoid the future of neurotic tendencies and also "deprive sexuality at once of its mystery and of a great part of its danger" (1–2). But her son had already signaled his distress; there was, in Klein's view, a certain inhibition of his curiosity. Originally Klein thought that Fritz's clinging to superstition, to the fantasy figure of "the Easter Bunny," and likewise to an absolute faith that his wishes could be granted, meant that he had stopped thinking. Indeed, Fritz did not want his wishes and theories tested by the knowledge of the adult: he did not want to be enlightened. Things get rather absurd. At one point, the five-year-old Fritz believes that he is a gourmet cook, can speak French fluently, and can fix any object that is broken. While Klein explains patiently that he does not yet know how to do these things—that he must learn—Fritz calmly replies: "If I am shown how just once, I can do it quite well" (3). He holds tightly to this great refrain as his last word. Something about having to learn is being skipped over, and Klein places what is missing under the ominous heading, "The child's resistance to enlightenment." It is possible, I think, to wonder still, what precisely is being resisted, given the fact that other divisions of this early paper gather Fritz's struggle under the grand theme of "existence." That is, Fritz wonders about the nature and qualities of reality and its judgments, the definitions of his rights and powers, the meaning of wishing and hoping, the nature of existence and death, and whether God exists.

These are heady questions, though not yet important news. They can become so if we consider how symbolization is made from encountering both reality and phantasy. If Fritz is now sounding a bit like the philosopher, Kant, trying to know things in themselves, and so bumping up against his own subjectivity, his position also forces Klein to move as close as she ever would to confronting her own wishes for enlightenment. Klein worried that Fritz was not interested in the difference between reality and phantasy, and so in collapsing these realms, he was holding himself back. Although Klein begins to think about infantile omnipotence, a mode of obdurate thoughts that even if buried by having to grow up is still preserved by our wishes for learning and existence, she also is on the way to her own education as an analyst and perhaps as a mother. After all, an early version of this paper qualified her as a member of the Hungarian Psychoanalytical Society in 1919, and she was reporting on the progress of analyzing her son, whom she disguised in the writing of this case. Some of her discomfort was admitted a few years after her admission to the society when she wrote a second chapter and bade a farewell to the promise of psychoanalytical education. And then by the time of the Controversial Discussions, her discomfort with education reaches fruition. In chapter 2 of this strange affair, Klein encountered the problems that Fritz originally offered in such a condensed and displaced form: the (unconscious) nature of existence as such.

Klein had difficulty figuring out the nature of curiosity—where it comes from, what it represents, how it loosens itself from its object and, so, what it means to urge *this* facility. These questions also animated something new about her own curiosity; Klein discovered, along with the child's resistance to enlightenment, her own resistance to what else the child asks. We are entering the psychoanalytic field of the transference: the exchange of unconscious wishes, the displacement of love and hate onto figures of authority, the index of a time before and the symbolic equivalences of old and repressed conflict onto new and unknown situations. Significantly, Sigmund Freud (1912) writes of transference as a dynamic and as a relation. He felt the transference in the very activity of theory; it emerges from "a compromise between the demands of [the resistance] and those of the work of investigation" (103). Something within the very work of investigation resists its own demands. And in psychoanalysis, the resistance may be a paradox: there is mystery to sexuality, and knowledge cannot take this away. But there also is mystery to knowledge, because we have sexuality.

In reading Klein's (1921) early study today, one may be struck by the unanswerable qualities of Fritz's questions. Indeed, Klein accepted a glimpse of this mystery. Fritz asks: "How do eyes stay in?" "How does a person's skin come on him?" When will I be a Mama?" (8–9). Yet even if Klein tried to answer (and we will soon learn the strange discussions her attempts made), her son refused to believe her. Thus Klein came to believe that proof neither was the criterion for a convincing reality nor even a prerequisite for receiving important news about the self. This child's questions defied the adult's imagination and conventional notions of time. After all, how would one answer the worry, where was I before I was born? The particular qualities of the questions Fritz tried to ask— such as, how do I keep together, and what will happen to me because I am me—can be gently grouped under the sign of existence as such and so as on the precipice of important news. The unconscious question may be: What can I make because I was made? Until this could be heard, the more the child asked, and the more the mother answered, the more anxious, repetitive, and stereotyped was the discourse. The very psychoanalytic education meant to open curiosity became something like an intellectual inhibition.

Listen to the conversation between Klein and her son on the topic of how babies are made. Klein offered these explanations in the child's language as a way to help her son leave behind his theory that children are made from milk. And listen to the child use language to sustain his first ingenious theories.

> When I begin once more about the little egg, he interrupts me, "I know that." I continue, "Papa can make something with his wiwi that really looks rather like milk and it is called seed; he makes it like doing wiwi only not so much. Mama's wiwi is different to papa's" (he interrupts) "I know *that!*" I say, "Mama's wiwi is like a hole. If papa puts his wiwi into mama's wiwi and makes the seed there, then the seed runs in deeper into her body and when it meets with one of the little eggs that are inside mama, then that little egg begins to grow and becomes a child." Fritz listened with great interest and said, "I would so much like to see how a child is made inside like that." I explain that this is impossible until he is big, because it can't be done till then but that then he will do it himself. "But then I would like to do it to mama." "That can't be, mama can't be your wife, for she is the wife of your papa, and then papa would have no wife." "But we could both do it to her." I say, "No, that can't be. Every man has only one wife. When you are big your mama will be old." . . . "Your mamma will always love you, but she can't be your wife." . . . At the end he said, "But I would just once like to see how the child gets in and out." (34)

There are some lovely moments of deja vu in all of this confusion of time and timing, and there also is the punctuation of Fritz's confidence: the "I know that!" and his wish that if he can just be shown once, he could do it himself. Klein places this conversation under the sign "The child's resistance to enlightenment." The resistance moves back and forth. It functions like grammar: the mother's knowledge is of the future perfect, and this timing is insufficient to the present tense and to the past perfect of the child's logic. And the resistance carries the transference: there also is the passion between mother and son, a mystery of vulnerability.

This vulnerability resides in and is carried by language. Even if the adult uses the same words as the child, the adult may well be assuming what Michael Balint (1992) calls "the Oedipal level of language," where "the analyst's interpretations are experienced as interpretations by the patient" (14). The tension is that, at times, the analyst's interpretation cannot be received by the analysand as interpretation. Instead, the utterances are felt as if they chastised and prohibited and so imposed compulsive reality. Balint compares the Oedipal level of language to *a time before:* terrible literalness, a collapse between the thing and that which tries to represent it, what Klein (1930a, 220) would call "symbolic equation." The problem is that there is, what Ferenczi (1988) noted, "a confusion of tongues" between adults and the child. The adult's language cannot gesture toward itself *as an interpretation,* and so language is received as if it is reality. Specifically, there can be no question-child when the adult resorts to premature explanations, defends conventionality, or wishes to enlighten.

One can say that where there is language, there is defense against language. This trajectory—a question is asked, an answer offered, and then feigned ignorance clouds over any attempt for a dialogue—is close to how Sigmund Freud (1900) described the kettle defense. There, a man borrows a kettle from his neighbor and returns it in damaged condition. "The defendant asserted first, that he had given it back undamaged; secondly, that the kettle had a hole in it when he borrowed it, and thirdly, that he had never borrowed a kettle from his neighbor at all. So much the better: if only a single one of these three lines of defense were to be accepted as valid, the man would have to be acquitted " (Freud 1900, 119–120). Look at Fritz's defense: your answer is damaged, I never asked that question, what you answer is not the truth. Alice Pitt's (2001) discussion of this kettle joke raises a key paradox in educational relations: "For speech to function as revelation, something happens that is completely new and unforeseen; revelation transforms the ego" (99). If the question is to transform into something meaningful and become important news, so too must the response. Klein eventually understood that the question-child transforms the adult's knowledge and, so too, her ego and its capacity for working through. The question-child questions the adult's desire, and there is no alibi for our desires.

Originally, Klein put great faith in the value of psychoanalytic education to cure ignorance and perhaps even the mistakes of existence. And she felt that rational persuasion could work to change her son's mind, to talk him out of his theories, and to solve the mysteries of sexuality. But as she studied her son's questions, she began to realize a certain repetition, and this brings us back to the problem of existence: "Where was I before I was born? . . . How is a person made? . . . What is a papa needed for? . . . What is a mama needed for?" (1921, 3). The more Klein explained, the less the child thought. Klein observed "that a certain 'pain,' an unwillingness to accept (against which his desire for truth was struggling), was the determining factor in his frequent repetition of the question" (4). Where there is existence, there is a certain pain, an ambivalence. To listen to the unconscious question meant, for Klein, to turn away from the idea that the purpose of knowledge is to extinguish phantasies and move as close as one could to the analysis of phantasies. Answering her son's questions with her own conventional truths gave way to interpreting the questions along two lines: along the lines of defense and the unconscious wishes of both the child and the mother.

What, then, are the qualities of the question-child? First, the question-child's questions are difficult. Against all odds, the question-child is capable of bizarre thoughts, of turning back to a time before. The question unnerves adult knowledge, returning to the adult her anxiety and the event of the transference. In Adam Phillips's (1998a) view, to meet what is unexpected requires noticing "something of value: an attentiveness to the irregular, to the oddity, the unpredictability of what each person makes of what he is given—the singularity born of each person's distinctive history" (40). The question-child is that singularity. The question-child offers the adult important news through an unusual reality test: use the child's question to find the truth of the adult's phantasy. If all goes well, "speech can function as revelation" (Pitt 2001), indeed, as the beginning of ever-new ways to interpret important news. What Klein noticed as "a certain pain," an unwillingness to accept truth *and* a desire for truth all at the same time, catches the adult in what Sedgwick (1997) sees as "the most stretched and ragged edges of [her] competence" (3). The particular truth at stake is, after all, our unpredictable singularity, and this truth, as Sedgwick suggests, can even be found while a poem is being written.

PHANTASIES OF THEORY

A startling assertion of psychoanalytic thought is that one can mean something far away from what one says. From this unmooring of meaning from its earliest context comes the theoretical force of the transference: we must act out our meanings before they can be known. With the insistence that there is something of a disagreement between affect and idea comes another shock: it is the affect that makes the idea, and not the other way around.[12] Theory is not just a substitution for that elusive first object, and it is not just sublimation, one far away from the expression of sexuality. More pointedly, it is a product and the activity of phantasy, and so can never be so far from sexuality. We are entering what

Sedgwick (1990) thought of as "the epistemology of the closet." And so we have theory because we have destruction.

Winnicott (1992a) also notices our first use of knowledge: it begins in aggressiveness, ruthlessness, the wish for omnipotence, and anti-concern. If knowledge and the self can survive this first attack and not retaliate, it will then be deemed worthy for our use. For Winnicott, creativity is made somewhere between the destruction of knowledge and the illusion that knowledge matters. It is a precarious balance, where omnipotence is both sustained and destroyed, and where the knowledge at stake can tolerate its breakdowns without ruining something else. This is learning in its most rigorous and demanding sense because, paradoxically, the learning comes from outside, from the other. Whereas Klein offers us the figure of the analyst who encounters the psychic suffering of the other by entering it, identifying with it, and giving it new words, for Winnicott, it is the figure of the "good enough mother." Hers is the work that contains the abstract qualities of reparative theory, and thus even makes for bad enough theory something that can be good enough. A good enough theory can survive the theorist's aggression, can move beyond her need to sustain anxiety through manic defenses, and it attempts, from this doubt, a capacity for concern and agony. Melanie Klein (1957) would call such concern for the other the desire for reparation and gratitude. It is a debt to the other that is never fully paid.

If we can somehow move from primal anxiety to aggression, then to depression, and then, to reparation, the timing of these positions is not developmental, at least in terms of how development is normally exposed, for at least four significant reasons.[13] Developmentalism resides in the terrible confines of normal psychology, where stages are linear and chronological and thus thought to be mastered and transcended. In developmental models, experience is discrete, discontinuous, and immune from more elaborate editions of older conflicts. Theories of developmentalism posit that anxiety becomes less and less prevalent, because reality testing becomes more and more adequate. For Klein, anxiety both allows and inhibits thought. The second reason has to do with how the ego itself feels about its own development, and what it means to learn from experience. According to Bion (1994b), there is a hatred of development, of having to learn, and this must be overcome. These implicit difficulties are expelled from developmentalism. The work of the ego is not developmental for a third reason: its work emanates from unconscious phantasies, and these forces belong neither to chronological time nor to the pressures of logic and convention. From the vantage of Klein, Bion, and Winnicott, it is development that makes experience, not the other way around. Anxiety does not just inhibit. Instead, in its uses of anxiety, the ego vacillates between the paranoid-schizoid and the depressive positions that are made from clusters or complexes of phantasies, defenses, and object relations. The fourth reason Kleinian theory cannot be developmental is that each of these positions requires its other, and there is no absolute boundary between them. The ego cannot evacuate itself from these positions because these positions, are constitutive of the ego. In Klein's view, the ego's use of knowledge and, hence, theory, occurs not just along the lines of object relations but because of object relations.

In those first relations with objects, both phantasied and actual—and indeed, in the beginning, thanks to projective identification, or the means by which the ego rids itself of unbearable anxiety and yet continues to identify with it—there is and can be no distinction between phantasy and reality, between the inside and the outside. This may well be the condition for any poem to be written, where the question-child, the writer, and the reader must create new playgrounds for affect and thought. "From the beginning," writes Melanie Klein (1957), "all emotions attach themselves to the first object" (234). Even the terms *good* and *bad* are unstable and subject to confusion. Because object relations occur before the infant has any access to a knowledge of them or, rather, because the knowledge the infant makes is unconscious phantasy, then the elaboration of psychical positions—the paranoid-schizoid and the depressive—is how the ego must struggle with the nature of reality and phantasy, with possessing and letting go and, with world relating. Even to think such positions requires an imaginative practice akin to what Sedgwick (1990, 1997) calls "risking the obvious" and, in her discussion of Melanie Klein, "reparative reading practices."

Try to imagine the destructive beginnings of our judgments, our earliest forms of theory kindergarten. This is what Sigmund Freud (1925a), in his essay "On Negation," suggests as our earliest experiences with judging good and bad, with introjection and projection, and with taking the side of "no." In Freud's words, "Expressed in the language of the oldest—the oral—instinctual impulses, the judgement is: 'I should like to eat this,' or 'I should like to spit it out'; and put more generally: 'I should like to take this into myself and to keep that out.' That is to say: 'It shall be inside me' or 'it shall be outside me' "(237). However elegantly wrapped, our intellectual judgment also may be saying something difficult, again to quote Freud: "This is something I should prefer to repress" (236). Or, in the case of the joke, another negation: "This is a place I will never step foot in, even if I built it."

Whereas for Freud the sentence that tries to make itself into a judgment is one of spitting and swallowing, "I shall spit this out and I shall eat this," for Klein, one must spit and split. Her imagined sentence is convulsive, bellicose, belligerent, and frightened, more along the lines of a preemptive paranoid talisman principle: "This is eating me because I have killed it, and so I shall kill it before it returns to eat me again." This rather vicious cycle, where cause and effect are confused through projection, is one that Joan Riviere (1936) also tries to put into words: "You don't come and help, and you hate me, because I am angry and devour you; yet I *must* hate you and devour you in order to make you help" (283, emphasis in original). Put as simply as possible, at the level of phantasy (and phantasy is where Klein plays), there is no boundary among identifications, projection, symbolization, and terror. There is no difference between help and harm. This is another aspect of theory kindergarten: our call for knowledge to help us may mean that we must make mincemeat of knowledge before it makes mincemeat of us. Klein is imagining the difficulties of becoming, reminding her readers that asking for help is like feeling terrible helplessness and that terrible helplessness is the response to fear of annihilation. This is how help and harm become collapsed.

If we can never be free of negation, if negation is one of those sticky ego defenses that protects the ego from that which it cannot bear to know and yet still taunts it to think, if even in what we discard there are still preserved an attraction and a wish to keep this hidden, it still takes a theory of affect to understand the subtlety of not choosing to notice psychical reality. Klein steps back from Freud's description of negation to focus on what comes before the spitting out, namely, the taking in, or the introjection, of the object. When it can be akin to nourishment, introjection serves as a nascent model for Klein's views on reparation. She returns to the work of introjecting the good object, not from the viewpoint of phantasies of invasions but from the position of curiosity and containing. Sedgwick (1997) sees something of this loving work in her description of the work of reading: "to read from a reparative position is to surrender the knowing, anxious paranoid determination that no horror, however apparently unthinkable, shall ever come to the reader *as new*: to a reparatively positioned reader, it can seem realistic and necessary to experience surprise" (24, emphasis in original). Reparative readings offer us a very different sense of reality testing, not that of the Freudian ego, where what is tested is the veracity of the object in terms of its refinding, rather, a reparative position tests the ethical reach of one's own theory, one's own phantasy of encountering the world. A reparative reading practice is one where the object is restored, indeed, revitalized, because of the reader's efforts. Surely we are back to "a question-child," Sedgwick's young reader who loves "the most stretched and ragged edges of [her] competence" (1997, 3).

Sometimes there can be no surprise, because the theory itself forecloses reparative readings, and because there is a hatred of development that severs theory from its own potential gratitude. When this occurs, there is no existence for the "question-child." Sedgwick (1991) analyzes these painful moves when she imagines a manual that is not yet written. "How to bring your kids up gay" considers one devastating form of homophobia in psychiatry. Perhaps it takes the loving reparation of the figure of the child's queer body, who catches, without reason, the shadow of the mother's femininity or the father's masculinity, even if these were not the first shadings of gender offered, to remind one of the chances nature can take. This is the queer relation, for surely when we encounter the other, our identities are just that, a gamble.

The figures of the sissy boy, the he-she girl, and the so-called gender disorder are lovingly held by Sedgwick and so are no longer poster children for pathology. One can look upon psychiatric theories of gender as saying something about our own stalled academic arguments over nature and culture. Sedgwick restages these debates, now along the lines of Kleinian positions. Like the paranoid-schizoid position that cannot recognize its own potential or, indeed, its need to injure, the anxiety that collapses gender with sexuality must foreclose the relation of sexuality to curiosity. There is, in these psychiatric theories, a terrible confusion: feelings of hatred, helplessness, and not knowing are mistaken for the object. Sedgwick urges psychiatry and gay activists toward a reparative reading practice, one that does not settle the nature/culture debates, since no theory can do that. She writes a theory that does not find itself securing its own presumptive ontology, *a theory that welcomes gay children:*

> In this unstable balance of assumptions between nature and culture, at any rate, under the overarching, relatively unchallenged aegis of a culture's desire that gay people *not be,* there is no unthreatened, unthreatening theoretical home for a concept of gay and lesbian origins . . . in the absence of a strong, explicit, *erotically invested* affirmation of some people's felt desire or need that there be gay people in the immediate world. (1991, 164, emphasis in original)

Eros can make of ontology, after all, something marvelous. In her introduction to *Novel Gazing* (1997), where finally the figures of Tomkins and Klein meet tentatively, Sedgwick raises for the nature/culture debates more dilemmas: Is there something within the human that is in excess of ontology and its knowledge representatives? And then, is there a knowledge that can represent its own blind spots, indeed, that tries to make reparation for its first destructive moment of knowing? Let us welcome Eros into this design. Surely more questions can be raised here, but one of the more interesting, because it harkens back to a moment in theory kindergarten where the preoccupation with being treated fairly was excruciatingly insisted upon, is asked by Adam Phillips (1999): "How does one take justice seriously if one takes nature seriously?" (10). Sedgwick offers us a variation on this theme: How does one take reading seriously if one takes psychical reality seriously?

THEORY'S CURIOSITY

One of the great originators of the idea of theory kindergarten and the story of how knowledge develops for the child was, of course, Sigmund Freud (1905b), who calls children "little sex researchers" (194). His second essay on infantile sexuality suggests that we have curiosity from the beginning of life, because we have sexuality. And because curiosity comes before knowledge, our earliest theories of sexuality must run from the ridiculous to the magical and from the paranoid to the sublime. Our little Fritz knows this from his first show. These sexual theories are, for Freud, representative not just of the instinct for pleasure but also of that other instinct, our drive to know, or the instinct to master. Klein's early analytic theories began with the principle that she called "the epistemophilic instinct"—but she stretched it to its limits by heightening not instinct but phantasy, not mastery but anxiety, and, not real angst but that which comes before it: the aggressive and sadistic defenses that collapse knowing with possessing. For Freud, the instinct to master is a part of one's curiosity toward the outside world and toward what other bodies look like.

Klein, however, directs curiosity back upon itself, to its own inside. She argues that the desire to know does not reside in rendering the visible as intelligible but, instead, curiosity's preoccupation is with trying to make sense of the invisible, with what, in fact, the baby cannot see, what is absent but intolerably so. It is the empty space within that the curiosity aims to fill and make present, and for the Kleinian baby, the empty space that must be filled with phantasies is the interior of the mother's belly. In Klein's (1930b) strange words: "In the earliest reality of the child it is no exaggeration to say that the world is a breast and a belly which is filled with dangerous objects, dangerous because of the child's own impulse to attack them" (233). At least initially, knowledge is equated to parts of the other body that must be possessed, and not having knowledge feels as though something was stolen. Having knowledge is also filled with danger, for at the level of phantasy, possessing is the same as injuring and stealing. In this world of concrete symbolization, where metaphors do not yet exist and where there is terrible exaggeration, these injured objects do not, at least in phantasy, take lightly being destroyed.

Another way that Klein describes the epistemophilic instinct is in the awkward phrase, "the highest flowering of sadism," or sadism at its height (Petot 1990, 187). It was her first attempt to convey the idea that the aim of sadism is, in phantasy, to annihilate the object that the phantasy has already injured. For both Klein and Freud, the instinct to master is tied to the ambivalent desire to both destroy and control and thus, in this strange logic, to preserve the object. And yet this work of preservation defies mastery, for at least in the Kleinian view, the injured object returns: it retaliates and persecutes. The desire to know, then, is felt as traumatic and painful, entangled in primal helplessness and paranoia, and it occurs too early to be clarified by language. In Klein's (1928) view, "One of the most bitter grievances which we come upon in the unconscious is that these many overwhelming questions, which are apparently only partly conscious and even when conscious cannot yet be expressed in words, remain unanswered. . . . In analysis these grievances give rise to an extraordinary amount of hate" (188). Klein's understanding of ignorance, then, particularly because it can be noticed only retrospectively, is extremely difficult to bear, and even the knowledge that attempts to assuage our having to learn is linked, by Klein, to the confusion made from a strange combination of affect: love and hate, traumatic frustration, the dread of injury, and helplessness.

Klein sketches the painfulness of learning through her theories of positions. In a late essay on the problem of thinking, she (1958) insists that this painfulness is there from the beginning:

> I recognized, in watching the constant struggle in the young infant's mental process between an irrepressible urge to destroy as well as save himself, to attack his objects and to preserve them, that primordial forces struggling with each other were at work. . . . I had already come to the conclusion that under the impact of the struggle between the two instincts [life and death], one of the ego's main functions—the mastery of anxiety—is brought into operation from the very beginning of life. (236)

Although Klein would later abandon her concept of "epistemophilic instinct" in order to move closer to that which she saw as inaugurating, shattering, and repairing the uses of knowledge, namely, positions within anxiety, she preserves a kernel of its negativity in trying to answer her lifelong question, "What holds the child back?" (Pontalis 1981, 95). How does the ego learn to tolerate its own constitution?

Klein makes some very startling and, for some, outrageous claims about where knowledge comes from, and about what comes before we have the tenacity to engage something like it. She claims to think with infants, entering their phantasies, finding negativity at the heart of their phantasy life, and constructing a very different version of theory kindergarten and a very surprising theorist. "Let's note," observes Jacqueline Rose (1993),

> that the genesis of the persecutory object in Kleinian thinking casts a shadow over interpretation, since, according to the logic of negation, interpretation comes as a stranger from the outside. And let's note too that if Klein makes of the analyst a fool and a fantast, it is from this place that the analyst has to try to speak . . . between the baby ignorant of the external world and the scientist aware of nothing else. (169–70)

Sedgwick, too, would occupy this very difficult space, "a stranger from the outside," bringing a gift of interpretation. She offers to readers both the fantastic returns to the shadowy world of literature and her sharp analyses of how the external and internal world tries to foreclose imagination. Are these the difficulties where the urge for reparation is lost and found?

LOVE'S THEORY

Surely it would be a terrible place if all that happened in theory kindergarten was learning how to defend oneself against the most violent and recursive attacks of anxiety. In her introduction to *Novel Gazing*, Sedgwick (1997) thoughtfully calls this mode of internal persecution "a position of terrible alertness" (8). She was speaking again about theory, but this time as a problem of paranoia, an intellectual example of Klein's paranoid-schizoid position. The position is one of preemptive retaliation, made from phantasies or, better, from an unbearable sense of not knowing and not being able to stand it. For Klein, we all begin in anxiety, and this difficult beginning inaugurates a second way to think, what Klein calls "reparation." There can be a desire to save the object from destruction, to consider the object not just from the vantage of introjection and

projection. There can be an allowance for the object and so for the self
to be whole. This work is one of mourning, of caring, and of gratitude.
In the strange calculus of Klein, we split in order to attempt integration,
and we project before we can see. Thus integrating the world into the self
is painful. In the strange calculus of Sedgwick (1997), we write and read
in order to surprise ourselves, and we think in order to love. "The desire
of a reparative impulse . . . is additive and accretive. Its fear, a realistic
one, is that the culture surrounding it is inadequate or inimical to its
nurture; it wants to assemble and confer plenitude on an object that will
then have resources to offer an inchoate self" (27–28).

Here are some resources we might use. Sedgwick's (1993c) haunting essay, "White Glasses," offers us a story of how identifications work
against all odds:

> Now, I know I don't "look much like" Michael Lynch. . . .
> Nobody knows more fully, more fatalistically than a fat woman
> how unbridgeable the gap is between the self we see and the
> self as whom we are seen . . . and no one can appreciate more
> fervently the act of magical faith by which it may be possible,
> at last, to assert and believe, against every social possibility,
> that the self we see can be made visible as if through our own
> eyes to the people who see us. (256)

There is, in this essay, a desire to honor the invisible and the contents of
our own belly. Putting on these glasses is a homage to a vision of loving
the self and the other, and the reader feels gratitude for the passionate
work of identifications. The choice made, which is, the allowance for the
free association of phantasy, is to release identification from the agonies
of ontology. It is, simply put, to choose to love and to make of that work
a certain relation that can take its residence, in the words of Sedgwick
(1993c), "across the ontological crack between the living and the dead"
(257).

It is, at some intimate level, very lonely to take residence in, to be
addressed by one's own phantasies, and to risk the work of loving. It
would not be until the end of her life that Klein (1963) would take on
an experience that her work hinted at all along, namely, feelings of loneliness. "On the Sense of Loneliness" is, for me, one of her most poignant
and suggestive essays. As in many of her essays, she reviews her key
theoretical efforts, but what seems to set this essay apart from others is
the poignancy of her own thinking, a certain grace. Here Klein acknowledges, in ways that may not be so apparent in her earlier work, the

difficulties and the sadness made when the ego tries to accept the work of integration. In staying with the ego's own feelings about itself, Klein brings the desire for reparation back to the self, who not only has the capacity to destroy the object but who can know that doing so would mean destroying the self as well. Leaving this vicious circle is, Klein admits, very painful for the ego: "The coming together of destructive and loving impulses, and of the good and bad aspects of the object, arouses the anxiety that destructive feelings may overwhelm the loving feelings and endanger the good object" (301).

The pain of integration also makes one lonely, for in accepting the good and the bad, omnipotence must be given up. And without the illusion of omnipotence, a certain sense of hope also is lost. What makes the work of integration so difficult, Klein suggests, is that it is also, paradoxically, a work of mourning. And yet, there will still be enjoyment:

> The capacity for enjoyment is also the precondition for a measure of resignation which allows for pleasure in what is available without too much greed for inaccessible gratifications and without excessive resentment about frustration. Such adaptation can already be observed in some young infants. Resignation is bound up with tolerance and with the feeling that destructive impulses will not overwhelm love, and that therefore goodness and life may be preserved. (1963, 310)

We can, I think, glimpse the painful work of integration in Sedgwick's (1999) record of her own analysis, the beautiful gift, *A Dialogue on Love*. There is no need to argue for the currency of affect, nor even to protect theory from that which makes it fall apart. And surely we can understand that we take reading seriously, precisely because we take psychical life seriously. If we are to make a work from our identifications, and not suppose our points of view, if the resources that the other offers are what allows one to deepen one's own reparative urges that also, after all, belong to the other, then *A Dialogue on Love* is one place where theory kindergarten plays. Still, what the careful reader might grasp is neither a better knowledge of Sedgwick nor even an understanding of the transitional space of that other theory kindergarten, analysis. More pertinent, more surprising, more intimate, and more reparative, the reader might read for important news about herself or himself, for noticing that her or his own destructive readings will not overwhelm the very new work of theory that Sedgwick proposes, the work of love.

CHAPTER SIX

LONELINESS IN EDUCATION: TOWARD A COMPASSIONATE INQUIRY

Long after the Controversial Debates between Melanie Klein and Anna Freud, something fortuitous emerged to exceed its formal resolutions. Twenty years later, there was a moment of agreement—recognition, really—that gave pause to their adversarial relations. This did not occur face-to-face but was recorded through the small regard of mutual citation. They met through a shared topic that, in its very literal qualities, might have separated them even further or else could have served only to punctuate the affective traces the Controversies left in their wake. Instead, these analysts converged theoretically when both happened to draw upon their own self-analysis to inquire into experiences of loneliness, speculating on its vicissitudes and psychical significance and questioning where else it might lead. Neither wanted loneliness to be a *cul-de-sac*, for they saw this affective experience as another metaphor for the fact of natality, and thus necessary to and even needed for the reach they both called "thinking." So they used it as an analogy to think about relations between reality and phantasy, self and other, Eros and aggression, and thinking and feeling. For both, loneliness became a fragile bridge necessary for thinking to cross from the emptiness of loss and anxiety to the poignant work of mourning and reparation. Turning to experiences of loss and reparation, of absence and presence, they argued, can both allow for the significance of configurations of conflicts made in human vulnerability and offer a way to accept, interpret, and learn from the emotional qualities of thinking itself. To notice these subtle ambiguities made from a sense of loneliness, compassionate inquiry is required.

In this last chapter, I turn to how each woman thinks about loneliness, and why their views illuminate the poignant means—*indeed, the psychoanalytic archive*—from which we can construct histories of learning after the experience of education. Their concept of loneliness invites us into a more intimate sense of education and the ongoing work of having to make education from experiences never meant to be educative. This very dynamic also is transferred to the question of history: we make history from events that were never meant to be history. To emphasize the accidental and idiomatic nature of becoming and of singularity also allows for a very different sense of education, gathered both from the surprising relations between reality and phantasy that make something from nothing, and from the novel question of our time—how does one encounter one's own history of learning through the learning of the other?[1]

Other analysts who were affected by Anna Freud and Melanie Klein, yet came to new views because of their work, such as Wilfred Bion, Donald Winnicott, and Edna O'Shaughnessy, are discussed because they too write compassionately when they emphasize responding thoughtfully to experiences of loneliness. They all notice loneliness as a constellation of affect: some call attention to loneliness as in contact with the incoherent, while others name it as a painful dialogue between phantasy and existence as such. The grammar of loneliness, they suppose, can only be transcribed indirectly: bodily symptoms communicate something missing, and there is a disturbance of dependency. From this absence we also can invoke the means to refine how loss can be encountered and made present differently by thinking. They all sketch a paradoxical geography of loneliness and imagine what it is to be in that place: one can run away from what seems difficult in life, but also one can walk away from what feels like clutter and move toward a welcome solitude. These analysts witness feelings of emptiness—their own and those of others—by encountering their own affectations, pulled through psychoanalytic interpretations of the transference. Then they all notice how they are affected, both by its estranging qualities and by the desires made into thinking when the sudden urgency of loneliness and its bare necessity meets the other. From this painful meeting, loneliness becomes a means for poignant thinking, a way to experience what Kristeva (2001b) calls "the fate of being a stranger" (194). This chapter, then, considers how these imagined scenes are sketched in theory. From this psychoanalytic vantage, the archaeology of education can be reconsidered by another construction, now through a novel history, whose very clues are in contact with the incoherent and so are used to notice when one must run away and when one can walk away in order to construct the poignancy of thinking.

An ordinary enough feeling of disconnection, isolation, abandonment, and strangeness, loneliness can take its furtive residency in the crowded space of education. It also may be the means to conjugate, in paradoxical ways, the desire for autonomy with the need for belonging: while loneliness requires a crowded world, its findings are utterly singular in combination.[2] Anna Freud and Melanie Klein offer to education ethical orientations for thinking with the vicissitudes of loneliness. If loneliness at times feels like its own education, and if education can make us lonely as well, then their surprising insights suggest that to encounter the loneliness in the self or in the other requires a thoughtfulness that exceeds the very educational impulse to correct. After all, one does not have to be taught to be lonely, since loneliness feels like its own instruction, even as Klein (1963) claims, "there remains an unsatisfied longing for an understanding without words" (301). Nor is it ever helpful to offer measures of what one should or should not do to avoid it, even as loneliness telegraphs an enigmatic message to the other. Meeting the necessity of loneliness then is not a problem of applying their theories to alter individual behavior. Instead, and perhaps more elusively, the significance of their sense of loneliness begins with how they propose loneliness to signify a relation necessary for thinking and for crafting a kind of freedom within one's inner world. Then we can use their speculations to rethink what becomes of education after the experience of education. Their view of loneliness—its subtle resonance, its sudden occurrence, its noisy symptom—opens up new questions: What is the significance that poignant loneliness brings to thinking of the self and others? What are the strange relations between loneliness as alienation and loneliness as solicitude? How can encountering loneliness lend poignancy to our thinking after education?

SENSES OF LONELINESS

Near the end of her life, Melanie Klein was planning a book on the topic of loneliness. A kernel of her thinking was developed in one of her last papers, published posthumously, "On the Sense of Loneliness (1963)."[3]

She had given an early version of this paper at the Twenty-First Psycho-analytic Congress in Copenhagen in 1959, and a few months before her death she had read, on February 17, 1960, another version to her colleagues in London. Klein also sent a draft for comment to Wilfred Bion, who responded in a birthday greeting dated only March 29.[4] Bion wondered whether his views were a "birthday subject but maybe it is very appropriate," implying that loneliness was a fine subject, even if it serves as a strange reminder that one is born alone, and that one dies alone. It was the ordinary sense of loneliness, albeit expressed extraordinarily, that interested him, yet he could find no term adequate for that feeling. Bion did have a "hunch"

> that loneliness of a particular kind may not be painful or misplaced but springs from the fact that some people of outstanding ability to tolerate the painful concomitants of a capacity to synthesis, live in a mental environment . . . but chiefly independent on their choice to live in contact with the un-synthesized and the in coherent with a view to bringing synthesis and coherence. They always confront the paranoid-schizoid position in its external form—namely the unknown which science has to make known.[5]

Even without finding a proper term—and Bion tried a few, such as "normal loneliness," "isolation," and "no friendship at the top," but discards them because they stung from grievance—his sense of loneliness was courageous and without resentment. A particular kind of loneliness is made from contact with the incoherent, with that which remains inexplicable, even as this relation to the unknown can threaten to disorganize what has, one hopes, already been settled in the compromise of a signification. Bion places his sense of loneliness between the hope for science to somehow make the unknown known and the psychical incurrence of splitting, persecution, and retaliation, or what can be thought of as too much that is known. Loneliness is a transitional space for the play of psychical positions that Klein would leave us with: the paranoid-schizoid and the depressive. What Bion would like to make known, without an adequate term or proper timing, is that these positions ripple throughout one's phantasy life, and that loneliness is that ripple. Both positions, however, are necessary and painful; the sense of loneliness reminds him that the Kleinian positions have no absolute boundaries, even as they must register, each in different ways, the difficulties implicit in conveying understanding and in being understood.

Grosskurth's (1986, 459) biography of Klein points out that while writing her essay on loneliness, Klein had been studying Donald Winnicott's, "The Capacity to Be Alone," and goes on to note that whereas Winnicott's view of aloneness is optimistic, Klein's formulation is "tragic." Winnicott's (1986) optimism may reside in the fact that his paper contemplates something positive, an existential problem that children face from the beginning of their lives: the fact of natality. He sees the ability to experience this dilemma as a sign of sophisticated development. Here is how Winnicott poses the paradox: "It is the experience of being alone while someone else is present" (30). His model for this experience is the infant, alone and satisfied, in the presence of mother. Later, this paradox returns in an achievement made from the sentence "I am alone" (32). This acknowledgment, for Winnicott, is the basis for constructing a personal life, and the ending in this paper offers a glimpse of the poignant thinking of the other that allows for the capacity to be alone: "Even so, theoretically, there is always someone present, someone who is equated ultimately and unconsciously with the mother, the person who, in the early days and weeks, was temporarily identified with her infant, and for the time being was interested in nothing else but the care of her own infant" (36). Winnicott's optimism resides in the sufficiency of beginnings made from the capacity of the other for attentiveness, love, and efforts to understand. This willingness of the other to be mindful allows for the beginning of thinking. Indeed, the other's mindfulness is, for the infant, the first resource for constituting both internal and external worlds.[6]

Klein, however, enters the fray of loneliness from other parts of life where the external world can feel *too constituted*: the loneliness of mental illness and the loneliness of growing old. The care of the other is still crucial, but in ways very different from that of the infant and mother. Klein uses the difference between infancy and old age to comment upon the end of life and on everyday experiences that accrue a share of loneliness and contribute to "the pain of integration" (1963, 304). This may be where she reverses Bion's insight: for Klein, it is not the toleration of the unknown outside that makes integration so painful but toleration of one's inside destructive impulses, the incoherence from within. Klein uses toleration to signify acceptance of the precarious work of trying to understand one's own psychical reality, and in this sense, it is close to her notion of "overcoming."[7] There one brings together the experience of feelings as raw and fragmented communications that contain the depths of inarticulate prehistory, a time before language, with thinking that might free oneself from the confines of the literal and its fear of psychological meaning. Toleration is made and found in trying to understand the creative and destructive depths of one's own psychical reality. In a note for her book on loneliness, Klein includes personal relations with others as being central to this work when she wrote a note to herself: "Tolerance also implies the acceptance of the fact that others are different from the self."[8] Through her consideration of the pain of integration, Klein adds something more to Winnicott's capacity to be alone, imagining integration as the efforts of accepting the destructive and loving aspects of one's life. She considers this process continuous, as always addressing two experiences: dispelling the power of splitting and sustaining one's capacity to relate to others.[9] Arriving after destruction, indeed, invoked by inner destruction, integration is on the side of reparation, and it is never complete.[10] Perhaps this is where Grosskurth places the tragedy: the very difficulty we meet is the self made from mistakes in judgment, hubris, and peripeteia. The very difficulty we meet is the incoherence within. These human qualities structure both psychical reality and external existence. Coming to terms with the frustrations of trying to know one's own psychical reality as one meets the unknown, within existence, constitutes the painfulness of the work Klein called "integration."

What, then, is the quest for trying to understand what is lost when destructive impulses can be admitted? Certain necessary illusions of the self—what Klein calls "idealization"—must be given up. Thus the loss is one of idealization, followed by a measure of resignation that accompanies, but cannot be a substitute for, the loss. Then the resignation made from acknowledging one's own vulnerability can be experienced neither as resentment nor as grievance. Because idealization can turn into fear of persecution, Klein moves counterintuitively when she proposes that the opposite of idealization is loneliness. To illustrate this dilemma, Klein (1963) draws from one analysis, quoting from a patient and then offering her thoughts: " 'The glamour has gone.' The analysis showed that the glamour which had gone was the idealization of the self and of the object, and the loss of it led to feelings of loneliness" (305). One might ask, why should one be lonely without idealization? And what is idealization that it can defend against loneliness? Klein suggests that idealization is a defense against a vulnerability startled by its own persecutory phantasies; it attempts to keep the self in good company, but the company is rather fickle, since it is a projection that must be protected from any difference in order to retain its goodness. The problem is that an understanding of the self and the other cannot be reached through mechanisms of idealization, even as this structure is necessary to the poiesis of psychical processes.

Yet idealization cannot admit difference or, to return to Klein's note, "that others are different from the self." At its least intrusive and in terms that do not repeat the defenses mobilized to hold the unknown at bay, understanding entails trying to account for the incoherent made in the double efforts of trying to understand the self and the other as one experiences the fragility of feeling understood. Idealization denies this very work, while a sense of loneliness, reminds Klein, also is an experience that allows one to reach out to the world. By the end of her essay, Klein maintains that there can be no cure for loneliness, because it "springs from internal sources which remain powerful throughout one's life" (1963, 313). That is, loneliness is a constant development in the internal human condition, as necessary to Winnicott's capacity to be alone and Bion's contact with the incoherent as it is for Klein's sense of the urge to make reparation. It also is part of our fact of natality, where the condition of being the only one becomes the event of being alone with others.

All that remains of Klein's plans for the book on loneliness are notes in the form of scraps of paper, pinned together in a file and stored in Box 20 at the Wellcome Contemporary Medical Archives Center in London. The straight pins, such as those found in a sewing kit, are now rusty; the typed notes, faded and ink smeared, are fragile and yellowed; and paper bits have now curled in on themselves. There are no complete pages, just strips of paper notes that Klein must have arranged and rearranged, perhaps to remind herself of the incoherence of the puzzle of loneliness. Sometimes four of these bits are held together by rusty clips. They make an odd-sized page. One of these patchwork notes is titled, in her handwriting, "Notes to Loneliness," as if Klein gave life to a new creature and then tried to send it a message. The message was tender, at least at first, and she may have been looking back on her Copenhagen trip when she typed: "The delight which I found in some people about being quite free from everybody's demands and going their own way, which was represented for instance by going to Norway and from there on to further snow fields where one would not meet anybody, or by the deep love of the desert." Here is her memory of walking away from one world in order to meet the solitude of another. Here too is the interest in being alone in the presence of love.

Walking away is not the end of her journey. Klein must have had second thoughts, perhaps made to remind herself that this creature called "loneliness" was something that she herself had created, when she penciled in another missive to loneliness, "link with hostility." That thought continued: "This links with following up one's own thoughts and even excluding the good internal object because it is a burden and makes demands. And the suddenness of loneliness which follows after such phantasies. Actually, it means death."[11] It also may mean that even good objects are difficult to accept. We have a hint of what comes after phantasy—not reality, but loneliness and feelings of remorse and mourning. Klein continued to add more complexity, turning as well to "the wish to be alone": "While one is longing to be understood and appreciated and gratified to find this in the external relations, there is also the feeling of wanting to be alone with one's thoughts, phantasies and feeling anything which would disturb this as an interference."[12] Perhaps this is where one can experience again, "an understanding without words" (1963, 301).

In another note titled, "Giving up Idealization," Klein again turns to the loss of glamour, this time to note its absence and perhaps strange compensation, namely, the acceptance of existence as such:

> The feeling of loss when you give up your idealized object is unavoidable. It means an experience of internal and external reality which means recognizing one's own deficiencies. "Glamour goes out with it." It is a great relief, but it is also part resignation. . . . That feeling of loss is overcome and counteracted by the relief that one is no longer driven to make such enormous demands on oneself and others. But it is nevertheless as loss. Adaptation to reality is always painful.[13]

Winnicott (1990b) also would stress the trouble with reality in his often-repeated observation that the reality principle is an insult to us all.[14] It is insulting not just because if we had our choice we would do anything we wished, or that feelings of omnipotence are hurt easily. Instead, Winnicott speculates on the difficulties of tolerating, without falling into bits, the frustrations and feelings of being thwarted that reality does bring. Indeed, for Winnicott, there are two dimensions of reality: psychical reality and existence. Reality, for Winnicott, is on the brink of illusion and disillusion, compliance and compromise, choice and inheritance. "The Reality Principle," writes Winnicott in an essay called "Living Creatively," "is the fact of the existence of the world whether the baby creates it or not" (1990b, 40). This fact of existence does not settle much, because the existence of the world also is the existence of the inchoate, and so we are returned to Bion's strange birthday greeting: contact with the inchoate both requires and creates the singularity called "loneliness." Klein implies that if one can tolerate reality without recourse to fix it through the phantasies of idealization and splitting, then one can accept reality and not be motivated by compliance. Here her interest is in the ways in which one can adapt to an unsettling freedom, crafted from the work of accepting loss and a willingness to be touched by reparative urges. In a late essay, "On Mental Health," Klein (1960) calls this adaptation to the external world "an adaptation which does not interfere with the freedom of our own emotions and thoughts" (269). That adaptation has two dimensions: the capacity to be reassured by actual people, and the idea that reality must still be interpreted: "What matters about external reality is not merely its actuality, but the fact that through it [we can] discover a version of events that are governed by alternative principles" (Likierman 2001, 127).

This interest in freedom, and that which constrains it, underlines Anna Freud's (1967) poignant discussion, "About Losing and Being Lost." The freedom to be made is drawn from the pleasures of belonging and being able to treasure one's own psychical belongings as worthy. It also is made from constructing a relationship to the past that is no longer but still exerts its force in the present. Whereas Klein considers loneliness through the loss of idealization, Anna Freud begins with losing history. Like Klein's paper, a series of revisions, according to Young-Bruehl's (1988) biography, spanned the difficulties of a twenty-year period. Anna Freud's paper was written in the wake of analyzing her own disturbing dreams, and her ideas developed more fully in the postwar period, amidst deep sadness: mourning her father's death, the deaths of many analysts close to her, and the deaths of family members left in Vienna who perished in concentration camps and, finally, with her forced exile, coming to terms with the loss of her home in Vienna, perhaps with the sad fact of being left behind, lending a new poignance to the sentence, "I am alone." With so much lost history, it is little wonder that she reached in her own psychoanalytic archive of losing and of being lost. And is it any wonder that there is mention in this paper of being haunted by ghosts and lost souls? These are questions of presence and absence, and Anna Freud describes their strange affectations with the figure of the chronic loser, the one who cannot hold onto her or his possessions and who unconsciously acts out, in relation to her or his belongings, feelings of abandonment and hostility. We have here a very different perspective on running away and walking away, threaded through the affective states of being left behind and feeling forgotten.

The heart of this paper is her sense of what the work of mourning entails. For Anna Freud, the work of mourning does not only proceed through the necessity of decathecting memories bit by bit in order to find new objects in the world, as Sigmund Freud (1917) emphasizes. The daughter takes a different route to reach the question of how the loss of the other who is no longer there can still participate in one's present life. Anna Freud focuses on allowing the past its significance and on the work, whereby the past can be taken inside to enrich the ego. While her father considered how mourning is interrupted for melancholia, or the more devastating qualities of identification, when the ego incorporates the lost object and in doing so splits itself into two warring parts, Anna Freud notes these qualities of melancholia but stresses how identification with the lost object can lend the ego comfort, and an understanding that there is always another.[15] She specifies the loving qualities of identification, the taking in of goodness as the beginning of sublimation, and then she speculates on the psychological knowledge crafted from and for an encounter with the inchoate: with ghosts and lost souls, and with feelings of being haunted in the present by knowledge that could not have been known in the past. Through her encounter with these phantasies on the way to thinking, what we can note as an "after education," Anna Freud acknowledges the importance of Klein's concept, "projective identification," seeing its very first fluttering of communication as the means for thinking of the self and the other.[16]

Anna Freud's (1967) sense of loneliness passes through her interpretation of how the ego tries to defend itself against feelings of loss and mourning. "About Losing and Being Lost" is perhaps the closest she would come to agreeing with Klein's views on phantasy: that feelings create objects, and so objects possess psychological capacities, including *overhearing, taking revenge,* and *being lonely.* And these feelings are a story of object relations. Anna Freud would see in these processes displaced feelings made from the complications of history, regression, and infantile wishes.[17] She augments feelings of loneliness by stressing an underlying aggression expressed in "the wish to lose something" (303), and then fill what is missed with accompanying guilt and mourning that takes its place. Here is where Kleinian hostility enters. The wish to lose something defies our conscious intentions but still communicates a need to remove something that encumbers without knowing the nature of the encumbrance. These material objects symbolize archaic emotional relations that Anna Freud also considers prehistory, a time before language. Paradoxically, losing may discard the object in order to preserve the feelings of the encumbrance, for throwing something away can be equated to being abandoned. Then loneliness might be a substitute, a placeholder for what is missing. Like Melanie Klein, Anna Freud begins from the psychoanalytic assumption that belongings are cathected with both aggression and libido, and so with ambivalence; depending upon our unconscious wishes both toward them and our bodies, we hold onto and preserve our belongings, or we discard and lose them. Losing, however, does not end the drama of the cathexis, and in this strange scenery, Anna Freud and Melanie Klein meet.

Sigmund Freud (1925a), too, was preoccupied with losing, and nowhere is this more poignant than in the model he offers for the act of creating perception and memory: refinding the lost object, and a game of fort/da, or here/gone.[18] Ostensibly, this may be one reason losing something so affects the loser. In acts of perception and memory, the reality principle plays a belated and strange role, not so much in adding insults to injury but instead as cathexis and as a way to configure new ideas and so to craft imaginative satisfactions from old losses:

> The antithesis between subjective and objective does not exist from the first. It only comes into being from the fact that thinking possesses the capacity to bring before the mind once more something that has been perceived, by reproducing it as a presentation without the external object having still to be there. The first and immediate aim, therefore, of reality testing is not to *find* an object in real perception which corresponds to the one presented but to *refind* such an object, to convince oneself that it is still there. . . . The reproduction of a perception as a presentation is not always a faithful one; it may be modified by omissions, or changed by merging of various elements. In that case, reality-testing has to ascertain how far such distortions go. But it is evident that a precondition for setting up of reality-testing is that objects shall have been lost which once brought real satisfaction. (1925a, 237–38)

Freud casts perception in the midst of desire affected again in a process of reality testing that repeats a prehistory Klein calls "phantasy." He proposes perception as a means for self-assurance and mastery, that the object is still there, even if its "thereness" refers not to its actual presence but to one's feelings toward it. In this way, perception moves back and forth, testing psychical reality and external reality. There is still thinking to be made from this: How far can such distortions go? But there is more. For if a sense of reality is lost, so too is the ego.[19] For the realness of reality to be felt, however, there must be some satisfaction and someone. This is where Winnicott's notion of the capacity to be alone enters. It also is the place where Anna Freud's and Melanie Klein's use of projective identification extends Freud's discussion. Through perception, more than the world is being perceived, because perception emerges from

projective identifications that also are the means for psychical development and for the ego to transform itself gradually as it relates to the
other. As we try to establish the objective world, our subjectivity is being
formulated; losing something outside is felt as loneliness inside, and loneliness inside is elaborated through projective identifications.

Sigmund Freud's discussion of perception contains a kernel of object relations, but it is in the contemporary theory of object relations that
one finds the elaboration of phantasy and thinking. Edna O'Shaughnessy's
(1996) discussion of thinking is useful here, because while she links
processes of perception to the development of thinking itself, the emotive
qualities of thinking and constructing reality are preserved, as is a respect
for psychical reality:

> Instead of a pleasure ego evacuating unpleasure, a new struc-
> ture is slowly achieved: a reality ego which has unconsciously
> internalized at its core an object with the capacity to think,
> i.e., to know psychic qualities in itself and others. In such an
> ego there is a differentiation between conscious and uncon-
> scious, and the potential so to differentiate between seeing,
> imagining, phantasizing, dreaming, being awake, being asleep.
> (179)

A psychoanalytic history of learning begins in the conflict that
perception contains and scatters affective experiences of love and hate,
and of losing and refinding. While we must differentiate, through acts of
perception, these differentiations still require integration for new modes
of meaning to be made. Indeed, how we see the world also is an intima-
tion of how we think of the self and the other, because perception carries
traces of and adjusts—through constant processes of fragmentation and
integration—our psychical reality. Anna Freud's (1967) essay, "About
Losing," considers these dilemmas by highlighting the perspective of what
our belongings unconsciously represent, specifically when a valued object
is lost and when an object loses its value. While she feels that "human
beings are flexible where their attachments are concerned" (305), this
very resiliency, she also notices, animates vulnerability and can buckle. A
cathexis can become displaced and withdrawn and even turn against the
self who desires. Some psychical responses to losing, then, include, for
Anna Freud, deprivation, sadness, withdrawal, abandonment, hostility,
and phantasies created through projection, personification, and
identification.

These last three dynamics—projections of the internal content to the outside, personification of this content as then a separate and hostile other, and identification with this content, since it still represents parts of the inner world—shadow Klein's psychical positions and so offer a variation on the theme of projective identification. One combination of projective identification invokes the paranoid-schizoid position where splitting, persecution, and retaliation index the aggression of object relating, while another combination invokes the depressive position, what O'Shaughnessy notes as "differentiation," the capacity to think of the other and the interest in thinking about thinking. In Anna Freud's view, aggressive feelings are projected onto the object that must then be discarded, but there also are feelings of love and guilt, and this allows the lost object to be personified, bestowed with a strange agency—it speaks, it hears, and it overbears, and thus it feels the hurt of being discarded. Once the object is personified, identification becomes split—with the discarded object and the actions of the one who discards.[20] In one of her few acknowledgments of Klein's contributions to psychoanalytic theory, Anna Freud notes this trajectory as projective identification, even as she introduces a new emphasis on splitting in identification, proposing ambivalence as a point of view.

Projection, personification, and identification are the psychical means from which to enact both displacements and attachments. This is where the flexibility and the vulnerability reside, and both are communicated, albeit unconsciously. For Anna Freud, when a libidinal tie is lost, it is marked in the strange shorthand of the unconscious by a symptom that repeats and reverses the original loss: losing love is felt as abandonment, and being abandoned accrues hostility. The symptoms that preoccupy her repeat the dilemma of losing: "early wandering, frequently getting lost, truanting, etc." (1967, 312). Whereas Melanie Klein sketched the pleasures of walking away, for Anna Freud running away offers glimpses of the psychical pain made from senses of loneliness. The chronic loser maintains double identification: "passively with the lost objects which symbolize themselves, actively with the parents whom they experience to be as neglectful, indifferent, and unconcerned toward them as they themselves are toward their possessions" (313). The pain of being discarded and the pleasure of throwing something away is the phantasy. It also is reminiscent of fort/da, the here/gone, or presence/absence that electrifies perception, memory, and history. In psychical reality, the conflict of loyalty to the past, and phantasy of a future that is overly anticipated, is a particular answer to questions such as: Where do I belong? Where can I put feelings of longing, loneliness, and desertion? How can I transform the passivity of my disclaimed actions into the activity of refinding the lost object?

Klein's (1963) position on the painful experience of not belonging is similar to Anna Freud's. For Klein, projective identifications lend to the work of integration both its pathos and its incompleteness:

> However much integration proceeds, it cannot do away with the feeling that certain components of the self are not available because they are split off and cannot be regained. Some of these split-off parts . . . are projected into other people, contributing to the feeling that one is not in full possession of one's self, that one does not fully belong to oneself or, therefore, to anybody else. The lost parts, too, are felt to be lonely. (302)

Klein's description of integration follows Anna Freud's trajectory: projection, personification, and identification. Integration, paradoxically, includes mourning lost parts of the self and poignant thinking about loneliness.

Perhaps one of the most difficult questions, then, is how one can think about responding to expressions of loneliness and containing the transition from emptiness to thinking. After all, so much of this drama is internal, and its symptoms are congealed. O'Shaughnessy (1996) offers a clinical example of a particular dialogue made when "lost parts" of the self are communicated through projective identifications:

> A nine-year-old girl, for example, while going swiftly and systematically from one activity to the next, at times projected into me a feeling of isolation. I felt the isolation intensely in myself, i.e., I contained and became momentarily identified with her projection. After thinking about what I had received, I interpreted that she wanted me to know her feeling of isolation. (179)

O'Shaughnessy's method is compassionate inquiry: she tries to understand what her young analysand conveys anxiously. Not being able to settle into an activity symbolizes for the analyst a sense that the young analysand herself is missing. But rather than asking to be found, the young girl offers the analyst her experience of losing. O'Shaughnessy receives the affectation and contains it through her interpretation. In trying to accept this knowledge of the inchoate, namely, the knowledge conveyed through loneliness,

O'Shaughnessy proposes another sense of projective identification, this time through the transference: the analyst uses her capacity for projective identification as a means for learning from the other's representation and returning it back to the other, because the communication itself must be refound. This play of subjectivity also is what lends psychoanalytic interpretation its significance and emotional force. O'Shaughnessy is willing to pass through and so identify with the miasma of the young analysand and return to the girl, not the mess or the concreteness of the projective identification but rather the significance of the young girl's feelings. In doing so, she offers to the young analysand a means to think about her thinking. We are in the realm of psychoanalytic histories of learning, where interpretation itself returns what Bion called "a view toward synthesis," what Winnicott conceptualized as "the experience of being alone while someone is present," and what Klein noticed as "the pain of integration."

Our attentiveness to the dynamics of losing and refinding, of running away and walking away, and of poignant thinking can now illuminate a problem that the Controversial Discussions could not settle. Some of the acrimonies associated with the Discussions emerge from the question of whether education and psychoanalysis can be practiced together and still maintain their respective autonomy. The problem is that while these fields may be in need of distinction, they also have something in common, namely, that their respective practices must try to connect to the unknown and the incoherent. This is demanding work, and controversies themselves may try to foreclose the painful dilemmas made from contact with the incoherence. Discussions on loneliness—the point where Anna Freud and Melanie Klein met—provide education with a different sense of how its efforts are received and used, and for what can now be included under the sign of education when experiences of loneliness are considered. We also can understand why in education we have didacticism and the idealization of knowledge. These mechanisms defend against the inchoate that also is education. Indeed, if we can think differently about the importance that loneliness offers thinking, then the work of education can begin in thinking about what qualifies as a thoughtful interpretation of education's own events, and so the work of after-education.

A hint of what education becomes is found in Sigmund Freud's (1916) concept of *Nacherziehung*, or "after-education," the point where he attempts to distinguish between education and psychoanalysis. Something has been missed in education, and the methods employed to address the emptiness are marked by the very absences that the methods try to cover over. Indeed, the strategies themselves are incoherent. Responding to loss and emptiness does not require filling in what is missing or adding new information to top off the old. These actions belong to a transmission model where feelings of emptiness cannot be noticed, because knowledge is assumed to fill in the gaps and defend against the inchoate. Contact with this inchoateness, however, would allow education its capacity for poignant thinking of the other. After-education proposes that education is not a prevention but a provocation. Yet if it is, there may be a need to walk away and run away, and there may be alienation and solitude.

Analyzing education after the experience of education requires that we notice errors, losses of judgment, feelings of emptiness, and harmful practices, paying particular attention to how these conflicts affect experiences of loneliness and the urge for reparation. This reconstruction of what has happened to an experience that is not quite experienced can be made in a way that does not repeat the original trauma but instead creates the conditions for its loss to be mourned, as we saw in O'Shaughnessy's response to her young analysand. We can find what Klein thinks of as "poignant thinking," and what Anna Freud calls "mourning," in the ways in which we conceptualize psychoanalytic histories of learning. This entails being able to lose not the object but its idealization: again, to borrow from Klein, it is the glamour that must go. But to reach this poignancy of understanding, and to see where education and psychoanalysis may freely associate, requires an interest in Bion's contact with the unknown.

CONTACT WITH THE INCOHERENT IN HISTORY

Within Bion's birthday greeting to Melanie Klein there is a kernel of method. He suggests the importance of being in contact with the incoherent "with a view to bringing synthesis and coherence." What can this work entail, and how does the history of the other allow the self to find new significance from old losses? Patrick Modiano's (1999) short meditation on history and its inconsolable losses, titled *Dora Bruder*, is an imaginative reconfiguration of how we might think of synthesis and coherence not as completion or totality but as being closer to Klein's painful work of integration and Anna Freud's work of mourning. Modiano's method of thinking depends upon his interest in bringing himself into contact with the incoherence of history, that is, history as phantasy and as holding these residues. He employs projective identification: projecting himself into the archive, personifying what he finds there, and identifying with the emotional qualities that this contact brings.

Dora Bruder is both a person and the title of Modiano's book. It also is the name of a stranger and her fate, stretched to signify Modiano's obsession with refinding the lost object of history. There is a certain desperation, for Modiano also understands what he has lost in himself when this particular history is lost. His inquiry tries to get in touch with this aporia and so can be read as a historical novel in that its narrative is an archaeology, a facsimile of fragments that arranges and rearranges how he understands his own affective biography, now reconstructed from his efforts to think of the other.[21] As such, this text is, among other things, a fictional account of object relations and a psychoanalytic inquiry into what history means for the psyche.

The story is deceptively simple and its outline stark: Modiano narrates his incomplete search, fifty-five years after she disappeared, for a Jewish adolescent girl, Dora Bruder, who lived in Paris until 1942 and happened to run away from the Catholic boarding school that her parents enrolled her in precisely at the same moment when the German occupation of Paris began organizing its mass deportations of Jewish French citizens. None of these details made explanatory sense to Modiano. Indeed, they were symptoms of social and private incoherence, and it took the narrator years to patch together a semblance of chronology, balancing his sense of loneliness with the preservation of what must remain unrepresentable. Like the analytic work of O'Shaughnessy, facts cannot cohere into linear relation and so signal something about history's incoherence. The question that haunts Modiano's inquiry, one made from the place of projective identification, is who and what is lost when history is lost?

It was an accident that he found traces of her existence at all. He was sitting in a library doing other research, and his attention roamed until it settled on an old newspaper classified advertisement; a grown-up Modiano learns that one teenage Dora Bruder was reported missing by her parents on December 31, 1941, having escaped from her school on December 14, 1941. She was missing for four months and found by the police on April 7, 1942. Dora was returned to her parents, but a short time later, on September 18, 1942, she was picked up again by the police, now to be deported, along with her father, to Auschwitz. Dora, her father, and later her mother died in Auschwitz. From these skeletal facts that could not be animated from staring at photographs of the family he acquired through some surviving cousin years later, Modiano constructs his own urges for reparation. The urge has two dimensions: refinding split off parts of his self, and acknowledging the loss of fragments of a world he would refind and mourn in the brief life of Dora Bruder.

Modiano rehearses all of the missing details, as though the rehearsal itself would bring them back to life. He cannot find out where Dora went over those wintry months, who she saw, or what she did to survive. The fragments of reality Modiano could construct are from the weather reports during the time she was missing: it was bitterly cold and snowy. But also, fragments of lost experiences returned in the form of official edicts for destruction: four Stars of David, to be affixed upon clothing, were supplied to Jewish adults; curfews were enforced to limit movement; edicts were issued that prohibited Jews from using bicycles, going to the theater, and owning radios; arrests were made; and people disappeared as though they were thrown away. Modiano documents this history, but his interest seems to be more in how to thread—through projective identification—through his own life the story of Dora Bruder. After all, in searching for what happened for Dora, he also is asking this question of himself. Yet he is careful not to take the synthesis as a presumption, that these two histories—his and Dora's—now resting side by side, are similar. They are not. While identification can become a means of foreclosing difference between the self and other, it also can be that fragile bridge made from compassionate inquiry and the desire to think of the other as separate. Still, he lets Dora's world remind him of his own, now pondering old disappointments, events he did not make but that are his.

Modiano imagines that her parents agonized over whether to report Dora to the police, the very institution that was assisting in the roundup and deportation of Parisian Jews. Their decision must have been even more painful, for Dora's parents had not registered her as a Jew when required to do so in 1940; instead, they sent her to a Catholic boarding school. Perhaps they hoped she could wait out the occupation there. Or maybe Dora had become wayward, difficult for her parents to control and in need of the discipline that they hoped the boarding school would offer. It was the parents' newspaper advertisement that accidently caught Modiano's interest, almost fifty years after they placed their notice.

This notice of a missing person reminded the narrator of something unresolved in himself: his roaming discontentment, his own conflicts with making sense of postwar France from his own childhood disappointments, and his incredulity toward his father's abandonment of him after the war. In the war, did Patrick's father know Dora? With so many reversals and with the condensation that is also found in the newspaper classified advertisement, Modiano began to think of Dora, wondering what had happened, why she left, where she went, and how she thought of her life. But he could only imagine his own questions: the more he searched for Dora, the more he confronted the inchoate in his own life.

His patient research could not answer the question, "What makes us decide to run away?" (1999, 46), except to note his own urge as a teenager: "But it seems that the sudden urge to escape can be prompted by one of those cold, gray days that makes you more than ever aware of your solitude and intensifies your feeling that a trap door is about to close" (47). His own running away—that strange mix-up of both running from and walking away—cannot compare to Dora's, and he knows this. Modiano could, after all, run away and not have history collapse upon him. And perhaps the fact that Dora was denied this very ordinary experience—the pleasure of fleeing and the opportunity to return—is also what he mourns with projection, personification, and identification. This is another way of thinking about the other without recourse to the glamour of idealization and certainty.

Most of the records that pertained to Dora Bruder and her family have been destroyed, and Modiano records these lacunae: "It takes time for what has been erased to resurface" (9). It took him four years to find Dora's date of birth: February 26, 1926. Originally the information was withheld from him, because he was not a family member. What resurfaced were not the registries that listed the dates of deportation but the letters that family members wrote to the police begging for news of their missing loved ones. Modiano's reconstruction of Dora's life is, in essence, a reconstruction of his own: his alienation from his father, who survived the war but abandoned him; his gratitude for writers no longer here—"So many friends I never knew disappeared in 1945, the year I was born" (81)—and his premonitions while walking in his own Paris neighborhood, that this also was Dora's everyday world. In the small book he wrote, the story of Dora Bruder is summarized continually, as though these fragmented details of her story could lend clarity to the incoherence that he met in the newspaper accounts of those years. No retelling is the same; small details reconfigure and lend poignancy to what at first is ordinary (a teenager runs away) and then sad (she runs into a terrible history) and, to what now belongs to the poignancy of Modiano's thought, the work of mourning. The glamour is of course gone, but because it was never there at all; the reality is too stark, and our efforts to understand this—our view of synthesis and coherence when in contact with the incoherent—are flawed.

Bion's birthday greeting to Klein ends with the idea that the extraordinary individual confronts the paranoid-schizoid position in its external form, and that it is science that "has to make the unknown known." Modiano, too, confronted the paranoid-schizoid position of history itself: its disclaimed murders, its absolute splitting of good and bad, and its preemptive retaliatory aggression. But his confrontation resided not in repeating the position but rather by a new reparative narrative for literacy, and so bringing back something of the lost significance of learning from this psychoanalytic history. What contact with the incoherent can come to mean also may be implied in Modiano's meditation on losing and finding, but this definition is modest: compassionate inquiry allows for the lost or disclaimed affect to return, and it is through the affect's return that the urge for reparation and mourning begins. Contact with the incoherent with a view toward synthesis, as Bion advised, may mean acknowledging that which exceeds knowledge, and from this excess the unknown is still required for knowledge to speculate upon its own limits. The work of integration is made from the fragments of history and from one's capacity to think poignantly of what is missing in the self, because the other is no longer here. The sense of loneliness that emerges from these thoughts is in no way predicative of any future, accept to say that the one who must keep time is changed. The very ambiguity of loneliness may become a transitional space where one can hold the past in memory, not by changing what has already occurred but by taking this occurrence through the construction of narratives that can be in contact with the incoherence made from this psychoanalytic history of learning.

AFTER-EDUCATION

The concept of "after-education," while originally used by Sigmund Freud to distinguish education from psychoanalysis, can now return to distinguish new work in our contemporary education. If we must ask what is education that it gives us such trouble, our answers can do no more than refine the creative nature of our dilemma. If in trying to understand the self, through the learning of the other, we must take a detour through the psychical qualities of projective identification, and if it is this very detour that accrues a sense of loneliness, then after-education also can be thought of as a means to inquire into this significance and what defends against acknowledging and working through the psychical consequences of education.

Late in his life, Wilfred Bion (1991) wrote three novels of psychoanalysis under the elegiac title, *A Memoir of the Future*. The novels are almost unreadable, for what Bion tried to do was enter subjective catastrophes and display them from the inside out. Affects are personified into characters, and these characters meet circumstances that they can change or that change them. Occasionally a Greek chorus chimes in to punctuate the tragic qualities of memory. There is an analyst everyone argues with and plenty of discussion over why psychoanalysis should be discarded, even if it manages to return. Still, characters freely associate and sometimes can make from this jumble a semblance of significance. Hinshelwood's (1991) description of Bion as a writer aptly portrays the experience of reading this psychoanalytic novel: "He perfected a trick of describing certain psychic processes, while at the same time engaging in just that process during the act of describing it. . . . The reader is required to fill Bion's words with his or her own experience" (235). Here then is another sense of after-education: we are required to fill in the meaning of education after the experience of education, it must still be interpreted, even if where interpretation was there education shall become.

Melanie Klein haunts these pages, as do Anna Freud and the Controversies. They retain something of their idiomatic difficulty in the novel, but they also are needed to remind the other characters of the ways that phantasy becomes thinking and the ways that thinking elaborates phantasy. Bion witnessed the Controversies, but his conern was with a psychoanalysis unbounded by disparate schools, a psychoanalysis in contact with its own inchoate, that is, the unconscious. Can education be in contact with its own unknowable qualities? Perhaps Bion's contact with incoherence leads him to a time before education, and that to understand what education is, one must go back to an original trouble: the problem of learning and not learning at all. There we may meet emptiness, a hatred of development, which Bion will call "Minus K." And he will use it to wonder what becomes of knowledge when knowledge cannot become itself, that is, cannot become the means for thinking. The indecipherable novel Bion offers to his puzzled reader contains a lifeline, in case the reader falls into the inchoate that he so strangely called upon. To conclude his experiment in a novel psychoanalysis, Bion conveys something of the difficulty in understanding and in being understood by offering readers a glossary.

Two of these glossary terms—*job* and *training*—are relevant to the concept of "after-education," although in their common usage it is possible to dismiss them. Meeting these thoughts can allow thinkers to bring back something of the missed timing in education and so magnify the difficulty and necessity of separating education from an anticipatory future. If such a separation can be made, then we can face what returns to alter education, but from a vantage beyond its control. There is a paradox as well: after-education occupies the time of education by his concept of "thoughts awaiting thinkers." We can put the paradox this way: education awaiting humans.

Bion's entry on the word "job" hints at one dilemma: "An analyst has no control over the use to which the analysand puts his experience.

He therefore has to be aware of accepting responsibility for a matter that is not his job" (1991, 626). To substitute educator for analyst suggests that educators are called upon to respond to symptoms of education—their own and those of others. To do so is to accept a matter that is not the job. We are obligated to answer for a responsibility that our work has set in motion without knowing in advance how education is received or even put to use. Still, a responsibility that obligates is something one must make: education awaiting responsibility.

Bion's definition of "training" comes closest to the difficult nature of that response:

> It is a commonplace that loving parents like to have their children correctly trained. Since we cannot foretell the future we do not know for what we need to be trained, or for what to train the child. We, therefore, fall back on memories of the past and assumptions about the future. Memory and desire can be seductively useful and as misleading as seductions are. (669)

Projective identification is that strange conflation when memories of the past shape our anticipations for the preconceptions of the future. But it also is the means from which we can begin to think about what we want from the self and from others. This desire, both useful and misleading, returns back to us the crisis of education. When the desire for continuity and correction by those already born meets the promise and vulnerability of the future, our fact of natality may be that first crisis of education. Perhaps this wishful constellation of time is where the Controversial Discussions and its fights over the currency of education stalled.

If our desire for education misleads, then education also can lead to desire a thinking subject. Where interpretation was, there education shall become. To leave our preoccupation with training and consider instead the question of why we have education at all may not so much prepare us for our job, assuage the force of a responsibility felt before it can be known, or even ease that sense of loneliness made when we can acknowledge that our hopes for the future are intimately bound by what we can understand as history. This psychic archive of education, constructed from psychoanalytic histories of learning, may help remind us that because education has psychical consequences it cannot be known in advance. Because education can make us nervous, and because education gives us such trouble, then there must be a responsibility that comes after education. Then we can think the thought that where education was, there our responsibility can become.

NOTES

CHAPTER ONE

1. My phrasing, where interpretation was, there education shall become, is a play on Freud's (1933) hope for the work of psychoanalysis: "Where id was, there the ego shall be" (80). In his early lectures, Freud (1915a) warns his audience that education can sustain illusions and even defend against the capacity to think. My rephrasing begins with the idea that the interpretation of knowledge is just the beginning material for the possibility of becoming a participant in one's education, and that after the experience of education, there is still the problem of thought. (See also note 7 of this chapter for additional discussion of Freud's phrasing.)

2. The misinterpretation of after-education is found in Freud's (1905a) early discussion "On Psychotherapy." At that time, Freud took great pains to separate psychoanalysis from hypnotic treatment. That early essay offers a series of rules about who is suitable for treatment, how old one should be, and which problems psychoanalysis can adequately address. Almost all of these rules were discarded except for the emphasis on analyzing resistance to cure. At this point, after-education was mistranslated as re-education. This association returns Freud to the problem of suggestibility, for re-education has a brainwashing ring to it:

> Psycho-analytic treatment may in general be conceived of as such a *re-education in overcoming internal resistances.* Re-education of this kind is, however, in no respect more necessary to nervous patients than in regard to the mental element in their sexual life. For no where else have civilization and education done so much harm as in this field, and this is the point, as experience will show you, at which to look for those aetiologies of the neurosis that are amenable to influence; for the other aetiological factor, the constitutional component, consists of something fixed and unalterable. (267)

171

The editors of the *Standard Edition* also note this mistranslation again in Freud's (1925c) preface to August Aichhorn's study, *Wayward Youth*. And yet there is a sense that psychoanalysis is a re-education, a concept stressed in Freud's (1915b) early introductory lectures, where he rehearses the public's objections to psychoanalysis and situates some of their resistance to their education: "Thus society makes what is disagreeable into what is untrue" (23).

I thank Susanna Luhmann for her discussion of *Nacherziehung* (after-education).

3. Marion Milner's (1996) talk to teachers, under the title, "1942: The Child's Capacity for Doubt," is perhaps one of the most explicit discussions on the importance of doubting to creativity and to resisting not only forces of conformity but even anti-democratic events in education.

4. Anna Freud's (1930) characterization of education as all forms of interference is first offered in "Four Lectures on Psychoanalysis for Teachers and Parents." Melanie Klein never defines education explicitly, although her early theories emerged from analyzing children's phobias of school and learning. She was always interested in the problem of what invokes the work of thinking and what she views as the work of love, or the desire for reparation. But because these processes are still affected by what comes before them, namely, anxiety, aggression, sadism, and so on, education, for Klein, is never complete or positive. Also see Kristeva (2001b). I discuss Klein's views on anxiety and reparation in chapter 5.

5. The term *phantasy* refers to unconscious processes and is therefore distinguished from such flights of imagination as daydreams, fantasy play, and games of "let's pretend." Hinshelwood's (1991) entry in his dictionary of Kleinian thought offers some provocative images of phantasy as "worried constructions" children experience as they try to understand sexuality, and as "mental representations of biological instincts" (33). For Klein, phantasy is an expression of primal anxiety; it is a borderline concept that allows for the relation between the mind and the body to be thought, but it also is a concept that allows for the development of thinking itself. Phantasies represent, in Hinshelwood's terms, "a small bellicose society of relationships with objects" (38). Anna Freud's earliest paper, "Beating Fantasies and Daydreams" (1922), suggests this view as well. For a thoughtful discussion on the differences between Klein and Sigmund Freud on the concept of phantasy, see Spillius (2001).

6. John Phillips's (1998) discussion of Melanie Klein's conception of knowledge is extremely useful regarding many of the points I am making. He describes Klein's view of knowledge as a knowledge of phantasy:

> The Kleinian notion of knowledge must be considered in terms of her account of its *possibility*. . . . A deeply objective knowledge in the Kleinian sense demands a knowledge of phantasy itself, as well as an understanding of the inhibiting power of authority. Without this the "reality principle" is just another tyrannous master, because the phantasy of omniscience remains undiminished. For Klein, objective knowledge is a step towards an understanding of phantasy. (163)

7. While it may be more accurate to speak of the wide-ranging differences within ego psychology and object relations, Roy Schafer (1997) offers a balanced account of some of the present differences and convergences between these schools of thought that are different branches of Freudian theory. He does offer a cogent difference between them as he considers what these orientations to psychoanalytic practice hold in common:

> [J]ust as superego factors are regularly part of traditional Freudian ego psychology, they are also that in contemporary Kleinian work. There, however, we find not so much reliance on the terms *atonement* and *undoing* as on *reparation*. The emphasis on reparation underscores the love or concern for the object that these Kleinians see as a vital and potentially constructive setting for guilt reactions in the depressive position; by contrast, the traditional Freudians present guilt in a more narcissistic and simply self-punitive light. For these Kleinians, therefore, superego action is always personified, never the abstract code that Freud conceptualized as the endpoint of superego development. (18)

Martin Bergmann's (2000) reconsideration of the history of Ego Psychology in North America, focusing on the theories of Hans Hartmann, suggests three models of psychoanalysis: Freud's, Klein's, and Hartmann's. His distinctions between these models consider their implications for practice and in terms of the extent of their optimism for self-change:

> In my view, Freud's model was designed to highlight the fact that man accepts the reality principle slowly, reluctantly, and incompletely. As the ego grows, so does the capacity of the person to accept reality. Hence the famous "where id was, there shall ego be." The Kleinian model implies that the margin of libido over aggression is slim at best, and a special psychic structure, the ego, is needed to defend man against his self-destructive tendencies. The purpose of the Hartmann model was to bring psychoanalysis out of its isolation and connect it with currents in biology and sociology. It was the most optimistic of the three, and implies the greatest trust in the human capacity to grow and develop. (24–25)

8. Psychoanalytic theory offers contradictory views on the meaning of homosexuality, even if Freud (1905b) first argued for an original bisexuality, and then that the meaning of heterosexuality also is a problem. One of the most sustained and interesting discussions on the dangers and potentials of using psychoanalytic theory to consider homosexuality without pathology is found in the edited volume of Dean and Lane (2001).

9. In thinking about my relationship with the work of Melanie Klein and Anna Freud, I have been influenced by Young-Bruehl's method of empathetic understanding with her subjects, particularly as she worked this out in writing

about the life of Anna Freud. Young-Bruehl (1998) argues that empathy is made from both identification and imitation but also from its opposite, from the strange work of not being able to relate to another. The latter difficulty, what she calls "overcoming antipathy" (21), was Young-Bruehl's problem; her relation to Anna Freud was ambivalent: "I could feel myself identifying with her lucid mind, but not with her very restricted sexuality; with her physical energy and her energy of mind, her wit, but not at all with her physical presence, her embodiedness; with her sense of tradition, but not with the severest parts of her superego" (21).

10. Kristeva's (2001b) first chapter of her study of Melanie Klein is titled "Introduction: The Psychoanalytic Century," which was ushered in by Sigmund Freud's (1900) *The Interpretation of Dreams* and by the insight of the unconscious. But there is more to this psychoanalytic century for Kristeva: "Mental illness, in fact, is what Freud and his 'accomplices' considered to be the royal road toward understanding and liberating the human soul" (7). And this would give rise, Kristeva continues, to a paradox: "How can pathology give voice to truth?" (8). This was the question developed by both Anna Freud and Melanie Klein, and then by those who extended their theories. This psychoanalytic century would allow us to see within in the social the psychosis of the individual and the depressive qualities of our culture, indeed, what Roudinesco (2001), in her defense of psychoanalysis, calls "the depressive society."

11. A few key studies of controversies in knowledge and institutions also make this point, although not with psychoanalytic theory. See Derrida (2002), Dosse (1999), Haver (1999), Smith (1997), and Readings (1996).

12. Christopher Bollas (1999) argues that the only goal of psychoanalysis, and what makes psychoanalysis distinct in its therapeutic practice, is free association. The radical rule of this mode of communication suggests how difficult it is to say whatever comes to mind without judgment of its importance, relevance, or even its meaning, and without censorship. Bollas also offers a more social implication: "To ask Western man to discover truth by abandoning the effort to find it and adopting instead the leisurely task of simply stating what crosses the mind moment to moment is to undermine the entire structure of Western epistemology" (63). And yet this undermining has an intimate side. In his study on hysteria Bollas (2000) suggests that free association is most like what goes on in our inner world, and that which is there before there is language: "The patient allowed simply to speak what came to mind seemed almost a maternal defiance of the demands to get to the truth; if so, then it only borrowed from the psychic reality that no truth could ever be imposed, but rather had to be created" (112).

13. While Melanie Klein (1957) is not often associated with ego defenses, years after her theoretical arguments with Anna Freud she wrote: "I have often described my approach to anxiety as a focal point of my technique. However, from the very beginning, anxieties cannot be encountered without the defenses against them . . . I even think it is likely that the primordial anxiety, engendered

by the threat of the death instinct within, might be the explanation why the ego is brought into activity from birth onwards" (215–16).

14. See Freud (1915a). Primary processes belong to the unconscious and can be thought of as the force of instinctual conflict. Freud's *The Interpretation of Dreams* (1900) describes the relation between primary processes (belonging to the unconscious and to dream processes) and secondary processes (belonging to consciousness, to ego functions and, hence, to inhibitions) as a relation and as a conflict between the pleasure principle and the reality principle. They are, for Freud, two forms of "thinking" but to very different aims:

> The primary process endeavors to bring about a discharge of excitation . . . it may establish a "perceptual identity" [with the experience of satisfaction . . .]. The secondary process, however, has abandoned this intention and taken on another in its place—the establishment of a *"thought"* identity [with experience]. All thinking is no more than a circuitous path from the memory of a satisfaction (a memory which has been adopted as a purposive idea) to an identical cathexis of the same memory which it is hoped to attain once more through an intermediate stage of motor experiences. Thinking must concern itself with the connecting paths between ideas, without being led astray by the *intensities* of those ideas. (602; brackets, emphases, and parentheses in original)

One might say that while primary processes are the intensities of affect, secondary processes attempt to represent and work through the force of affect. For a sustained discussion of affect and instinct in Freud's work, see Green (1999a).

Laplanche's and Pontalis's (1973, 339–41) entry under "primary processes" offers a thoughtful distinction: whereas primary processes cannot care for logic, rationality, and control of associations, secondary processes seek "thought identity" or clarity of relations. Secondary processes can ask, what does this have to do with that? Primary processes can tolerate not knowing, because knowledge itself is not yet a goal or an object to be apprehended.

15. Anna Freud (1965) would return to the hope that psychoanalysts would, given their preoccupation with childhood, "become experts on childhood, even when they were engaged in the therapy of adults only" (3). She did see some advancement in understanding actual children, but she also notes, "in spite of many partial advances, psychoanalytic education did not succeed in becoming the preventative measure that it set out to be" (8).

16. August Aichhorn and Siegfried Bernfeld were analysts in Vienna, and their focus was on psychoanalytic education for youth. Both worked closely with Anna Freud. For a history of psychoanalytic influences on education, see Rodriguez (1999). For discussion on the history of psychoanalysis in the United States, see Hale (1995a, 1995b). For discussions on psychoanalytic histories in South Africa, see Sachs (1947) and Rose (1996). Lawrence Friedman's (1999) biography

of Erik Erikson offers an interesting assessment of Anna Freud's psychoanalytically designed education for children. But also see Edgcumbe (2000) for a discussion on Anna Freud's views of psychoanalytic education, and why Anna
Freud continues to be relevant for ordinary education.

17. Freud's (1937b) essay, "Constructions in Analysis," offers a poignant
discussion on the work of the analyst and the analysand. Freud calls the analytic
dialogue a "preliminary labor" in the construction or reconstruction of one's life
history. If one cannot change what happened, one might create a new construction from what is gone yet still exerts pressure. "That work would consist in
liberating the fragment of historical truth from its distortions and its attachments to the actual present day and in leading it back to the point in the past
to which it belongs" (268). For a discussion on the fragility of this work of
memory, see Freud (1925b, 1939) and for contemporary debates, see the edited
volume of Belau and Ramadanovic (2002).

18. D. W. Winnicott (1896–1971) was a British pediatrician and psychoanalyst affiliated with the "Independent School," and he was able to work with
both Melanie Klein and Anna Freud. Between 1935 and 1939, Winnicott analyzed Melanie Klein's son, Eric, and Melanie Klein, years later, analyzed Winnicott's
second wife, Clare. Klein also supervised Winnicott. Winnicott was able to bring
together in his theories, and so revise significantly, Anna Freud's views on the
importance of the actual parents and Melanie Klein's views on aggression in
psychical life. For a study of Winnicott, see Phillips (1988).

19. Recent books by analysts suggest the rich potential of psychoanalysis
for understanding problems in history: see Benjamin (1998); Bollas (1999);
Chodorow (1999); Kohon (1999b); Kristeva (2000, 2001a, 2001b); Phillips
(1999) and Roudinesco (2001).

20. Wilfred Bion (1897–1979) was a British psychoanalyst analyzed by
Melanie Klein. He did not take sides during the Freud–Klein Controversies—
the topic of chapter 2—but he is considered as one of the most creative Kleinian
thinkers. He is known for his studies on the problems of thinking in groups,
where many of his views were formulated from his World War I experience as
a soldier and his work with soldiers suffering from war trauma. I discuss his
group theories in chapter 4. Much of my discussion considers two of Bion's texts
(see 1994a, 1994b) and his autobiographical work (1991, 1997a). Also, see
Jacobus's (1998, 1999) studies of Bion's psychoanalytic work and Bléandonu
(1994).

Reading Bion is a strange affair, in that his efforts to put into language the
felt experiences of emotional life require that he work with language as though its
material were combustible. In some of his sort texts he numbers each paragraph
and offers an alchemy notion of affective states. I focus on his concept of "Minus
K" in this chapter and again in chapter 4. Other texts of his read as though Bion
wrote in free association. His short transcribed book, *Taming Wild Thoughts*, begins:
"If a thought without a thinker comes along, it may be what is a 'stray thought,'
or it could be thought with the owner's name and address upon it, or it could be

a 'wild thought.' The problem, should such a thought come along, is what to do with it" (1997a, 27). This problem emerges because of Bion's and Klein's view that psychological knowledge, by which they mean phantasies, comes before knowledge of the world (see O' Shaughnessy, 1996). I try to give a sense of Bion's strange discourse in chapters 5 and 6.

21. Klein insisted that object relations were the beginning of life, and so she centered the absolute and imaginary power of the maternal and the role of femininity for both females and males on the infant's development. This diverged significantly from Freud's emphasis on castration and the father's authority. See Kristeva (2001b) for a sustained and an inspired account of Klein's contribution.

22. The concept of splitting spans, for Klein, two related areas: splitting of the object into good and bad, and splitting of the ego. Klein sees splitting as a defense against overwhelming anxiety, felt as fear of annihilation but also transforming into fear of persecution. She argues that because the breast is the baby's first external object, it also is the place where these destructive impulses are played out. Her (1946) essay, "Notes on Some Schizoid Mechanisms," describes the relation made between the ego and the object in splitting: "I believe that the ego is incapable of splitting the object—internal and external—without a corresponding splitting taking place within the ego. . . . It is in phantasy that the infant splits the object and the self, but the effect of this phantasy is a very real one, because it leads to feelings and relations (and later on, thought processes) being in fact cut off from one another" (6).

23. "Columbine Students Talk of the Disaster and Life," *New York Times*, April 30, 1999, p. A25. What is known as "the Columbine Massacre" resulted in the violent loss of fifteen lives on April 20, 1999. Over that year alone, a series of violent murders took place in elementary and high schools in the United States and provoked for education a rash of new surveillance methods, school uniforms, discussions of the importance of bringing religion into classes, gun control, and so on.

24. Kristeva (2000) makes this claim in her study on art and the possibility of revolt. In turning to Freud's study of the violent origins of civilization, she writes:

> *Totem and Taboo* (1912) . . . emphasizes the difference between acts that are repeated without having psychological representatives (in particular the murder of the father), on the one hand, and, on the other an assimilation-identification with the agency of power represented by the father that is effected through the totemic meal, which generated the symbolic pact between the brothers. (44)

That which cannot be symbolized, not in the sense of making a linguistic equivalent but in the sense of cathexis between idea and affect, does return, as traumatic repetitions.

25. Freud's *Civilization and Its Discontents* was originally published in 1929; a second version with new footnotes and a new final sentence appeared in 1931, when the rise of Hitler and the Nazi movement was becoming obvious. Freud (1930) raises his difficult question at the end of the essay: "The fateful question for the human species seems to me to be whether and to what extent their cultural development will succeed in mastering the disturbance of their communal life by the human instinct of aggression and self-destruction" (145). The added sentence that the editors of *The Standard Edition* footnote as 1931 opened readers to Freud's uncertainty: "But who can foresee with what success and with what result?" (ibid.). Between 1933 and 1939, large numbers of Jewish analysts would leave Germany and Austria. Many of these analysts in exile went to London. By 1939, it would no longer be possible to practice psychoanalysis as Freud knew it in Germany and Austria, under the Third Reich. For a study of the Third Reich's destruction of Freudian psychoanalysis, see Goggin and Goggin (2001) and Falzeder et al. (2000), *The Correspondence of Sigmund Freud and Sándor Ferenczi*, vol. 3.

CHAPTER TWO

1. The list of participants is impressive and begins Pearl King's (1991) compilation of the meeting notes and papers. Three schools of thought were represented: the Anna Freudians, the Kleinians, and the Independents (see King and Steiner 1991, xi–xxv). These schools came to symbolize what King called "a gentleman's agreement" (see note 18 of this chapter). King also identifies the main protagonists: "for scientific purposes, the main argument was between Edward Glover, Melitta and Walter Schmideberg, Willi and Hedwig Hoffer, Barbara Low, Dorothy Burlingham, Barbara Lantos, and Kate Friedlander, who, along with Anna Freud, opposed the new ideas of Melanie Klein, whose main supporters were Susan Isaacs, Joan Riviere, Paula Heinmann, Donald Winnicott, and John Rickman" (1991, 3). Melitta Schmideberg was Melanie Klein's daughter. For a discussion of their difficult relations, see Kristeva (2001b).

2. Kristeva (2001b) offers the view that the institutional splits within psychoanalysis were not only because the analysts came as close to madness as possible. "Rather, and more significantly, a nuanced analysis reveals that the infighting within the analytic movement reflects the cruelty that is endemic to all of human culture precisely because innovations occur only at the outer bounds of possibility" (7). That cruelty goes hand in hand with innovation also is the basis of Melanie Klein's sense of development.

3. For a discussion on how the Second World War affected the preparation of Freud's *Standard Edition*, see Ilse Grubrich-Simitis (1996). For a discussion of historical anxieties that informed the British context of psychoanalysis and modernism, see Stonebridge (1998). For a discussion on the Nazification of psychoanalysis during the Third Reich, see Goggin and Goggin (2001). And, for

a personal account of psychoanalysis during the First World War and its encounter with the Second World War, see volumes 1, 2, and 3 of *The Correspondence of Sigmund Freud and Sándor Ferenczi* (Brabant et al. 1993; Falzeder et al. 1996, 2000).

4. Melanie Klein was born in Vienna on March 30, 1882, to a middle-class Jewish family. While she never published an autobiography, in 1953 she began writing one, working on it intermittently until her death on September 22, 1960. The manuscript is held by the Melanie Klein Trust; it is available to read at the Wellcome Library for the History and Understanding of Medicine in London. Klein's fragment of autobiographical reflection romanticizes her early years, her stormy relationships with her mother and her own children, and her feelings of warmth toward being Jewish. In this way, it resembles a *Bildungsroman*. Grosskurth's (1986) biography of Melanie Klein begins with this fragment, as does Kristeva's (2001b) study, and she uses it to ponder the unanswerable question of why Klein glossed over her painful losses and disappointments. Likierman's (2001) reappraisal of Klein's life work also draws from this fragment.

Anna Freud, the youngest of the Freud's six children, was born in Vienna in December 1895. She too was a daughter of the Jewish Enlightenment. In 1982, she died at age eighty-seven in London. Young-Bruehl's (1988) biography of Anna Freud is the central source for discussions on her long life. Freud did not write an autobiography, but over the course of her writing and in interviews, one gleans snippets of her life and her keen humor. See, for example, Coles (1992) and Sandler, with Freud (1985).

5. At first, Melanie Klein was against Jones's decision to bring the Freud family to London (see Steiner 1991, 227–63). Klein was not supportive of the Viennese analysts' move to London, and their sense of not being welcome surely added fuel to the Controversies.

6. Derrida (1996) wonders how today's technologies of communication might have killed off the archive of Freud:

> One can dream or speculate about the geo-techno-logical shocks which would have made the landscape of the psychoanalytic archive unrecognizable for the past century if, to limit myself to these indications, Freud, his contemporaries, collaborators and immediate disciples, instead of writing thousands of letters by hand, had access to MCI or AT&T telephonic credit cards, portable tape recorders, computers, printers, faxes, televisions, teleconferences, and above all E-mail. (16)

7. This approach is not original; many contemporary discussions use the Controversies as a lens to magnify controversies of our own present. See, for example, Phillips (1998b); Rose (1993); Schafer (1994); Steiner (1985, 1995a, 1995b).

8. Laplanche's and Pontalis's (1973, 112) entry on "deferred actions" notes three characteristics of *Nachträglichkeit*: an experience that cannot be

assimilated into lived experience, a revision of the first event because of a second event, and uneven development. The term suggests a revision and a repetition of time because of a quality of experience itself: events are not and cannot be immediately assimilated by meaning, and this aspect disrupts the possibility that the meaning of an event is set by its chronological order. Indeed, chronology is lost and found through an affective logic, and experience may emerge from a kernel of incomprehensibility. Caruth (1996) calls this uneventfulness "unclaimed experience," where reclamation requires a confrontation "with the possibility of a history that is no longer straightforwardly referential (that is, no longer based on simple models of experience and reference)" (11). This is recognition as belated and, hence, not as projective. From the vantage of *Nachträglichkeit*, we also might begin to reconsider the problem of how experiences or practices in the human sciences become a means of both insight and blindness. Also see Laplanche (1992) and his discussion on "afterwardness." I bring this dynamic of "afterwardness" to the question of after-education.

9. The Freud–Jones Correspondence, edited by R. Andrew Paskauskas (1995), spanned the period 1908–1939, until Freud went into exile and joined Jones in London. This correspondence is a touchstone for contemporary discussions of the Freud–Klein Controversies. See, for example, Rose (1993); Steiner (1985, 1995a, 1995b); Stonebridge and Phillips (1998).

10. Grosskurth's (1986) discussion of this exchange asks the provocative question, "Did Jones suspect that Freud had analyzed Anna?" (172).

11. Laplanche (1989) describes Freud's term, *Hilflosigkeit,* in two ways. It refers to the profound helplessness of the infant, who if left to her or his own accord could not survive. Second, the need for help confronts an absence of help. "*Hilflosigkeit* must not be reduced to meaning panic or abandonment. The child's inability to help itself is not restricted to the search for positive values such as subsistence, food and drink; it also comes into play at the level of avoiding danger, or in other words in what is known as the fright reaction" (98).

12. Klein's (1923, 1930a) theory of the epistemophilic instinct emerges from her early case studies on intellectual inhibition and learning difficulties. From this tension she would develop her views on symbolization and intellectual development. What gives this instinct urgency is sexuality, and what gives this instinct its aggressive qualities is sadism. Klein felt that in the beginning of life, the infant cannot distinguish between knowing and taking possession of a thing. She attributed to this struggle a psychological knowledge. The drive to know composes this frustration and is emotional. Klein would, in her later views, drop this theory. For a thoughtful discussion on the difficulties of this term and its links to Klein's notion of the early Oedipal complex, see Petot (1990, 190–96). For a critique of its problems, see Bass (2000, 173–77). I return to this concept in chapter 5.

13. For a discussion of Anna Freud's centrality to ego psychology, see Bergmann (2000). Bergmann dates the beginning of ego psychology to Sigmund

Freud's (1926a) monograph, *Inhibitions, Symptoms, and Anxiety* and to Anna Freud's (1936) study, *The Ego and The Mechanisms of Defense*.

14. Whereas Anna Freud published many of her lectures to teachers over the course of her career, Klein's lectures to teachers in London's Institute of Education are unpublished. However, Anna Freud had a larger public persona during her life, perhaps because she was in charge of Freud's writings, and perhaps because she was active in bringing psychoanalytic theory to the practices of law, education, and medicine. Today there is a contemporary return to the work of Melanie Klein in the humanities, the arts, and in social theory and feminism, although Klein rarely wrote on these topics. I could not locate a comparable return to Anna Freud, except in the work of Young-Bruehl (1996) on prejudice and in Fanon's (1986) study, where he speaks approvingly of Anna Freud's ego defense mechanism, "identification with the aggressor," as useful to the study of the psychical consequences of colonization.

15. Ricardo Steiner's (1985) discussion on how psychoanalytic research differs from other forms of human studies is quite clear on this point: "Psychoanalytical discussion and development aim to provide a better understanding of the affective and phantasamic processes which lie at the root of neurotic and psychotic disturbances. They are also concerned with understanding these problems as they appear amongst researchers who are concerned with them" (55).

16. Philosophically, the German word *Aufklärung* refers to the Enlightenment, but it also means "clearing up, solution, information, and explaining the facts of life to children" (*Collins German Concise Dictionary,* 3rd ed., s. v.). As it was used in the early history of child analysis, education was thought to remove inhibitions and repressions caused by social pressures and adult mythology offered in answering the child's sexual questions. I discuss some of the tensions associated with this in chapter 5 (see also Pontalis 1981).

Michel Foucault's (1997) discussion of Kant's "*Was ist Aufklärung?*" argues that the Enlightenment is best thought of as an attitude, "a way out, an exit" (305) from immaturity rather than a discrete periodization of time. A new question Kant asked, "What differences does today introduce with respect to yesterday?" (ibid.), allows for Kant's interest in reason's reconstruction of authority, will, and obligation. This question also is relevant to the analytic session, and it supports, as discussed later in this chapter, Freud's notion of construction in analysis.

17. Otto Kernberg (1996) published a parody of psychoanalytic training under the title "Thirty Methods to Destroy the Creativity of Psychoanalytic Candidates." His second method states: "It is important for the instructor to keep in mind that it is the *conclusions* Freud arrived at that have to be taught and memorised, not the *process of Freud's thinking*" (1032, emphasis in original).

18. Pearl King (1994) has described the compromise made to hold the society together as "a gentleman's agreement" (341). Three schools of thought emerged from the Controversies: the Anna Freudians, the Kleinians, and the Independents. The "gentleman's agreement" was unwritten, and it required

representatives from all three orientations to sit on the main committees of the Society. Steiner (1985) argues that the accommodation of these three orientations within one Society is a tribute to the Society's capacity to live with internal differences. But also, it is worth noting that the concept of a gentleman's agreement also refers to Gentiles' unwritten agreement to maintain restricted access in businesses, clubs, schools, and real estate, refusing entry to Jews. It now connotes secret disturbances that are felt but not narrated.

19. There are important exceptions to the rule of normal development. See, for example, Grumet (1988); Silin (1995); Tobin (1997).

20. For this first history of child analysis, see Geissmann and Geissmann (1998).

21. See Maclean and Rappen (1991).

22. Hug-Hellmuth (1991) argued that children under age seven or eight were not ready for analysis, but even then, the analyst must understand the differences between child and adult analysis. She identified three differences: the child is not in analysis voluntarily but is brought by the parents; the child does not have a past to explore but is in the midst of the difficulties; and the child has no desire to change herself or himself.

23. Anton von Freund, a wealthy Jewish Hungarian, was a patron supporting the institutions of psychoanalysis in Budapest. He was an analysand of both Freud and Sándor Ferenczi, and one gets a flavor of his idiom and the regard in which he was held in *The Correspondence of Sigmund Freud and Sándor Ferenczi, vol. 2, 1914–1919* (Falzeder et al. 1996) and in vol. 3, 1920–1933 (Falzeder et al. 2000). Klein (1921) describes the conversation with him in her discussion of the "Fritz" case.

24. Almost forty years later, Anna Freud (1966) would characterize the lectures given to the Vienna Institute of Psychoanalysis as "a step forward in the line toward more systematic development. . . . I consider it in line with later developments that even in these early days the new venture into the area of childhood did not remain restricted to therapy but was carried further into the fields of application and prevention by means of a Course for Educators, founded by Willie Hoffer" (50–51).

25. Joan Riviere (1883–1958) was the first lay analyst in England, an early translator of Freud from German to English, and an analyst of D.W. Winnicott. She met Klein in Berlin in 1924 and helped with her English. Riviere was first analyzed by Ernest Jones in 1916 and then, in 1922, by Freud. For a biographical note and her work, see Hughes (1991).

26. Sigmund Freud's (1909) "Little Hans" case is written in three parts. Freud writes a description, based upon the child's father's notes and conversations, of Little Hans' worries, fears, and sexual research. The second part is Freud's analysis. While Freud only met with "Little Hans" once during the analysis, the figure of "Professor Freud" looms large in discussions between the father and the son. Hans used this figure as a way to signal his own psychoanalytic thoughts. For example, Hans' father wrote the following to Freud: "On

May 1st Hans came to me at lunchtime and said: 'D'you know what? Let's write something down for the Professor' " (97). Hans wanted his father to record a phantasy. The third part of the case is a postscript, added in 1922, when nineteen-year-old Hans seeks out Freud; this time to say that he had read Freud's case but hardly recognized himself there. "So the analysis," Freud wrote, "had not preserved the events from amnesia, but had been overtaken by amnesia itself" (148–49).

27. For a discussion on Freud's use of this case and the ethical issues involved in understanding the child through questions of interiority, see Benzaquen (1998).

28. This title eventually was published in English as "Four Lectures on Child Analysis" (1926) in volume 1 of Anna Freud's collected writings.

29. Joan Riviere's (1991) contribution to "Symposium on Child Analysis (1927)" is more blunt. Upon reviewing Anna Freud's insistence on bringing education to the analysis of a child, Riviere has this to say: "The analysis of a child, however small, is a process by which it learns, just like an adult, to *tolerate the bitterness* of frustrated and disappointed desires; it can never enjoy gratification of them—that is, of the Oedipus wishes and the essential part of the pregenital phantasies" (86, emphasis in original).

30. Friedländer (1997) describes the shift in Nazi policy in 1933 from economic boycott and destruction of Jewish businesses to attacks on culture:

> On the evening of May 10 [1933], rituals of exorcism took place in most of the university cities and towns of Germany. More than twenty thousand books were burned in Berlin, and from two to three thousand in every other major German city. In Berlin a huge bonfire was lit in front of the Kroll Opera House, and Goebbels was one of the speakers. After the speeches, in the capital as in the other cities, slogans against the banned authors were chanted by the throng as poisonous books (by Karl Marx, Ferdinand Lassalle, Sigmund Freud, Maximilian Harden, and Kurt Tucholsky, among many others) were hurled, batch after batch, into the flames. (57)

31. Pearl King (1991) reports that the following Berlin analysts left for London in 1933: Paula Heimann, Heinz Foulkes, Kate Friedlander, Eva Rosenfeld, and Hans Thorner. The Freuds went into exile and left for London on June 6, 1938. On September 23, 1939, almost to the day that Britain declared war on Germany, Freud died. After war was declared, analysts who had lived in Germany but who now resided in London were declared enemy aliens and were not allowed free travel beyond London. As for the psychoanalytic project in Germany and Austria, for an analysis of its destruction and why Freudian psychoanalytic theory and practice cannot exist in totalitarian countries, see Goggin and Goggin (2001).

32. Ester Bick (1996) also would return to the problem of what analysis demands of the analyst in her overview of child analysis delivered in 1961 to the 22nd International Psycho-Analytical Congress in Edinburgh. There, Bick lamented the secondary role of child analysis to the field, discussed the particular difficulties that countertransference makes for the analyst working with children, and advocated for those in training to be in analysis during their education. Many analysts' anxieties that Bick notes are comparable to teachers': emotional overinvolvement and identification with the child, worries over one's effects upon the child, anxiety over relations with the child's parents, and questions about the nature and reach of one's responsibility to the child. I return to these issues in chapter 3. Countertransference, or the ways in which the analyst is affected by her or his work also is present because of the content of the child's material: "The intensity of the child's dependence, of his positive and negative transference, the primitive nature of his phantasies tend to arouse the analyst's own unconscious anxieties. . . . Also the child's suffering tends to evoke the analyst's potential feelings, which have to be controlled so that the proper analytic role can be maintained" (171).

CHAPTER THREE

1. Anna Freud's (1936) work on the ego and its defenses draws from Sigmund Freud's (1926a) discussion on anxiety and his shift from repression to defenses. "Anxiety," writes Freud, "is a reaction to danger" (151). The large discussion in psychoanalysis is, however, over which danger matters. If all agree that anxiety is an anguished perception, then the source of anxiety is not settled. Freud could not answer why we have anxiety and neurosis: "Whence does neurosis come—what is its ultimate, its own raison d'être? After tens of years of psychoanalytic labour, we are much in the dark about this problem as we were at the start" (149).

2. Anna Freud (1936) elaborated on and added to Sigmund Freud's discussions of the ego's work. If, as the latter Freud (1926a) argued, the ego is the seat of anxiety, then it also has strategies of defense. For Freud, anxiety has two simultaneous functions: "Anxiety is therefore, on the one hand an expectation of trauma, and on the other a repetition of it in mitigated form" (166). Defenses are best thought of as dynamics that take on specific content and its events. Anna Freud discussed twelve mechanisms: repression, regression, reaction formation, isolation, undoing, projection, introjection, sublimation, turning against the self, reversal, identification with the aggressor, and altruistic surrender.

3. Anna Freud (1952) presupposed many questions that teachers asked about the role of psychoanalysis and education. Her lecture, "Answering Teachers' Questions," is perhaps her most direct attempt. It begins by noting "three great dangers that threaten the school teacher" (560): not seeing the child's developmental trajectory over the life cycle; getting caught up in the lives of children and so losing their adult world; and feeling as though the student was

the teacher's own child or, the child the teacher once was. The questions she raises and answers are an odd combination of information and worries that emerges from these dangers. The key worry that Anna Freud engages is: What can it mean for the teacher to consider a more neutral and distanced understanding of the child?

4. In 1927, Erikson moved to Vienna, invited by Peter Blos, now known for his writing on adolescence and psychology. Together, from 1927 to 1933, they worked at a school run by Anna Freud. Erikson also was in analysis with her. Friedman's (1999) biography of Erikson describes his relation with Anna Freud as very conflicted. There were tensions between working in the school, having philosophical differences with both the school's philosophy and with aspects of her theories on the ego, and in being analyzed by Anna Freud. In 1933, alarmed by Nazi policy, Erikson and his wife, Joan, left Vienna to settle in the United States (see chapter 2 in Friedman).

5. Winnicott's (1992a) concept, "fear of breakdown," is linked to the problem of defense mechanisms, although not from the vantage of ego psychology but object relations. "I contend," writes Winnicott, "that clinical fear of breakdown is *the fear of a breakdown that has already been experienced.* It is a fear of the original agony which caused the defense organization which the patient displays as an illness syndrome" (90, emphasis in original).

6. In this work, I proposed three cultural myths of teaching: everything depends upon the teacher; the teacher is the expert; and the teacher is self-made. I now believe that these myths work as psychical prohibitions to acknowledging the ego's various phantasies of omnipotence and mastery, even as they defend against helplessness in learning. See also Britzman (1998).

7. Simon's (1995) discussion of the uses of the teacher's body suggests that the politics of presence passes through and is constituted by projecting phantasies of love and hate. This is the case for the teacher and the student. Pitt (In Press) considers thoughtfully these dynamics of implication, where teaching is identified with breakdown. From a different context, Watney (1991) discusses fear of libidinality in school.

8. Melanie Klein's view of projection raises very different difficulties, for she views projective identification as both a process of externalizing and internalizing, as this defense mechanism works to define both the self and the not self. Joseph Sandler's (1986) discussion of Klein's views on projection centers on two problems: phantasy and splitting. See his chapter 5, "The Concept of Projective Identification," for a discussion on Klein's views. I return to the question of projective identification and where Melanie Klein and Anna Freud may have been in closer agreement in chapter 6.

CHAPTER FOUR

1. These are qualities that Freud (1915c) discusses in his essay, "The Unconscious." In his Freud Memorial Lecture, André Green (1986) summarizes the

unconscious by its actions as primary processes, or the obeying of the pleasure principle: "Its main characteristics are that it ignores time; it does not take negation into account; it operates by condensation and displacement; and it does not tolerate any expectation or delay" (18).

2. The idea that one can have an experience without "experiencing it" belongs to Winnicott's (1992a) discussion in "Fear of Breakdown [1963?]," also discussed in chapter 3. There are, however, additional qualities of this concept to keep in mind when thinking about group psychology. The fear of breakdown, while future directed, is actually tied to the past, to previous experience that was felt but could not be encompassed by the ego. The paradox is that while this traumatic event occurred in the past, its details feel as though they return from the future. The fear of breakdown anticipates what has already occurred but could not be integrated. In Winnicott's words, "The patient needs to 'remember' this but it is not possible to remember something that has not yet happened, and this thing of the past has not happened yet because the patient was not there for it to happen to. The only way to 'remember' in this case is for the patient to experience this past thing for the first time in the present, that is to say, in the transference" (92). Because such a fear can only be encountered through the transference, group psychology is one scene that seems to invite the returned experience of fear of breakdown.

3. The psychical process of "splitting" is elaborated on in Freud (1940b). The ego splits between the demands of instinct and reality. Freud suggests that there are ingenious compromises made from this conflict: "On the one hand, with the help of certain mechanisms he rejects reality and refuses to accept any prohibition; on the other hand, in the same breath he recognizes the danger of reality, takes over the fear of that danger as a pathological symptom and tries subsequently to divest himself of the fear" (275). These compromises then structure the ego as "a to and fro between disavowal and acknowledgement" (278). I discuss Klein's view of splitting in chapters 1, 2, and 5.

4. That groups cannot think, or that their first task is other than thought, is drawn from two key works in group psychology: Sigmund Freud's (1921) study, "Group Psychology and the Analysis of the Ego" and Elias Canetti's (1962) *Crowds and Power*. Freud opens his study with the difficulty of separating the individual from the social: "It is true that individual psychology is concerned with the individual man and explores the paths by which he seeks to find satisfaction for his instinctual impulses; but only rarely and under certain exceptional conditions is individual psychology in a position to disregard the relations of this individual to others" (69). Early in this study, Freud characterizes these social relations in groups as subject to illusions, herd mentality, and unreality. Canetti's work begins with the claim that if the deepest fear of an individual is being touched by the unknown, then joining a crowd "is the only situation in which the fear changes into its opposite. The crowd he needs is the dense crowd, in which body is pressed to body; a crowd, too, whose psychical constitution is

also dense, or compact, so that he no longer notices who it is that presses against him" (15).

5. See W. R. Bion (1997b), *War Memoirs 1917–19*.

6. Also see Lipgar's (1998) discussion of "thoughts awaiting thinkers."

7. "Minus K" is encountered in chapter 1. "K" stands for knowledge, the group's capacity to tolerate symbolization and abstract discussion. "Minus K" is an emotional state for the group made from the group's defense. The group can only accept literal knowledge, has no tolerance for abstraction or interpretation, and it attacks psychological meaning.

8. Bion proposes three basic assumptions that emerge from the emotional state in any group: dependency, flight-fight, and pairing. For a discussion of these assumptions, see Bion (1994a).

9. For a rich discussion of the history of social science's concern with the problem of prejudice, authoritarian modes of social life, and the psychical problems of working through forms of prejudice, see Young-Bruehl (1996).

10. Contemporary psychoanalytic research in education has enlarged the concept of subjectivity in education by taking into account such problems as: learning from traumatic knowledge and social catastrophe (Britzman 1998; Felman and Laub 1992; Simon et al. 2000); analyzing the unconscious dynamics of resistance and transference in the research relationship (Pitt 1998, In Press); encountering the uses of fantasy in constituting the teacher's persona (Roberston 1997); making insight into the underside of teaching (Appel 1999; Pajak 1998); and tracing the unruly play of desire in making pedagogical identifications (Todd 1997). Other educational researchers raise important questions about the qualities of address and the inherent difficulties of dialogue in educational life (Ellsworth 1997); social-psychoanalytic orientations to the study of place in curriculum theorizing (Kincheloe and Pinar 1991); sexuality and its discontents (Pinar 1998); and student and teacher transferential relations in reading literature and responding to others (Britzman and Pitt 1996). Appel (1996) details extensively the psychical difficulties of changing educational institutions, and the institutional denial of aggression and love in group psychology. He also suggests— echoing Bion's insight into hatred of development—that even at the level of theory, as critical sociology, one can find a wish for a rational, noncontradictory subject who can apply, without difficulty, the theory's insights. Appel argues that this wish defends against acknowledging both the aggressive qualities of social theory and the aggressive psychical events that also are formative of institutional life.

11. Schmuck and Schmuck (1983) also note in the 1960s the popularity of discussion on group process at American Educational Research Association meetings, although in our own time, contemporary program meetings seem to all but ignore psychoanalytic views on groups.

12. For a history of the dominance of experimental forms of psychology in education and the mode of rationality and subjectivity produced, see Popkewitz

(1998). Popkewitz analyzes contemporary uses of constructivist theory for teaching and relates school knowledge to systems of power. Theories of self-governance and development of new modes of normalcy are a part of this history, as are the particular exclusions and inclusions made from this governance. My orientation to depth psychology offers a different sense of construction, working within the assumptions of psychoanalysis. Advocating for the unconscious to be included in education is other to the production of new mechanisms of control, confessional incitements, and so on. Indeed, much of my argument concerns the question of irrationality as working within organizations, knowledge, authority, and even theory.

13. Hannah Segal (1997a) suggests in her discussion of public responses to the possibility of nuclear war that the refusal to know is made not from a conflict between an intellectual knowledge of possibility of war but from the individual's dissociation and divestment of the emotional significance of this knowledge. Molnos (1990) observed a similar dynamic in her study of professionals attempting to talk amongst each other about the AIDS crisis. Within some groups, the more anxious and fearful the group became, the more the group intellectualized and distanced itself from its emotional response.

14. While it is beyond my discussion to examine whether in fact Freud could reject hypnotic suggestion and still maintain that individuals are susceptible to the other (see, e.g., chapter 7 in "Group Psychology," where Freud [1921] compares falling in love to being hypnotized, in that when in love one seems to suspend all critical activity), there is always the question of what influence means in the analytic encounter, specifically because of the psychoanalytic concepts of resistance, transference, and countertransference. For an extremely thoughtful commentary on this dilemma, see Jacobus (1999), who likens reading to becoming hypnotized, or susceptible to the imagined other. For a provocative sense of the uses of hypnosis beyond the popular conception of it, see Roustang (2000).

15. This subtitle is borrowed from Anna Freud's (1951) conclusion, where she describes her work with the children as "an experiment staged by fate, in the sense that it accentuates the actions of certain factors in the child's life" (225). For a very different experiment in psychoanalytic education, see Mannoni (1999).

16. Terezin is a small, walled-off city close to Prague that was made into a transit camp for deported Jews by the Nazis. It served as a transit camp from 1941 to 1945, and initially it was made to represent what Hitler called "a model camp" for the outside world. Many Jewish intellectuals, artists, composers, children, and elderly people were arrested and confined to Terezin until further deportation to extermination camps. According to Moskovitz (1983), 58,000 people died in Terezin, of which 15,000 were children. By the end of the war, only 100 children survived, and twelve of these children were resettled to the United Kingdom. For discussions on Terezin, see Dwork (1991), Krizkova et al. (1995), Sebald (2001), and Troller (1991).

17. Sarah Moskovitz's (1983) work, *Love Despite Hate: Child Survivors of the Holocaust and Their Adult Lives,* describes the work of Alice Goldberger, who

was in charge of one of Anna Freud's War Nurseries. Moskovitz interviewed Goldberger and many of the adults who were brought to the nursery as young children. I am indebted to Professor Miriam David for many discussions about this book and her thoughts on friendships with a community of survivors associated with the Nursery that has yearly reunions in London.

CHAPTER FIVE

1. Silvan Tomkins (1911–1991) was an American psychologist known for his studies and grand theories of emotional life. He was one of the designers of the Thematic Apperception Test, a set of drawings on everyday life that provoked the viewer to free associations interpreted as emblematic of emotional states. For an introduction to Tomkins, see Demos (1995) and Sedgwick and Frank (1995).

2. The figure of the "question-child" belongs to Pontalis (1981) and his discussion of how Melanie Klein's work with children transformed her understanding of Freud and made more evident her difference from Anna Freud's use of education in the psychoanalysis of children. Pontalis's characterization of Klein's own theoretical transformation allows for the otherness of "question-child":

> If in her first text, Melanie Klein's attention was held above all by the child's inhibitions, it was because they assumed an exemplary value for her: the child had more to say for himself than what he actually said. . . . She therefore chose not to define the conditions which should be fulfilled by child analysis, but to submit psychoanalytic theory and methods to the disconcerting test of the child's speech . . . a matter of coming to meet the child's psychic reality and measuring adult knowledge against it "in the spirit of free and unprejudiced research." (95–96)

3. For a thoughtful discussion on the uses of Kleinian theory as offering new ways to work through contemporary debates between modernity and postmodernity, see Steuerman (2000). For a discussion of how Kleinian theory might affect more intimately the question of politics and freedom, see Kristeva (2001b).

4. This dilemma is one that Eve Sedgwick acknowledges when she considers the teaming up of psychoanalysis with queer theory. She raises the question "which psychoanalysis?" and then answers, not the one that posits sexual difference as an ontological exclamation. In Sedgwick's (1997) view:

> From such often tautological work, it would be hard to learn that—from Freud onward, including for example the later writings of Melanie Klein—the history of psychoanalytic thought offers richly divergent,

heterogeneous tools for thinking about aspects of personhood, consciousness, affect, filiation, social dynamics, and sexuality that, while
relevant to the experience of gender and queerness, are not centrally
organized around "sexual difference" at all. (11)

Sedgwick goes on to observe that while psychoanalytic categories are certainly
not immune from the history of psychoanalysis, the desire for a pure theory that
can somehow "guarantee a nonprejudicial . . . beginning" (12) may well be a
symptom of a paranoid defense against the capacity to be surprised. From another vantage, this wish for a pure theory also may be a symptom of the desire
for omnipotence, surely a force in theory kindergarten.

5. Sedgwick's (1990) terminology, "minoritizing" versus "universalizing," is
an alternative to thinking about the nature/nurture debates from the view of
essentialist versus constructivist understandings. "I prefer," she writes, "the former
terminology because it seems to record and respond to the question, "In whose
lives is homo/heterosexual definition an issue of continuing centrality and
difficulty?" (40).

6. Klein's concept of phantasy is discussed in chapter 2, where a great deal
of the debate in the Freud–Klein Controversies consisted of whether her propos-
als for the centrality of phantasy for the infant's inner world would be acceptable
to psychoanalytic theory and practice and in agreement with Freud's views.
Likierman's (2001) discussion of the implication of Klein's concept of unconscious phantasy considers how shocking Klein's views were to the analytic community and, more generally, to a theory of object relations: "It portrays the basis
of our mental operations as relational in nature, and suggests that we cannot
make sense of our experiences, nor indeed our identity, without referring continually to an internal scenario in which meaning is actualized in an exchange
between a subject and an object" (140).

7. The paranoid-schizoid position is an outcome of what, for Klein, is a
primal struggle that inaugurates the ego's capacity to feel itself: the fight between
the death drive and the life drive. What the infant projects is this struggle, that
is, fragments of her or his internal world. But this process of projection, felt as
capable of invading the body of the mother, also splits the ego into fragments,
and so the ego's fear of annihilation, made from its own death drive, is sustained
in the very attempt to console itself. Here is Klein's (1946) description:

I hold that anxiety arises from the operation of the death instinct
within the organism, is felt as fear of annihilation (death), and takes
the form of fear of persecution. The fear of the destructive impulse
seems to attach itself at once to an object—or rather it is experienced as the fear of an uncontrollable overpowering object. . . . Even
if these objects are felt to be external, they become through introjection internal persecutors and thus reinforce the fear of the destructive impulse within. (4–5)

8. In the depressive position, the ego is able to feel distressed about its phantasies. Klein (1935) has a lovely description of this first poignant and also manic attempt to think about the other:

> The ego then finds itself confronted with the psychic reality that its loved objects are in a state of dissolution—in bits—and the despair, remorse and anxiety deriving from this recognition are at the bottom of numerous anxiety situations. To quote only a few of them: there is anxiety how to put the bits together in the right way and at the right time; how to pick out the good bits and do away with the bad ones; how to bring the object to life when it has been put together; and there is the anxiety of being interfered with in this task by bad objects and by one's own hatred, etc. (269)

At the level of phantasy, everything is in bits. That is, the ego's worries are over its integrity and also what Kristeva (2001b, 84) identifies as "a phobia of being."

9. The distinction between the symbol and what it represents is discussed by Hannah Segal (1988), who extends Klein's (1930) discussion on the failure to symbolize, where the ego cannot distinguish, cannot gain any perspective on phantasy and reality, and instead it collapses the symbol with the original object. Segal offers the example of the man who could not play the violin in public, because he equated this activity with masturbation. This symbolic equation is emblematic of the paranoid-schizoid position, where "the concept of absence hardly exists" (164). In her summary of Ernest Jones's work in the area of symbolization, Segal offers a cogent observation on the painful efforts that symbolization attempts to assuage: "One might say that when a desire has to be given up because of conflict and repressed, it may express itself in a symbolical way, and the object of the desire which had to be given up can be replaced by a symbol" (162). And yet precisely because the symbol is a substitution, and therefore marks an absence and a loss, it also is tied to the work of mourning and to the working through of the depressive position.

10. In her work with the early theories of Freud, Julia Kristeva (2000) makes the point that we have sexuality before we have language. Even in learning language, what the young baby learns is the mother's love of and erotic tonality in communication. Sedgwick's (1993a) "A Poem Is Being Written" makes this point as well. Yet putting our sexuality into language will always be an insufficient project, because there is a constitutive conflict between sexuality and language. Kristeva puts the dilemma this way: "The particularity of our species, immature at birth, with an initial linguistic incapacity, carves out the asymptote between the sexual and the verbal and prevents the gap between them from one day being filled" (2000, 32–33).

11. For an insightful discussion of how the personal dynamics of "hide and seek" play out in educational spheres, see Pitt (2000).

12. See chapter 4 for a discussion of Bion (1994b) and his counterintuitive theory, that it is thought that makes the thinker.

13. For a discussion of Kleinian understandings of "development," see Hinshelwood (1991). He notes six interactive aspects: "(1) physiological maturation; (2) phases of the libido; (3) the reality principle; (4) the development of object-relations; (5) development of the ego; and (6) the sequence of anxiety-situations" (277). Thus development, in Klein's view, is no longer a question of individual growth but of uneven relations between the inside and the outside, self and other, and phantasy and reality.

CHAPTER SIX

1. The question "how does one make a history of learning from the history of other's learning?" is a central leitmotif in contemporary literature and education. Felman's and Laub's (1992) work on the crisis of witnessing in psychoanalysis, literature, and history, and Haver's (1996) work on marking the limit and grounds of historical consciousness in the time of AIDS, for instance, have been central to my thinking on this question. But so too have the novelists and their reconceptualization of the crisis of fiction by animating the utter difficulty, indeed, the loneliness of learning from absence and erasure. One fine example of this orientation is the haunting work of W. G. Sebald (1944–2001), particularly his last novel on the deceptions of history and the working through of the traumatic perception that overtakes the significance of history and identity. From the accidental dialogue of two men over a thirty-year period, Sebald's (2001) novel, *Austerlitz*, is the dream of history's archive and the risk of its interpretation (see Sebald 2001).

2. Bion (1991) describes how Klein imagined psychical reality as a "crowded world": "Take the individual, for example: Melanie Klein, thinking in terms of visual imagery, regarded a single human individual as if he were a world in himself" (208). Kristeva's (2001b) discussion of Melanie Klein's views suggests the other side: "Not content with being incredibly foolhardy, our inner world is also wholly solitary" (111). This is where loneliness takes its residency, somewhere between the internal crowd and the sense of aloneness this world invokes.

3. Edna O'Shaughnessy (1975, 335–36) wrote an explanatory note to the paper "On the Sense of Loneliness (1963)" in the *Envy and Gratitude* collection, reminding readers that Klein was not yet ready to publish it and that the paper, presumably, was not yet finished.

4. Wilfred Bion to Melanie Klein, March 29. The year of Bion's birthday greeting is not recorded. It may have been written in either 1959 or 1960. Klein was born on March 30, 1882, and died on September 22, 1960. Bion's birthday greeting may have been for Klein's seventy-seventh birthday. Her last years are described by Segal (1991).

5. Bion's birthday greeting to Melanie Klein, March 29, 1959 or 1960, (underline in original). Melanie Klein Archives, Wellcome Library, London.

6. Hinshelwood's (1991, 301–302) entry on "external world" makes the point that, for Klein, the external world is amendable and always in flux. In Klein's view, it also is partly constituted through phantasy, so one of the tensions in trying to understand the world concerns the intrusive qualities of subjectivity, where omnipotent phantasies, fear of annihilation, and idealization, for example, foreclose encountering difference in the world and in the self. Yet another tension belongs in the world, and Klein saw this external reality as coercive and intrusive as well.

7. Likierman's (2001) discussion of Klein's work emphasizes the notion of "overcoming":

> "Overcoming" means that an internal scenario of tragedy ceases to dominate experience, but not that its significance recedes altogether. While tragic anxieties become gradually overlaid in the process of growth, their presence in the primitive strata of the psyche continues to give them the power of an emblematic tale of warning. This tale is essential to a moral framework that protects the good internal object, even though in its essence it represents a negation of the security and progress achieved through morality. (124)

Thus overcoming is akin to Freud's "working through."

8. Klein, note, n.d., Melanie Klein Archives, Wellcome Library, London.

9. Klein (1946) argues that the ego's process of splitting alters not just the object but the ego as well. She considers idealization in relation to splitting:

> Idealization is bound up with the splitting of the object, for the good aspects of the breast are exaggerated as a safeguard against the fear of the persecuting breast. . . . However, the bad object is not only kept apart from the good one but its very existence is denied, as is the whole situation of frustration and the bad feelings (pain) to which frustration gives rise. This is bound up with denial of psychic reality.
>
> It is, however, not only a situation and an object that are denied and annihilated—*it is an object-relation* which suffers this fate; and therefore a part of the ego, from which the feelings towards the object emanate, is denied and annihilated as well. (7, emphasis in original)

10. Integration is best thought of as a work in progress. In his account of the concept of affect in psychoanalytic theory, André Green (1999b) states the dilemma forcefully: "But one should be under no illusion as to the power of integration, which is never acquired definitively. *No one completes the integration of their ego*" (76, emphasis in original).

11. Klein, notes, Melanie Klein archive, n.d., Wellcome Library, London.

12. Ibid.

13. Ibid.

14. Winnicott (1990b) insists in his essay, "Living Creatively (1970)," that the reality principle is an insult, and if it were not, all we would do is comply. His collection of essays, *Home Is Where We Start From*, includes in his index entry under "reality principle" the subheading "as an insult."

15. Young-Bruehl (1988) offers a thoughtful description of Anna Freud's discussion on identification: "Anna Freud portrayed displaced feelings recaptured in an experience of identification; not a severance, but a form of perpetual oneness or assimilation of the lost one into the loser's psychical structure, a form of sublimation" (292). In that way, Anna Freud seemed to cast identification on the side of memory, a reconstruction made through the preservation of libidinal ties.

16. Klein developed the concept of "projective identification" in 1946 as a clarification of the paranoid-schizoid position but also was dissatisfied with the term, since it referenced a complex set of events, developmental cycles, and structures of phantasy. For discussion of the trajectories of how this term is used, see, for example, Sandler (1986), Anderson (1995), and the collected papers of Betty Joseph, edited by Feldman and Spillius (1997).

17. This view of Kleinian theory is developed in Stein (1999).

18. Pitt's (2000) consideration of the importance of the game "hide and seek" brings losing and finding to the very act of communication: "Communication itself is experienced as an urgent game of hide and seek" (65). Sigmund Freud (1920) notes an early form of this game of "disappearance and return" (15) as "fort/da." This was a game that his young grandson played, making his toys disappear and finding them again. In one version, played after his mother had left for an errand, the young boy threw a cotton reel under the bed and then retrieved it. Freud noticed that his grandson took a great delight in sending the toy away: "Throwing away the object so that it was 'gone' might satisfy an impulse of the child's, which was suppressed in his actual life, to revenge himself on his mother for going away from him. In that case it would have a defiant meaning: 'All right, then, go away! I don't need you. I'm sending you away myself.' " (16). This is where the pleasure of throwing something away is linked to hostility and the compulsion to repeat, but it also is a way to free oneself, at least at the level of phantasy, from the fact of being alone.

19. For a discussion of the mutually constitutive features of ego and reality, see Loewald (2000), "The Ego and Reality (1951)," where he develops the psychoanalytic claim that "the psychological constitution of the ego and the outer world go hand in hand" (5). In Loewald's view, what is lost when reality is lost is the other and the ego's capacity to make boundaries. For a thoughtful discussion on Loewald's contributions to a different and less hostile sense of reality in psychoanalytic thinking, see Bass (2000).

20. The split identification that Anna Freud describes also is the model for her thinking on "identification with the aggressor," a complex ego defense that suggests the contradictory, partial, and ambivalent qualities of identification. A

discussion of this defense is found in Anna Freud (1936). Given the ways in which identification is split (both with the aggressive action and the pain of feeling the other's aggression), it can be compared to Klein's paranoid-schizoid position.

21. In his review of *Dora Bruder*, Michael Woods (2000) reads the text as a "novel," not because the events that Modiano writes about did not happen, but perhaps because the events are emotional ones and so must pass through phantasies, haunting losses, and contact with the incoherent. This leads Woods to speculate: "History doesn't run parallel to fiction, it runs through it. And vice versa" (31).

BIBLIOGRAPHY

Adorno, Theodor W. 1998. *Critical Models: Interventions and Catchwords.* Translated by Henry W. Pickford. New York: Columbia University Press.

Adorno, Theodor W., with Else Frenkel-Brunswik, Daniel J. Levinson, and R. Nevitt Sanford. 1950. *The Authoritarian Personality.* New York: Harper and Row.

Agamben, Giorgio. 1999. *Remnants of Auschwitz: The Witness and the Archive.* Translated by Daniel Heller-Roazen. New York: Zone Books.

Anderson, Robin, ed. 1995. *Clinical Lectures on Klein and Bion.* London: Routledge.

Anzieu, Didier. 1984. *The Group and the Unconscious.* Translated by Benjamin Kilborne. London: Routledge.

Appel, Stephen. 1996. *Positioning Subjects: Psychoanalysis and Critical Educational Studies.* Westport, Conn.: Bergin and Garvey.

———. ed. 1999. *Psychoanalysis and Pedagogy.* Westport, Conn.: Bergin and Garvey.

Arendt, Hannah. 1993. *Between Past and Present.* New York: Penguin.

Balint, Michael. 1992. *The Basic Fault: Therapeutic Aspects of Regression.* Evanston: Northwestern University Press.

Bass, Alan. 1998. "Sigmund Freud: The Question of Weltanschauung and Defense." Pp. 412–46 in *Psychoanalytic Versions of the Human Condition: Philosophies of Life and Their Impact on Practice,* ed. by Paul Marcus and Alan Rosenberg. New York: New York University Press.

———. 2000. *Difference and Disavowal: The Trauma of Eros.* Stanford: Stanford University Press.

Belau, Linda and Peter Ramadanovic, eds. 2002. *Topologies of Trauma: Essays on the Limit of Knowledge and Memory.* New York: Other Press.

Benjamin, Jessica. 1998. *Shadow of the Other: Intersubjectivity and Gender in Psychoanalysis.* New York: Routledge.

Benzaquen, Adriana. 1998. "Freud, Little Hans, and the Desire for Knowledge." *Journal of Curriculum Theorizing* 14(2): 43–52.

Bergmann, Martin, ed. 2000. *The Hartmann Era.* New York: Other Press.

Bernfeld, Siegfried. 1971. *Sisyphus or the Limits of Education.* Translated by Frederic Lilge. Berkeley: University of California Press.

Bick, Ester. 1996. "Child Analysis Today (1962)" Pp. 168–76 in *Melanie Klein Today, vol. 2, Mainly Practice,* ed. Elizabeth Bott Spillius. London: Routledge.

Bion, Wilfred R. 1991. *A Memoir of the Future*. London: Routledge.

———. 1993. *Second Thoughts*. London: Maresfield Library.

———. 1994a. *Experiences in Groups and Other Papers*. London: Routledge.

———. 1994b. *Learning from Experience*. Northvale: Jason Aronson.

———. 1997a. *Taming Wild Thoughts*. Edited by Francesca Bion. London: Karnac Books.

———. 1997b. *War Memoirs 1917–19*. Edited by Francesca Bion. London: Karnac Books.

Bléandonu, Gerard. 1994. *Wilfred Bion: His Life and Works 1897–1979*. Translated by Claire Pajaczkowska. London: Free Association Books.

Bloom, Allan. 1979. "Introduction." Pp. 3–29 in *Emile or On Education*. Jean-Jacques Rousseau, trans. Allan Bloom. New York: Basic Books.

Bollas, Christopher. 1987. *The Shadow of the Object: Psychoanalysis of the Unthought Known*. New York: Columbia University Press.

———. 1999. *The Mystery of Things*. London: Routledge.

———. 2000. *Hysteria*. London: Routledge.

Brabant, Eva, Ernst Falzeder, and Patrizia Giamperi-Deutsch, eds. 1993. *The Correspondence of Sigmund Freud and Sándor Ferenczi, vol. 1, 1908–1914*. Translated by Peter Hoffer. Cambridge: Belknap Press of Harvard University Press.

Brierley, Marjorie. 1991. "Memorandum on Her Technique, October 25th, 1943." Pp. 617–28 in *The Freud–Klein Controversies 1941–45*, ed. Pearl King and Riccardo Steiner. London: Routledge.

Britzman, Deborah. 1991. *Practice Makes Practice: A Critical Study of Learning to Teach*. Albany: State University of New York Press.

———. 1998. *Lost Subjects, Contested Objects: Toward a Psychoanalytic Inquiry of Learning*. Albany: State University of New York Press.

Britzman, Deborah P., and Alice J. Pitt. 1996. "Teaching As Transference: Casting the Past of Learning into the Presence of Teaching." *Theory into Practice* 35(2): 117–23.

Canetti, Elias. 1962. *Crowds and Power*. Translated by Carol Stewart. New York: Farrar, Straus, and Giroux.

Caruth, Cathy. 1996. *Unclaimed Experience: Trauma, Narrative and History*. Baltimore: Johns Hopkins University Press.

Chodorow, Nancy. 1999. *The Power of Feelings: Personal Meaning in Psychoanalysis, Gender, and Culture*. New Haven: Yale University Press.

Cohen, Richard A. 2001. *Ethics, Exegesis and Philosophy: Interpretation After Levinas*. Cambridge: Cambridge University Press.

Coles, Robert. 1992. *Anna Freud: The Dream of Psychoanalysis*. Reading, Mass.: Addison Wesley.

Dean, Tim, and Christopher Lane, eds. 2001. *Homosexuality and Psychoanalysis*. Chicago: University of Chicago Press.

Demos, E. Virginia, ed. 1995. *Exploring Affect: The Selected Writings of Silvan S. Tomkins*. New York: Press Syndicate of the University of Cambridge.

Derrida, Jacques. 1996. *Archive Fever: A Freudian Impression*. Translated by Eric Prenowitz. Chicago: University of Chicago Press.

———. 2002. *Who's Afraid of Philosophy? Right to Philosophy I*. Translated by Jan Plug. Stanford: Stanford University Press.

Dosse, François. 1999. *Empire of Meaning: The Humanization of the Social Sciences.* Translated by Hassan Melehy. Minneapolis: University of Minnesota Press.

Dwork, Deborah. 1991. *Children with a Star: Jewish Youth in Nazi Europe.* New Haven: Yale University Press.

Edgcumbe, Rose. 2000. *Anna Freud: A View of Development, Disturbance and Therapeutic Techniques.* London: Routledge.

Eigen, Michael. 1997. "Musings on O." *Journal of Melanie Klein and Object Relations* 15: 213–26.

Ellsworth, Elizabeth. 1997. *Teaching Positions: Difference, Pedagogy, and the Power of Address.* New York: Teachers College Press.

Falzeder, Ernst, and Eva Brabant, with collaboration of Patrizia Giampieri-Deutch, eds. 1996. *The Correspondence of Sigmund Freud and Sándor Ferenczi, vol. 2, 1914–1919.* Translated by Peter Hoffer. Cambridge: Belknap Press of Harvard University Press.

———. 2000. *The Correspondence of Sigmund Freud and Sándor Ferenczi, vol. 3, 1920–1933.* Translated by Peter Hoffer. Cambridge: Belknap Press of Harvard University Press.

Fanon, Frantz. 1986. *Black Skin, White Masks.* Translated by Charles Lam Markmann. London: Pluto Press.

Feldman, Michael, and Elizabeth Bott Spillius, eds. 1997. *Psychic Equilibrium and Psychic Change: Selected Papers of Betty Joseph.* London: Routledge.

Felman, Shoshana. 1987. *Jacques Lacan and the Adventure of Insight: Psychoanalysis in Contemporary Culture.* Cambridge: Harvard University Press.

———. 1992. "Education and Crisis, or the Vicissitudes of Teaching." Pp. 1–56 in *Testimony: Crises of Witnessing in Literature, Psychoanalysis and History,* Shoshana Felman and Dori Laub. New York: Routledge.

Felman, Shoshana, and Dori Laub. 1992. *Testimony: Crises of Witnessing in Literature, Psychoanalysis, and History.* New York: Routledge.

Ferenczi, Sándor. 1988. "Confusion of Tongues between Adults and the Child: The Language of Tenderness and Passion (1933)." *Contemporary Psychoanalysis* 24(2): 196–206.

Finkielkraut, Alain. 2000. *In the Name of Humanity: Reflections on the Twentieth Century.* Translated by Judith Friedlander. New York: Columbia University Press.

Foucault, Michel. 1997. "What Is Enlightenment?" Pp. 303–20 in *The Essential Works of Foucault, vol. 1, 1954–1984, Ethics, Subjectivity and Truth,* ed. Paul Rabinow. New York: New Press.

Freud, Anna. 1961–1981. *The Writings of Anna Freud.* 7 vols. Madison: International Universities Press.

———. "Beating Fantasies and Daydreams." 1922. Pp. 137–57 in *The Writings of Anna Freud, vol. 1, 1922–35, Introduction to Psychoanalysis.*

———. "Four Lectures on Child Analysis." 1926 [1927]. Pp. 3–69 in *The Writings of Anna Freud, vol. 1.*

———. "The Theory of Child Analysis." 1928 [1927]. Pp. 162–75 in *The Writings of Anna Freud, vol. 1.*

———. "Four Lectures on Psychoanalysis for Teachers and Parents." 1930. Pp. 73–136 in *The Writings of Anna Freud, vol. 1.*

————. *The Ego and the Mechanisms of Defense.* 1936 [1966]. *The Writings of Anna Freud, vol. 2, 1936.*

————. "An Experience in Group Upbringing." 1951. Pp. 163–229 in *The Writings of Anna Freud, vol. 4, 1945–1956, Indications for Child Analysis and Other Papers.*

————. "Answering Teachers' Questions." 1952. Pp. 560–68 in *The Writings of Anna Freud, vol. 4.*

————. "*Normality and Pathology in Childhood: Assessments in Development.*" 1965. *The Writings of Anna Freud, vol. 6, 1965.*

————. "A Short History of Child Analysis." 1966. Pp. 48–58 in *The Writings of Anna Freud, vol. 7, 1966–1970, Problems of Psychoanalytic Training, Diagnosis, and the Technique of Treatment.*

————. "About Losing and Being Lost." 1967 [1953]. Pp. 302–16 in *The Writings of Anna Freud, vol. 4.*

Freud, Sigmund. 1953–1974. *The Standard Edition of the Complete Psychological Works of Sigmund Freud.* Edited and translated by James Strachey, in collaboration with Anna Freud, assisted by Alix Strachey and Alan Tyson. 24 vols. London: Hogarth Press and Institute for Psychoanalysis.

————. *The Interpretation of Dreams: First Part.* 1900. SE 4, 1–338.

————. *The Interpretation of Dreams: Second Part.* 1900. SE 5, 339–627.

————. "On Psychotherapy." 1905a [1904]. SE 7, 257–70.

————. "Three Essays on Sexuality." 1905b. SE 7, 125–243.

————. "Analysis of a Phobia in a Five-Year-Old Boy." 1909. SE 10, 5–149.

————. " 'Wild' Psycho-analysis." 1910. SE 11, 221–27.

————. "Formulations on the Two Principles of Mental Functioning." 1911. SE 12, 213–26.

————. "The Dynamics of Transference." 1912. SE 12, 97–108.

————. "On Beginning the Treatment." (Further Recommendations on the Technique of Psychoanalysis I). 1913. SE 12, 123–44.

————. "Remembering, Repeating, and Working Through" (Further Recommendations on the Technique of Psychoanalysis II). 1914a. SE 12, 145–56.

————. "On Narcissism." 1914b. SE 14, 67–102.

————. "Instincts and Their Vicissitudes." 1915a. SE 14, 117–40.

————. *Introductory Lectures on Psychoanalysis, Parts I and II.* 1915b. SE 15.

————. "The Unconscious." 1915c. SE 14, 161–216.

————. *Introductory Lectures on Psychoanalysis, Part III.* 1916. SE 16.

————. "Mourning and Melancholia." 1917. SE 14, 243–58.

————. "On the Teaching of Psycho-analysis in Universities." 1919 [1918]. SE 17, 159–74.

————. "Beyond the Pleasure Principle." 1920. SE 18, 7–66.

————. "Group Psychology and the Analysis of the Ego." 1921. SE 18, 65–143.

————. "On Negation." 1925a. SE 19, 235–42.

————. "A Note on the 'Mystic Writing Pad.' " 1925b [1924]. SE 19, 227–34.

————. "Preface to Aichhorn's *Wayward Youth.*" 1925c. SE 19, 273–75.

————. "Inhibitions, Symptoms, and Anxiety." 1926a. SE 20, 77–174.

————. "Psycho-Analysis." 1926b. SE 20, 263–70.

————. "The Question of Lay Analysis: Conversations with an Impartial Person." 1926c. SE 20, 183–258.

————. *Civilization and Its Discontents.* 1930 [1929]. SE 21, 59–148.

————. *New Introductory Lectures on Psycho-Analysis.* 1933. SE 22, 3–182.

————. "Analysis Terminable and Interminable." 1937a. SE 23, 209–54.

————. "Constructions in Analysis." 1937b. SE 23, 255–70.

————. "Moses and Monotheism: Three Essays." 1939. SE 23, 7–140.

————. "An Outline of Psychoanalysis." 1940a. SE 23, 141–208.

————. "Splitting of the Ego in the Process of Defence." 1940b [1938]. SE 23, 275–78.

————. *Indexes and Bibliographies.* 1974. SE 24.

Friedländer, Saul. 1997. *Nazi Germany and the Jews, vol. 1, The Years of Persecution, 1933–1939.* New York: HarperCollins.

Friedman, Lawrence. 1999. *Identity's Architect: A Bibliography of Erik H. Erikson.* New York: Scribner.

Gardner, M. Robert. 1994. *On Trying to Teach: The Mind in Correspondence.* Hillsdale, N.J.: Analytic Press.

Geissmann, Claudine, and Pierre Geissmann. 1998. *A History of Child Psychoanalysis.* London: Routledge.

Goggin, James, and Eileen Brockman Goggin. 2001. *Death of a "Jewish Science": Psychoanalysis in the Third Reich.* West Lafayette, Ind.: Purdue University Press.

Green, André. 1986. *On Private Madness.* Madison: International Universities Press.

————. 1999a. *The Fabric of Affect in the Psychoanalytic Discourse.* Translated by Alan Sheridan. London: Routledge.

————. 1999b. *The Work of the Negative.* Translated by Andrew Weller. New York: Free Association Books.

————. 2000. "Experience and Thinking in Analytic Practice." Pp. 1–15, in *André Green at the Squiggle Foundation,* ed. Jan Abram. London: Karmac Books.

Greene, Maxine. 1973. *Teacher As Stranger: Educational Philosophy in the Modern Age.* Belmont, Calif.: Wadsworth Press.

Grinberg, Leon, Dario Sor, and Elizabeth Tabak de Bianchedi. 1993. *New Introduction to the Work of Bion.* Rev. ed. Northvale, N.J.: Jason Aronson.

Grosskurth, Phyllis. 1986. *Melanie Klein: Her World and Her Work.* Cambridge: Harvard University Press.

Grubrich-Simitis, Ilse. 1996. *Back to Freud's Texts: Making Silent Documents Speak.* Translated by Philip Slotkin. New Haven: Yale University Press.

Grumet, Madeline. 1988. *Bitter Milk: Women and Teaching.* Amherst: University of Massachusetts Press.

Hale, Nathan. 1995a. *Freud and the Americans: The Beginnings of Psychoanalysis in the United States, 1876–1917.* Vol. 1. New York: Oxford University Press.

————. 1995b. *The Rise and Crisis of Psychoanalysis in the United States, 1917–1984.* Vol. 2. New York: Oxford University Press.

Haver, William. 1996. *The Body of This Death: Historicity and Sociality in the Time of AIDS.* Stanford: Stanford University Press.

————. 1999. "Another University, Now: A Practical Proposal for a New Foundation of the University." Pp. 25–37 in *Equity and How to Get It,* ed. Kay Armatage. Toronto: Inanna Publications and Education Inc./University of Toronto Press.

Hinshelwood, R. D. 1991. *A Dictionary of Kleinian Thought.* London: Free Association Books.

Hoggett, Paul. 1998. "The Internal Establishment." Pp. 9–24, in *Bion's Legacy to Groups*, ed. Pathenope Bion Talamo et al. London: Karnac Books.

Hollander, Nancy Caro. 1997. *Love in a Time of Hate: Liberation Psychology in Latin America.* New Brunswick: Rutgers University Press.

Hug-Hellmuth, Hermine. 1991. "On the Technique of Child-Analysis (1920)." Pp. 138–53 in *Hermine Hug-Hellmuth: Her Life and Work*, ed. George Maclean and Ulrich Rappen. New York: Routledge.

Hughes, Athol. 1991. "Joan Riviere: Her Life and Work." Pp. 1–46 in *The Inner World and Joan Riviere, Collected Papers 1920–1958*, ed. Athol Hughes. London: Karnac Books.

Jacobus, Mary. 1998. "The Pain in the Patient's Knee." *Diacritics: A Review of Contemporary Criticism* 28(4): 99–110.

———. 1999. *Psychoanalysis and the Scene of Reading.* New York: Oxford University Press.

James, William. 1983. *Talks to Teachers on Psychology and to Students on Some of Life's Ideals: The Works of William James.* Edited by Frederick Burkhardt. Cambridge: Harvard University Press.

Jersild, Arthur. 1955. *When Teachers Face Themselves.* New York: Teachers College Press.

Kernberg, Otto. 1996. "Thirty Methods to Destroy the Creativity of Psychoanalytic Candidates." *International Journal of Psycho-Analysis* 77: 1031–39.

———. 1998. *Ideology, Conflict, and Leadership in Groups and Organizations.* New Haven: Yale University Press.

Kincheloe, Joe, and William Pinar, eds. 1991. *Curriculum As Social Psychoanalysis: The Significance of Place.* Albany: State University of New York Press.

King, Pearl. 1991. "Background and Development of the Freud–Klein Controversies in the British Psycho-Analytical Society." Pp. 9–36 in *The Freud–Klein Controversies, 1941–1945*, ed. Pearl King and Riccardo Steiner. London: Tavistock/Routledge.

———. 1994. "The Evolution of Controversial Issues." *International Journal of Psycho-Analysis* 75: 335–42.

King, Pearl, and Riccardo Steiner, eds. 1991. *The Freud–Klein Controversies, 1941–1945.* London: Tavistock/Routledge.

Klein, Melanie. "Development of a Child." 1921. Pp. 1–53 in *Love, Guilt and Reparation.*

———. "The Role of the School in the Libidinal Development of the Child." 1923. Pp. 59–76 in *Love, Guilt and Reparation.*

———. "Symposium on Child Analysis." 1927. Pp. 139–69 in *Love, Guilt and Reparation.*

———. "Early Stages of the Oedipus Conflict." 1928. Pp. 186–98 in *Love, Guilt and Reparation.*

———. "The Importance of Symbol-Formation in the Development of the Ego." 1930a. Pp. 219–32 in *Love, Guilt and Reparation.*

———. "The Psychotherapy of the Psychoses." 1930b. Pp. 233–35 in *Love, Guilt and Reparation.*

———. "A Contribution to the Psychogenesis of Manic-Depressive States." 1935. Pp. 262–89 in *Love, Guilt and Reparation.*

———. "Notes on Some Schizoid Mechanisms." 1946. Pp. 1–24 in *Envy and Gratitude.*

————. "The Psycho-Analytic Play Technique: Its History and Significance." 1955. Pp. 122–40 in *Envy and Gratitude*.

————. "Envy and Gratitude." 1957. Pp. 176–235 in *Envy and Gratitude*.

————. "On the Development of Mental Functioning." 1958. Pp. 236–46 in *Envy and Gratitude*.

————. "On Mental Health." 1960. Pp. 268–74 in *Envy and Gratitude*.

————. "On the Sense of Loneliness." 1963. Pp. 300–314 in *Envy and Gratitude*.

————. *Envy and Gratitude and Other Works, 1946–1963*. 1975a. London: Delacorte Press/Semour Lawrence.

————. *Love, Guilt and Reparation and Other Works, 1921–1945*. 1975b. London: Delacorte Press/Semour Lawrence.

Knoblock, Peter, and Arnold Goldstein. 1971. *The Lonely Teacher*. Boston: Allyn and Bacon.

Kohon, Gregorio. 1999a. "The Greening of Psychoanalysis: André Green in Dialogues with Gregorio Kohon." Pp. 10–58 in *The Dead Mother: The Work of André Green*, ed. Gregorio Kohon. New York: Routledge.

————. 1999b. *No Lost Certainties To Be Recovered*. London: Karnac Books.

Kristeva, Julia. 2000. *The Sense and Nonsense of Revolt: The Powers and Limits of Psychoanalysis*. Translated by Jeanine Herman. New York: Columbia University Press.

————. 2001a. *Hannah Arendt, vol. 1, Female Genius: Life, Madness, and Words— Hannah Arendt, Melanie Klein, Collete*. Translated by Ross Guberman. New York: Columbia University Press.

————. 2001b. *Melanie Klein, vol. 2, Female Genius: Life, Madness and Words— Hannah Arendt, Melanie Klein, Collete*. Translated by Ross Guberman. New York: Columbia University Press.

Krizkova, Marie, Rut Kotuoc, Jiri Kurt, and Ornest Zdenek, eds. 1995. *We Are Children Just the Same: Vedem, the Secret Magazine by the Boys of Terezin*. Prague: Aventinum Press.

Laplanche, Jean. 1989. *New Foundations for Psychoanalysis*. Translated by David Macey. Cambridge: Basil Blackwell.

————. 1992. "Notes on Afterwardness." Pp. 217–24 in *Jean Laplanche: Seduction, Translation, Drives*, comp. John Fletcher and Martin Stanton. London: Institute for Contemporary Arts.

Laplanche, Jean, and J. B. Pontalis. 1973. *The Language of Psychoanalysis*. Translated by Donald Nicholson-Smith. New York: W. W. Norton.

Lebovici, Serge. 1998. "Foreword." Pp. xii–xv in *A History of Child Psychoanalysis*, ed. Claudine Geissmann and Pierre Geissmann. New York: Routledge.

Likierman, Meira. 2001. *Melanie Klein: Her Work in Context*. London: Continuum.

Lipgar, Robert. 1998. "Beyond Bion's *Experiences in Groups*: Group Relations Research and Learning." Pp. 25–38 in *Bion's Legacy to Groups*, ed. Parthenope Bion Talamo et al. London: Karnac Books.

Loewald, Hans W. 2000. *The Essential Loewald: Collected Papers and Monographs*. Hagerstown, Md.: University Publishing Group.

Lyotard, Jean-François. 1991. *The Inhuman: Reflections on Time*. Translated by Geoffrey Bennington and Rachel Bowlby. Stanford: Stanford University Press.

Maclean, George, and Ulrich Rappen. 1991. "A Biography." Pp. 2–44 in *Hermine Hug-Hellmuth: Her Life and Work*, ed. George Maclean and Ulrich Rappen. New York: Routledge.

Mannoni, Maud. 1970. *The Child, His "Illness," and the Others.* New York: Pantheon Books.

———. 1999. *Separation and Creativity: Refinding the Lost Language of Childhood.* Translated by Susan Fairfield. New York: Other Press.

Milner, Marion. 1996. "The Child's Capacity for Doubt (1942)." Pp. 12–15 in *The Suppressed Madness of Sane Men: Exploring Forty-Four Years of Psychoanalysis,* London: Routledge.

Mitchell, Juliet. 1998. "Introduction to Melanie Klein." Pp. 11–31 in *Reading Melanie Klein,* ed. John Phillips and Lyndsey Stonebridge. New York: Routledge.

Mitscherlich, Alexander, and Margarete Mitscherlich. 1975. *The Inability to Mourn: Principles of Collective Behaviour.* Translated by Beverley R. Placzek. New York: Grove Press.

Modiano, Patrick. 1999. *Dora Bruder.* Translated by Joanna Kilmartin. Berkeley: University of California Press.

Molnos, Angela. 1990. *Our Responses to a Deadly Virus: The Group-Analytic Approach.* London: Karnac Books.

Moskovitz, Sarah. 1983. *Love Despite Hate: Child Survivors of the Holocaust and Their Adult Lives.* New York: Schocken Books.

New York Times. 1999. "Columbine Students Talk of the Disaster and Life." April 30, p. A25.

O'Shaughnessy, Edna. 1975. "Explanatory Notes." Pp. 324–36 in *Envy and Gratitude and Other Works, 1946–1963,* Melanie Klein. Delacorte Press/Seymour Lawrence.

———. 1996. "W. R. Bion's Theory of Thinking and New Techniques in Child Analysis (1981)." Pp. 177–90 in *Melanie Klein Today: Developments in Theory and Practice, vol. 2, Mainly Practice,* ed. Elizabeth Bott Spillius. London: Routledge.

Pajak, Edward. 1998. "Exploring the 'Shadow' Side of Teaching." *Journal of Curriculum Theorizing* 14(2): 8–14.

Paskauskas, Andrew R., ed. 1995. *The Complete Correspondence of Sigmund Freud and Ernest Jones, 1908–1939.* Cambridge: Harvard University Press.

Petot, Jean-Michel. 1990. *Melanie Klein, vol. 1, First Discoveries and First System, 1919–1932.* Translated by Christine Trollope. Madison: International Universities Press.

———. 1991. *Melanie Klein, vol. 2, The Ego and the Good Object, 1932–1960.* Translated by Christine Trollope. Madison: International Universities Press.

Phillips, Adam. 1988. *Winnicott.* Cambridge: Harvard University Press.

———. 1993. *On Kissing, Tickling and Being Bored: Psychoanalytic Essays on the Unexamined Life.* Cambridge: Harvard University Press.

———. 1998a. *The Beast in the Nursery: On Curiosity and Other Appetites.* New York: Pantheon.

———. 1998b. "Bombs Away." *History Workshop Journal* 45: 183–98.

———. 1999. *Darwin's Worms.* London: Farber and Farber.

Phillips, John. 1998. "The Fissure of Authority: Violence and the Acquisition of Knowledge." Pp. 160–78 in *Reading Melanie Klein,* ed. Lyndsey Stonebridge and John Phillips. London: Routledge.

Pinar, William, ed. 1998. *Queer Theory in Education.* Mahwah, N.J.: Lawrence Erlbaum.

Pitt, Alice. 1998. "Qualifying Resistance: Some Comments on Methodological Dilemmas." *International Journal of Qualitative Studies in Education* 11(4): 535–55.

————. 2000. "Hide and Seek: The Play of the Personal in Education." *Changing English* 7(1): 65–74.

————. 2001. "The Dreamwork of Autobiography: Felman, Lacan, and Freud." Pp. 89–108 in *Feminist Engagements: Reading, Resisting, and Revisioning Male Theorists in Education and Cultural Studies*, ed. Kathleen Weiler. New York: Routledge.

————. In Press. *The Play of the Personal: Psychoanalytic Narratives of Feminist Education.* New York: Peter Lang.

Pontalis, J. B. 1981. *Frontiers in Psychoanalysis: Between the Dream and Psychic Pain.* Translated by Catherine Cullen and Philip Cullen. New York: International Universities Press.

Popkewitz, Thomas. 1998. "Dewey, Vygotsky, and the Social Administration of the Individual: Constructivist Pedagogy As Systems of Ideas in Historical Spaces." *American Educational Research Journal* 35(4): 535–70.

Readings, Bill. 1996. *The University in Ruins.* Cambridge: Harvard University Press.

Riviere, Joan. 1991. "On the Genesis of Psychical Conflict in Earliest Infancy (1936)." Pp. 272–300 in *The Inner World and Joan Riviere: Collected Papers: 1920–1958*, ed. Athol Hughes. London: Karnac.

————. 1991. "Symposium on Child Analysis (1927)." pp. 80–87 in *The Inner World and Joan Riviere: Collected Papers: 1920–1958*, ed. Athol Hughes. London: Karnac.

Robertson, Judith. 1997. "Fantasy Confines: Popular Culture and the Education of the Female Primary School Teacher." *Canadian Journal of Education* 22(2): 123–43.

Rodriguez, Leonardo S. 1999. *Psychoanalysis with Children: History, Theory and Practice.* New York: Free Association Books.

Rose, Jacqueline. 1993. "Negativity in the Work of Melanie Klein." Pp. 137–90 in *Why War? Psychoanalysis, Politics, and the Return to Melanie Klein.* Oxford: Blackwell Press.

————. 1996. *States of Fantasy.* Oxford: Clarendon Press.

Roudinesco, Elisabeth. 2001. *Why Psychoanalysis?* Translated by Rachel Bowlby. New York: Columbia University Press.

Rousseau, Jean-Jacques. 1979. *Emile or On Education.* Introduction, Translation and Notes by Allan Bloom. New York: Basic Books.

Roustang, François. 2000. *How to Make a Paranoid Laugh Or, What is Psychoanalysis?* Translated by Anne C. Vila. Philadelphia: University of Pennsylvania Press.

Sachs, Wulf. 1947. *Black Anger.* Boston: Little, Brown.

Safouan, Moustapha. 2000. *Jacques Lacan and the Question of Psychoanalytic Training.* Translated by Jacqueline Rose. London: Macmillan Press.

Sandler, Joseph. 1986. "The Concept of Projective Identification." Pp. 13–26 in *Projection, Identification, Projective Identification*, ed. Joseph Sandler. London: Karnac Books.

————, ed. 1992. *The Harvard Lectures: Anna Freud.* Madison: International Universities Press.

Sandler, Joseph, with Anna Freud. 1985. *The Analysis of Defense: The Ego and the Mechanisms of Defense Revisited.* New York: International Universities Press.

Saramago, Jose. 1997. *Blindness*. Translated by Giovanni Pontiero. New York: Harcourt Brace.

Sarason, Seymour B. 1982. *The Culture of the School and the Problem of Change*. 2d ed. Boston: Allyn and Bacon.

Schafer, Roy. 1994. "One Perspective on the Freud–Klein Controversies 1941–45." *International Journal of Psycho-Analysis* 75: 359–65.

———. 1997. "The Contemporary Kleinians of London." Pp. 1–26 in *The Contemporary Kleinians of London*, ed. Roy Schafer. Madison: International Universities Press.

Schmuck, Richard, and Patricia Schmuck. 1983. *Group Processes in the Classroom*. Dubuque, Iowa: Wm. C. Brown.

Sebald. W. G. 2001. *Austerlitz*. Translated by Anthea Bell. Toronto: Knopf Canada.

Sedgwick, Eve Kosofsky. 1990. *Epistemology of the Closet*. Berkeley: University of California Press.

———. 1991. "How to Bring Your Kids Up Gay." *Social Text* 29: 18–27.

———. 1993a. "A Poem Is Being Written." Pp. 177–214 in *Tendencies*, Durham: Duke University Press.

———. 1993b. "Privilege of Unknowing: Diderot's *The Nun*." Pp. 23–51 in *Tendencies*, Durham: Duke University Press.

———. 1993c. "White Glasses." Pp. 252–66 in *Tendencies*, Durham: Duke University Press.

———. 1997. "Paranoid Reading and Reparative Reading; Or, You're So Paranoid, You Probably Think This Introduction is About You." Pp. 1–40 in *Novel Gazing: Queer Reading in Fiction*, ed. Eve Kosofsky Sedgwick. Durham: Duke University Press.

———. 1999. *A Dialogue on Love*. Boston: Beacon Press.

Sedgwick, Eve Kosofsky, and Adam Frank. 1995. "Shame in the Cybernetic Fold: Reading Silvan Tomkins." Pp. 1–28 in *Shame and Its Sisters: A Silvan Tomkins Reader*, ed. Eve Kosofsky Sedgwick and Adam Frank. Durham: Duke University Press.

Segal, Hannah. 1988. "Notes on Symbol Formation." Pp. 160–78 in *Melanie Klein Today, vol. 1, Mainly Theory*, ed. Elizabeth Bott Spillius. London: Routledge.

———. 1991. *Klein*. London: Karnac Books.

———. 1997a. *Psychoanalysis, Literature, and War: Papers 1972–1995*. Edited by John Steiner. London: Routledge.

———. 1997b. "Phantasy and Reality." Pp. 75–96 in *The Contemporary Kleinians of London*, ed. Roy Schafer. Madison: International Universities Press.

Shelley, Mary. 1996. *Frankenstein; Or, The Modern Prometheus (1818)*. Edited by J. Paul Hunter. New York: W. W. Norton.

Silin, Jonathan G. 1995. *Sex, Death and the Education of Children: Our Passion for Ignorance in the Age of AIDS*. New York: Teachers College Press.

Simon, Roger I. 1992. *Teaching against the Grain: Texts for a Pedagogy of Possibility*. New York: Bergin and Garvey.

———. 1995. "Face to Face with Alterity: Postmodern Jewish Identity and the Eros of Pedagogy." Pp. 90–105 in *Pedagogy and the Question of Impersonation*, ed. Jane Gallop. Bloomington: Indiana University Press.

———. 2000. "The Paradoxical Practice of Zakhor: Memories of 'What Has Never Been My Fault or My Deed.' " Pp. 9–25 in *Between Hope and Despair: Pedagogy and the Remembrance of Historical Trauma*, ed. Roger Simon, Sharon Rosenberg, and Claudia Eppert. Lanham: Rowman and Littlefield.

Simon, Roger, Sharon Rosenberg, and Claudia Eppert, eds. 2000. *Between Hope and Despair: Pedagogy and the Remembrance of Historical Trauma.* Lanham: Rowman and Littlefield.

Smith, Barbara Herrnstein. 1997. *Belief and Resistance: Dynamics of Contemporary Intellectual Controversy.* Cambridge: Harvard University Press.

Spillius, Elizabeth Bott. 2001. "Freud and Klein on the Concept of Phantasy." Pp. 32–46 in *Kleinian Theory: A Contemporary Perspective*, ed. Catalina Bronstein. New York: Brunner-Routledge.

Stein, Ruth. 1999. *Psychoanalytic Theories of Affect.* London: Karnac Books.

Steiner, Riccardo. 1985. "Some Thoughts about Tradition and Change Arising from an Examination of the British Psychoanalytical Society's Controversial Discussions (1943–1944)." *International Review of Psychoanalysis* 12: 27–71.

———. 1991. "Background to the Scientific Controversies." Pp. 227–63 in *The Freud–Klein Controversies, 1941–1945*, ed. Pearl King and Riccardo Steiner. London: Tavistock/Routledge.

———. 1995a. "Introduction." Pp. xxi–xlix in *The Complete Correspondence of Sigmund Freud and Ernest Jones, 1908–1939*, ed. Andrew R. Paskauskas. Cambridge: Harvard University Press.

———. 1995b. " 'ET IN ARCADIA EGO . . . ?' Some Notes on Methodological Issues in the Use of Psychoanalytic Documents and Archives." *International Journal of Psycho-Analysis* 76: 739–58.

Steuerman, Emilia. 2000. *The Bounds of Reason: Habermas, Lyotard and Melanie Klein on Rationality.* London: Routledge.

Stonebridge, Lyndsey. 1998. *The Destructive Element: British Psychoanalysis and Modernism.* New York: Routledge.

Stonebridge, Lyndsey, and John Phillips. 1998. "Introduction." Pp. 1–31 in *Reading Melanie Klein*, ed. John Phillips and Lyndsey Stonebridge. London: Routledge.

Symington, Joan, and Neville Symington. 1996. *The Clinical Thinking of Wilfred Bion.* London: Routledge.

Talamo, Parthenope Bion. 1997. "Aftermath." Pp. 309–12 in *War Memoirs 1917–19*, ed. Francesca Bion. London: Karnac Books.

Taylor, Kate. 1998. "A Choke Hold on Destiny." *The Globe and Mail,* Saturday, October 24, p. C9.

Tobin, Joseph, ed. 1997. *Making a Place for Pleasure in Early Childhood Education.* New Haven: Yale University Press.

Todd, Sharon, ed. 1997. *Learning Desire: Perspectives on Pedagogy, Culture and the Unsaid.* New York: Routledge.

Troller, Norbert. 1991. *Theresienstadt: Hitler's Gift to the Jews.* Edited by Joel Shatzky and translated by Susan E. Cernyak-Spatz. Chapel Hill: University of North Carolina Press.

Volkan, Vamik. D. 1994. *The Need to Have Enemies and Allies: From Clinical Practice to International Relationships.* Northvale, N.J.: Jason Aronson.

Waller, Willard. 1961. *The Sociology of Teaching.* New York: Russell and Russell.

Watney, Simon. 1991. "School's Out." Pp. 387–401 in *Inside/Out: Lesbian Theories, Gay Theories*, ed. Diana Fuss. New York: Routledge.

Winnicott, D. W. 1986. "The Capacity to Be Alone (1958)." Pp. 29–36 in *The Maturational Processes and the Facilitating Environment: Studies in the Theory of Emotional Development*, New York: International Universities Press.

———. 1988. *Human Nature*. Bristol, Penn.: Brunner/Mazel.

———. 1990a. "Aggression, Guilt, and Reparation (1960)." Pp. 80–89 in *Home is Where We Start From: Essays by a Psychoanalyst*, ed. Clare Winnicott, Ray Shepherd, and Madeleine Davis. New York: Norton.

———. 1990b. "Living Creatively (1970)." Pp. 39–54 in *Home Is Where We Start From: Essays by a Psychoanalyst*, New York: Norton.

———. 1990c. "The Price of Disregarding Psychoanalytic Research (1965)." Pp. 172–82 in *Home Is Where We Start From: Essays by a Psychoanalyst*. New York: Norton.

———. 1990d. "Thinking and the Unconscious (1945)." Pp. 169–71 in *Home Is Where We Start From: Essays by a Psychoanalyst*, New York: Norton.

———. 1992a. "Fear of Breakdown [1963?]." Pp. 87–95 in *Psychoanalytic Explorations*, ed. Clare Winnicott, Ray Shepherd and Madeleine Davis. Cambridge: Harvard University Press.

———. 1992b. "Transitional Objects and Transitional Phenomena [1951]." Pp. 229–43 in *Through Paediatrics to Psycho-Analysis: Collected Papers*. New York: Brunner/Mazel.

———. 1994. "Some Psychological Aspects of Juvenile Delinquency." Pp. 113–19 in *Deprivation and Delinquency*, ed. Clare Winnicott, Ray Shepherd, and Madeleine Davis. New York: Routledge.

———. 1996. "Yes, but How Do We Know It's True? (1950)." Pp. 13–20 in *Thinking about Children*, ed. Ray Shepherd, Jennifer Johns, and Helen Taylor Robinson. Reading, Mass.: Addison-Wesley.

Woods, Michael. 2000. "J.xxDrancy 13/8/42." *London Review of Books* 22:23 (November 30): 30–31.

Young, Robert. 1999. "Phantasy and Psychotic Anxieties." Pp. 65–82 in *The Klein–Lacan Dialogues*, ed. Bernard Burgoyne and Mary Sullivan. New York: Other Press.

Young-Bruehl, Elizabeth. 1988. *Anna Freud: A Biography*. New York: Norton.

———. 1996. *The Anatomy of Prejudices*. Cambridge: Harvard University Press.

———.1998. *Subject to Biography: Psychoanalysis, Feminism, and Writing Women's Lives*. Cambridge: Harvard University Press.

INDEX